Praise for *Donor-Centered P*[...]

"I would like to see nonprofit leaders, fundrais[...]   [...]bers embrace the essential knowledge this book co[...] [...]ow to create and improve a most critical component to every organization's development effort—a donor-centered planned gift marketing program."

> —H.F. (Gerry) Lenfest, entrepreneur and philanthropist

"Never has there been a better time to talk about planned giving. It is an effective tool for developing resources for an organization and it is a meaningful way to truly engage with one's donors. This book provides a thorough roadmap for both the nonprofit that needs to start and the nonprofit that needs to expand their efforts in developing an effective, well-planned, and successful development effort using planned giving."

> —R. Andrew Swinney, President, The Philadelphia Foundation

"Michael's book is the first of its kind to place the emphasis on the planned giving donor right from the start. In marketing our planned giving programs, we traditionally focus on promoting the organization, then we spotlight the donors. Jumpstart or enhance your planned giving program with this book and, no doubt, your organization will be in a wonderful position to get the planned gifts it deserves."

> —Laura Fredricks, JD, author of *The ASK:*
> *How to Ask for Support for Your Nonprofit Cause,*
> *Creative Project, or Business Venture*

"Rosen has artfully crafted an insightful, inspirational, and comprehensive road map for discerning planned gift donor engagement. By using the strategies and stories in *Donor-Centered Planned Gift Marketing*, professionals at all levels of proficiency can optimally engage and steward a donor's passion and purpose for a better world through significant and heart-felt gift planning that will last more than their lifetime. This is a win-win book for all who care about future generations and vibrant communities."

> —Margaret May Damen, CFP, CLU, ChFC, CDFA founder,
> The Institute for Women and Wealth, Inc.; coauthor of *Women,*
> *Wealth and Giving: The Virtuous Legacy of the Boom Generation*

"Rosen writes with a clarity that displays his depth of knowledge and breadth of experience. He articulates principles that will benefit everyone from CEOs and chief development officers to experienced gift planners and part-time fund raisers. Vivid illustrations from colleagues throughout the United States make the concepts very real and practical. *Donor-Centered Planned Gift Marketing* is an indispensible handbook for anyone who wants to achieve planned giving success."

—Robert E. Fogal, PhD, ACFRE, CAP, Minister of Philanthropy, Pennsylvania Southeast Conference of the United Church of Christ

"This is one of those rare books that delivers more than it promises, and it will appeal to the specialist and generalist alike. It not only makes a case for a new approach to marketing, as the title would suggest, but it is also a practical guide for the entire process of planned giving, easy to understand because of the clear style and numerous examples, and with exercises to implement what is learned."

—Frank Minton, Senior Advisor, PG Calc; founder, Planned Giving Services; Past Chair, American Council on Gift Annuities

"The number one training topic requested by PPP members is planned gift marketing. Michael Rosen answers that need with a well-organized approach, interesting anecdotes, a reader-friendly writing style, and a wealth of practical information."

—Tanya Howe Johnson, CAE, President and CEO, Partnership for Philanthropic Planning

"*Donor-Centered Planned Gift Marketing* by Michael Rosen is a comprehensive, well-researched and practical guide to the marketing of planned gifts via a donor-centered process. The book will be of interest to both those new to planned giving and those seeking to take their program to a higher level."

—Philip B. Cubeta, CLU, ChFC, MSFS, CAP, The Sallie B. and William B. Wallace Chair of Philanthropy, The American College

"Michael Rosen's *Donor-Centered Planned Gift Marketing* should become the Bible for anyone seeking to raise money from planned gifts. His donor-centered approach combined with useful examples and a wealth of practical tips and helpful hints, makes the book a must-have reference for anyone working in gift planning."

—Phyllis Freedman, President, founder, SmartGiving; The Planned Giving Blogger

Donor-Centered
Planned Gift Marketing

The AFP Fund Development Series

The AFP Fund Development Series is intended to provide fund development professionals and volunteers, including board members (and others interested in the nonprofit sector), with top-quality publications that help advance philanthropy as voluntary action for the public good. Our goal is to provide practical, timely guidance and information on fundraising, charitable giving, and related subjects. The Association of Fundraising Professionals (AFP) and Wiley each bring to this innovative collaboration unique and important resources that result in a whole greater than the sum of its parts. For information on other books in the series, please visit:

http://www.afpnet.org

The Association of Fundraising Professionals

The Association of Fundraising Professionals (AFP) represents over 30,000 members in more than 207 chapters throughout the United States, Canada,

Mexico, and China, working to advance philanthropy through advocacy, research, education, and certification programs.

The association fosters development and growth of fundraising professionals and promotes high ethical standards in the fundraising profession. For more information or to join the world's largest association of fundraising professionals, visit www.afpnet.org.

2010-2011 AFP Publishing Advisory Committee

CHAIR: D. C. Dreger, ACFRE

Director of Campaigns for the Americas, Habitat for Humanity International

Angela Beers, CFRE

Director of Development, Devereux Pocono Center

Nina P. Berkheiser, CFRE

Principal Consultant, Your Nonprofit Advisor

Linda L. Chew, CFRE

Development Consultant

Stephanie Cory, CFRE, CAP

Director of Development, The Arc of Chester County

Patricia L. Eldred, CFRE

Director of Development, Independent Living Inc.

Samuel N. Gough, CFRE

Principal, The AFRAM Group

Larry Hostetler, CFRE

Director of Marketing and Fund Development, Sierra Vista Child & Family Services

Audrey P. Kintzi, ACFRE

Director of Development, Courage Center

Steven P. Miller, CFRE

Director of Individual Giving, American Kidney Fund

Robert J. Mueller, CFRE

Vice President, Hospice Foundation of Louisville

Maria Elena Noriega

Director, Noriega Malo & Associates

Paula K. Parrish, CFRE

Director of Advancement, Fort Worth Country Day

Michele Pearce

Director of Development, Consumer Credit Counseling Service of Greater Atlanta

Leslie E. Weir, MA, ACFRE

Director of Family Philanthropy, The Winnipeg Foundation

Sharon R. Will, CFRE

Director of Development, South Wind Hospice

Timothy J. Willard, PhD, CFRE

Vice President for Development, Ranken Technical College

John Wiley & Sons, Inc.:

Susan McDermott

Senior Editor

AFP Staff:

Rhonda Starr

Vice President, Education and Training

Reed Stockman

AFP Staff Support

Donor-Centered
Planned Gift Marketing

Michael J. Rosen, CFRE

WILEY

John Wiley & Sons, Inc.

Published by John Wiley & Sons, Inc., Hoboken, New Jersey.
Published simultaneously in Canada.

For general information on our other products and services or for technical support, please contact our Customer Care Department within the United States at (800) 762-2974, outside the United States at (317) 572-3993 or fax (317) 572-4002.

Wiley also publishes its books in a variety of electronic formats. Some content that appears in print may not be available in electronic books. For more information about Wiley products, visit our web site at www.wiley.com.

Library of Congress Cataloging-in-Publication Data:
Rosen, Michael J.
 Donor-centered planned gift marketing/Michael J. Rosen.
  p. cm. – (The AFP fund development series)
 Includes index.
 ISBN 978-0-470-58158-2 (pbk); ISBN 978-0-470-91531-8 (ebk);
 ISBN 978-0-470-91532-5 (ebk); ISBN 978-0-470-91533-2 (ebk)
 1. Deferred giving–United States. 2. Deferred giving. 3. Fund raising. I. Title.
 HV41.9.U5R67 2011
 658.15'224–dc22

                                                                2010018597

Printed in the United States of America

10 9 8 7 6 5 4 3 2 1

This book is dedicated to my parents, Evelyn and Bernard, who were the first to teach me about the transformative power of philanthropy.

It is also dedicated to my best friend and wife, Lisa, who is both my motivation and inspiration. She reminds me every day of what is most important. "All the world . . ."

Contents

The AFP Fund Development Series   iv

Foreword   xv

Preface   xxi

Acknowledgments   xxvii

1   Introduction to Donor-Centered Marketing   1

Take Care of Donors: A Lesson from Aesop   2

Planned Gift Marketing for All Organizations   4

Percentage of Americans with a Planned Gift   5

Five Common Myths about Planned Giving   9

There Has Never Been a Better Time   13

An Illustration of Donor-Centered Fundraising   15

Proactive versus Reactive Planned Giving   17

Stepping Stones to a Successful Planned Giving Program   19

Summary   22

Exercises   23

2   Identify Who Makes Planned Gifts   25

Everyone Is a Planned Gift Prospect   26

General Characteristics of Planned Givers   27

The Priority-Prospect Equation   31

Factors That Impact Ability   33

Factors That Impact Propensity   38

Factors That Impact Social Capital   45

Pros and Cons of Information   49

Contents

Basic Prospect Data   50

Prospect Rating   52

Summary   55

Exercises   55

3 Identify What Motivates Planned Gift Donors   59

Manipulation versus Motivation versus Inspiration   60

What People Want   61

Demographic Factors Impacting Motivation   70

General Individual Motives   75

Organizational Factors   79

Bequest-specific Motives   81

Demotivating Factors   84

Summary   87

Exercises   88

4 Educate and Cultivate Planned Gift Prospects   89

The Need for Education and Cultivation   90

Create a Planned Giving Brand Identity   92

Fundamental Strategic Approach   95

Words Matter   96

Keep Messages Meaningful and Memorable   103

Existing Materials   109

Direct Mail   111

Telephone   116

Newsletters   120

Web Site   126

E-mail   134

Social Networking Technology   139

Events   142

Face-to-Face Visits   145

Advertising   151

Contents

	Summary	153
	Exercises	155
5	**Educate and Cultivate Professional Advisors**	**157**
	Build Win-Win Relationships with Donor Advisors	158
	Six Exchanges of Value	161
	The Planned Giving Advisory Council	169
	Defining and Evolving Roles	176
	The Planned Gift Advisory Council and Its Members	177
	Five Practices for Working with Donor Advisors	180
	Summary	184
	Exercises	184
6	**The Ask**	**185**
	Good Things Come to Those Who Ask	186
	Using Direct Mail to Ask for Gifts	187
	Using the Telephone to Ask for Gifts	192
	Meeting Face-to-Face for the Ask	200
	Different Ask Scenarios When Meeting with a Prospective Donor	220
	Donors Make Marketing Recommendations	229
	Summary	230
	Exercises	231
7	**Stewardship**	**233**
	Stewardship Closes the Circle	234
	Thank Donors Quickly and Frequently	237
	Recognize Planned Gift Donors	240
	Reporting to Donors	245
	Internal Stewardship	246
	Summary	251
	Exercises	251

8   Getting Started   **253**

Is Your Organization Ready?   254

Getting Organizational Acceptance   255

Case for Support   257

Gaining Staff Acceptance   263

Building the Marketing Plan   265

Evaluating the Marketing Effort   270

Summary   274

Exercises   275

Appendix A   Planned Gift Program Potential Worksheet   **277**

Appendix B   Bequest Confirmation Form   **283**

Appendix C   Sample Internal Case for Donor-Centered

Philanthropic Planning: GPD Academy   **285**

Appendix D   Cost to Raise a Planned Gift Dollar Worksheet **291**

Notes   295

Glossary   305

References   313

About the Author   321

AFP Code of Ethical Principles and Standards   325

A Donor Bill of Rights   327

Model Standards of Practice for the Charitable Gift Planner 329

Index   331

Foreword

Gerry Lenfest

Throughout my life—whether serving as an officer in the U.S. Navy, a lawyer for Walter Annenberg's Triangle Publications, or a cable television entrepreneur—I learned that achievement comes not only from hard work but from working effectively with others. In my life, I have been very fortunate. I have been surrounded by many talented people and have enjoyed success. In more recent years, I have had the opportunity to share a fine portion of my good fortune and also share some of my insights to benefit many worthwhile nonprofit organizations. It is my hope that they were both equally valuable in advancing these various good causes.

I have seen firsthand how the staff and volunteers at most nonprofit organizations work tirelessly to improve our society whether through education, art and culture, health care, conservation, social action, or other causes. Most of these dedicated people also realize, as did I, that they cannot achieve their goals alone. Most understand that they must work effectively with staff and volunteers, of course, but also with their donors.

Through my voluntary work with nonprofit organizations, I have seen the tremendous power of planned giving. I have always known that some of the most prominent names in philanthropy—for example, Rockefeller, Carnegie, Astor and, more recently, Annenberg—have left lasting philanthropic legacies through significant planned gifts that have established or transformed nonprofit institutions. But I have also seen that the impulse to support worthwhile causes is present and also acted upon by those of more modest means.

Planned gifts are the major gifts of the middle class and such gifts, cumulatively, have a significant impact. Such gifts also have great meaning for the donors themselves. When it is part of estate planning, planned giving can offer a means to help donors take care of their families in ways not otherwise available to them, and yet still provide added support to the charitable causes they cherish.

No organization is too small to benefit from having a planned gift endeavor as a critical component of its development program. It can be very tempting for charities to focus limited resources only on immediate, annual giving, or short-term pledges such as for capital campaigns. However, for any nonprofit organization to achieve long-term sustainability, it must incorporate, at the very least, the fundamentals of a planned gift program.

Part of the beauty of planned giving is that virtually any organization and any donor can participate. While the largest nonprofit organizations may offer comprehensive gift planning programs, even the smallest charities can encourage donors to make a gift of appreciated stock, a contribution from a retirement fund, or to leave something to the organization in their will. Planned giving is not something that should be restricted to the wealthiest of philanthropists or the largest of organizations. Enabling such giving opportunities creates a win-win scenario for organizations and their donors.

So, I have long asked: If planned giving is so good for both nonprofit organizations and the donors who support them, why don't more organizations have a planned giving program? And, among those that do, why are those programs not more effectively presented? Why do they often target only a handful of the organization's wealthiest donors when smaller, steady donors are proven to be among the best candidates for a planned gift?

Donor-Centered Planned Gift Marketing is a book that addresses the myths that might be holding back some organizations. It encourages all organizations to engage in some level of planned giving. And then, in a well-researched and comprehensive way, the book provides useful information that will help charities new to planned giving get started. It also provides practical tips about how existing gift planning programs can achieve even greater results. This is complex information presented in a readable, compelling, and useful format. And there are some great anecdotes from professionals in the field sprinkled throughout the chapters.

Success in a planned giving program starts with a potential donor's interest in the organization and its work. If what the organization does is not personally meaningful to the potential donor, all the planned giving techniques do not matter. This book is right on target in terms of "donor-centered marketing."

Knowing your prospects and understanding what motivates them are two critical steps in the process. Quite simply, you cannot skip cultivation and relationship building and expect a successful outcome.

To inspire planned gift support, charities must be truly committed to a planned giving program, regardless of how sophisticated the initial structure is. This means that boards of directors must support development teams with the necessary staff and budget resources. It also means that board members and senior staff should commit to making their own planned gifts. Showing true support for planned giving by making such gifts is leadership by example. It is essential.

When my own business success and good fortune became public knowledge, the charitable causes I had been supporting were swift to include me on their short lists of important planned gift prospects. I suddenly had a lot of requests for face-to-face meetings. But I was no less inclined to create a planned gift to benefit these organizations at other steps along my career path—yet rarely did my moderate but steady support trigger an approach to discuss planned gift options. That was a lost opportunity for many of these charities. Such opportunities are lost by organizations of all sizes every day when they neglect to learn more about their steady donors of all levels and what it would take to inspire them to do something more than write an annual check.

This book underscores my own belief that the propensity to give to an organization (that is, the frequency and consistency of gifts) may be more important than the capacity to give (the wealth of the donor). In short, everyone can "leave a legacy," not just the wealthy. And each one of those gifts will add up to some major support for an organization in the long run. So, everyone should be given the opportunity to do so. All charities need to help people understand the importance of planned giving, let people know that planned gifts are for everyone, educate people about how to make planned gifts, and ask more people for such gifts.

Once gifts are secured, it is essential that institutions find creative ways to "credit" and celebrate each planned gift donor. Remember, any planned gift donor is a major gift donor. Those of us who make planned gifts do not expect, nor do we want, lavish thank-you presents or excessive recognition. However, we do want to know that the organizations we support appreciate our philanthropy and will use our gift in the way we intend. So, do not make the mistake of forgetting about us once you receive our gift commitment. We may truly appreciate how efficiently and effectively you handle contributed funds so much that we entrust you with another planned gift. We are also in a position to influence others to do the same, so bringing together current and prospective planned gift donors for an informational event may have a very good outcome. Publishing stories—with or without the use of the donor's name—can show prospects the many backgrounds of planned gift donors. Even a reluctant philanthropist may be urged to serve as an example for others to follow.

As you read this book, remember that if more nonprofit organizations engage in gift planning, and if those who already do begin to do a more effective job, then dramatically more dollars will be made available to charities to do their good work—now and in the future. Organizations need to commit to planned giving, put donors first, and ask more people in the right way to make planned gifts. Working together, nonprofit organizations and donors can ensure the sustainability of organizations that make our communities, our nation, and our world a better place.

I would like to see nonprofit leaders, fundraisers, and their key board members embrace the essential knowledge this book contains on how to create and improve a most critical component to every organization's development effort—a donor-centered planned gift marketing program.

About the Foreword Author

H.F. (Gerry) Lenfest is a philanthropist and businessman who lives in the Philadelphia area. Mr. Lenfest graduated from Mercersburg Academy, Washington and Lee University, and Columbia University Law School. After practicing law as an estates and trusts attorney in New York, Mr. Lenfest joined Walter Annenberg's Triangle Publications in 1965 where he eventually became publisher of *Seventeen* magazine and managed the company's cable television operations.

In 1974, Mr. Lenfest purchased Triangle's two cable franchises with 7,600 customers and built the new company, Suburban Cable, into one of the largest in the country with over 1 million subscribers. In 2000, the Lenfest family sold Suburban Cable to Comcast Corporation and since that time Mr. Lenfest has devoted his efforts to philanthropy and leading nonprofit organizations.

Mr. Lenfest is Chairman of the Board of The Lenfest Foundation, which he and his wife, Marguerite, founded in 2000. Through the Foundation and personally, the Lenfests have made charitable grants and gift commitments of over $800 million as of the time of this writing.

Mr. Lenfest is Chairman of the Board of the Curtis Institute of Music in Philadelphia and is Chairman of the James Madison Council of the Library of Congress in Washington, DC. He is the founding Chairman of the Board of The American Revolution Center, which will be located in Philadelphia and will be the definitive museum of the American Revolution.

Mr. Lenfest just completed nine years of service as Chairman of the Board of the Philadelphia Museum of Art and continues to chair its planned giving donors' recognition organization, The Fiske Kimball Society.

Mr. Lenfest is a member of the Board of Trustees of Columbia University and chairs the university's 1754 Society, its honorary society for those who have made planned gifts to the university.

Preface

Once upon a time in the long, long ago, I began to learn about philanthropy and fundraising. I was eight years old, and wanted my parents to buy me some comic books. My mother said that she would get me any "real" book I wanted but, if I wanted comic books, I would have to spend my allowance. Well, in those days, an allowance was not an entitlement; I had to earn it by doing household chores. Sadly, I was already at my maximum earning capacity. And, I had no more money for the latest edition of Superman.

Because I simply had to have the latest Superman comic book, I asked my mother if I could sell my old comic books and open up a lemonade stand to generate some quick cash. Fortunately, she granted her permission.

My first entrepreneurial effort was a terrific success. I generated what in today's dollars would be about $150. As an eight-year-old kid, I was rich! Recognizing that I did not need to buy quite that many comic books, my mother suggested I give half of it away to charity. She further said that, if I agreed with her suggestion, I could pick whatever charity I wanted.

At the time, our local newspaper operated a fund to send "poor, inner-city" kids to summer recreational camp. I grew up in the suburbs. However, my cousin grew up in the big city. I knew how miserable summertime in the city could be for a kid. I knew how good I had it, even with our meager working-class lifestyle. I wanted other kids to enjoy the clean air and open spaces that I enjoyed. So, I took my coffee can with half of my earnings and marched into that local newsroom. The editor was so moved that he had my picture taken and put me on the front page! My little eight-year-old ego swelled. I was inspired for each of the next several summers to run a front-yard fair for that summer camp fund. The only changes were that I gave 100 percent of the revenue to the charity and the event got bigger each year. It even inspired similar efforts in other neighborhoods.

Part of my success with the fairs came from learning what the other neighborhood kids wanted and then delivering it. For example, I developed a game that allowed the older kids to purchase wet sponges. For 25 cents, they could hurl three soaking sponges at my friends and me. We taunted the big kids mercilessly. They knew they were not allowed to beat us up, so they just kept buying wet sponges to exact their vengeance. Sure, we got wet, but it was good, summertime fun and we were exacting more support from kids who enjoyed the chance to have at us. It was a win-win scenario.

I can trace the roots of both careers I have had in my adult life—journalism and development—back to that little boy's experience. I learned a great deal about fundraising in those days, especially about what it takes to inspire donors to support a good cause. I also learned how good it feels to be philanthropic.

Even at eight years old, I instinctively knew to be donor-centered. Of course, I did not know that was what I was doing. But, I was doing it nevertheless. Throughout my professional fundraising career, I have purposely and routinely adopted a donor-centered orientation. Stephen F. Schatz, CFRE and I successfully employed donor-centered fundraising principles at Temple University in 1980, long before it was popular to do so. We felt compelled to expand and build on the model we created, and so we later cofounded The Development Center (originally known as Telefund Management, Inc.). We achieved our tremendous results, for clients across the nation, by remaining donor-centered.

Now, I want to share with you how such donor-centered gift marketing can help your prospective planned gift donors, your organization, and you.

Before I tell you what valuable tools and insights this book will provide for you, I want to share with you what this book will not do. This book will not provide a comprehensive description of how to run a planned giving program. It will not discuss how to staff a planned giving program. It will not cover how to hire and train gift planning professionals. It will not even detail the many gift planning vehicles, though it will briefly touch upon some.

I am not a planned giving expert. In fact, when I began preparations in 1993 for the Certified Fund Raising Executive exam, the one area that I had to study, in particular, was planned giving. Until then, my career had focused quite successfully on annual giving, capital campaigns, and membership marketing. As I left the CFRE exam room in 1994, the only thing I remember thinking was, "Thank goodness that's over! Now, I can forget all that planned giving stuff I studied so hard." I could not have been more wrong. My career as a fundraising and marketing innovator naturally evolved into planned gift marketing as I saw the opportunity to apply the principles that had worked so dramatically well in other areas of fundraising. I have now spent the last several years helping nonprofit organizations throughout the United States enhance their planned gift marketing efforts. But, I am still not a gift planning expert; what I am is a highly effective planned gift marketer whose efforts have helped nonprofit organizations generate potentially hundreds of millions of dollars in planned gifts. So, through my own expertise and that gleaned from dozens of recognized leaders in the field, what I will teach you is how to effectively market planned giving.

This book will help you understand the differences between donor-centered planned gift marketing and traditional marketing. Whether you read this book cover to cover or use it as a reference, you will learn useful ideas that will dramatically enhance your fundraising results.

If you are new to gift planning, this book will help you build an effective planned gift marketing program from the start. If your organization is already engaged in gift planning, this book will help you enhance your efforts. As you read this book, you may find it describes some techniques you are currently using; this will validate your efforts and help you justify them to those within your organization. You will also find many fresh ideas that you can put to use with confidence to enhance your results.

This book is organized according to the stages of the marketing process. Following an introductory chapter in which the donor-centered concept is presented and defined, there are chapters dealing with prospect identification, prospect motivation, education and cultivation of prospects, education and cultivation of professional advisors, the ask, stewardship, and putting it all together so you can implement your own, highly effective donor-centered planned gift marketing effort.

As you read each chapter, you will come across *In the Real World*, a feature box that contains true stories and examples, many generously contributed by planned giving professionals from around the nation. You will also come across Key Concepts that will provide quick tips and Executive Insights that will include important quotes offering further perspective. These "extras" have been inserted into the text at appropriate points and are intended to be read in-line to illustrate the points of the text. At the end of each chapter, you will find a number of Exercises that will help you to begin to put the material into practical use. The appendices and supplemental inclusions will provide you with additional material that you will also find of value and use.

After reading this book, I hope you will be inspired to adopt or maintain a donor-centered approach. If you do, you will have much happier, more trusting donors who will give more often and more generously than would otherwise be the case. I also hope you will be encouraged to actually ask more prospects to make a planned gift commitment. If you want more gifts, you have to ask more people. With relatively minor enhancements to the way we do planned gift marketing, we can raise dramatically more money for our organizations.

In my faith tradition, Judaism, we have the precept of *tikkun olam*, "repair the world," which is incumbent upon each of us to incorporate into our everyday lives. Virtually all faiths advocate a similar concept of doing good works and helping those in need. All of us who serve the nonprofit community are doing something to improve the quality of life, now and into the future. We are repairing the world one small step at a time. Whether our organizations educate, entertain, inspire, heal, provide hope, feed, build, or work in numerous other ways, they make our communities, our country, and our world a better place. When we more successfully secure the resources necessary for these organizations to do their essential jobs more effectively, we practice *tikkun olam* in its many incarnations.

This book has been written to help you to be a more effective planned gift marketer. It is designed to show you how to more successfully secure the resources your organization needs by recognizing that putting the donor's needs first will pave the way to inspiring them to make the philanthropic commitments they truly would like to make. Together, I hope we will be able to do more to make a brighter future. *Tikkun olam.* Together, let us always work toward achieving increased success in our endeavors to repair the world and to show others a clear path to allow them to do the same.

MICHAEL J. ROSEN, CFRE
President
ML Innovations, Inc.
mrosen@mlinnovations.com

Acknowledgments

Writing this book has been the single greatest challenge of my professional life. I never would have undertaken such an ambitious project were it not for the invitation of Nina P. Berkheiser, CFRE, Chair, and her AFP Publishing Advisory Committee colleagues. I thank the Committee for the confidence they showed in me and the opportunity they provided for me to give back to a profession I care about so passionately.

I also want to thank legendary fundraiser and author James M. Greenfield, FAHP, ACFRE, President and CEO of J.M. Greenfield & Associates who most recently co-authored *Internet Management for Nonprofits: Strategies, Tools and Trade Secrets*. Jim was the first person to respond to my public call for planned giving stories and helpful tips. In addition to graciously providing material for this book, Jim also offered some simple words of encouragement that came at just the right times.

Many others have also been of enormous assistance to me on this project, offering both advice and material. Those who have been extraordinarily generous have been Roger Ellison, CFP, West Texas Rehabilitation Center Foundation; Laura Fredricks, JD, Laura Fredricks LLC and author of *The Ask*; Scott R.P. Janney, EdD, CFRE, RFC, PlannedGiving.com and Main Line Health; Bruce Makous, CFRE, CAP, ChFC, Barnes and Roche; Viken Mikaelian, Planned Giving.com; James Pierson, PlannedGiving.com; Brian M. Sagrestano, JD, CFRE, Gift Planning Development; Larry Stelter, The Stelter Company and author of *How to Raise Planned Gifts by Mail*; Nathan Stelter, The Stelter Company; and Robert E. Wahlers, MS, CFRE, Meridian Health Affiliated Foundations.

These fundraising experts have enriched this book by kindly sharing significant amounts of material which will enormously benefit readers. I thank them for their materials, their support, their open collegiality, and their friendship.

This book has also been enriched by the many stories, useful insights, and helpful tips that have been contributed by Mindy Aleman, CFRE, APR, Kent State University; Ann Barden, Oregon Health & Science University Foundation, Doernbecher Children's Hospital Foundation; Leslie D. Bram, Esq., the University of Florida Foundation; Susan Blair Brandt, CFRE, Jupiter Medical Center Foundation; Jim Brozo, CFRE, CSPG, Grossmont Hospital Foundation; Robert J. Crandall, CFRE, Robert J. Crandall and Associates; Tom Cullinan, Schola Donum Inc.; Margaret May Damen, CFP, CLU, ChFC, The Institute for Women and Wealth and author of *Women, Wealth and Giving*; Elizabeth Tice Eiesland, JD, Youth & Family Services Foundation; Heather Gee, CFRE, CAP, The Philadelphia Foundation; John Gillon, Wake Forest University Baptist Medical Center; Steven C. Greaves, Quinnipiac University; Ed John, United Way Worldwide; John B. Kendrick, The George Washington University; Jane B. Kolson, The George Washington University; Donald W. Kramer, Esq., Montgomery McCracken Walker and Rhoads and Editor of "Nonprofit Issues®"; Anne T. Melvin, Harvard University; David B. Moore, Chapman University; Michelle Mulia-Howell, Natural Resources Defense Council; Philip J. Murphy, Zimmerman Lehman; Lisa A. Rosen, ML Innovations, Inc.; Rebecca Rothey, CFRE, Catholic Charities; Mark R. Seeley, University of South Carolina; Katherine Swank, JD, Target Analytics; David C. Troutman, Wabash College; Justine Van Wie, The George Washington University; Larry C. Woodard, CFRE, FAHP.

I also want to express my deep gratitude to the community of researchers who have added to our knowledge and have made this book more meaningful than it otherwise would have been. They include John J. Havens, PhD, Center on Wealth and Philanthropy at Boston College; Russell N. James, III, JD, PhD, CFP, formerly at the Institute for Nonprofit Organizations at the University of Georgia and now director of Graduate Studies in Charitable Planning at Texas Tech University; Elaine Jay, PhD, Henley Management College; Patrick M.

Rooney, PhD, Center for Philanthropy at Indiana University; Adrian Sargeant, PhD, Center for Philanthropy at Indiana University; Paul G. Schervish, PhD, Center on Wealth and Philanthropy at Boston College; Jen Shang, PhD, Center for Philanthropy at Indiana University. I must also thank the Giving USA Foundation, publishers of *Giving USA*. I also want to express my appreciation to Adrian, Patrick, Paul, and Russell for their personal assistance with this project and, above all, their patience with me.

Barbara Yeager, Partnership for Philanthropic Planning, was very helpful to this book project. She pointed me in the right direction on a number of occasions, helped me track down material, generously granted permission for use of certain materials, and made me laugh when I needed it most. I thank her for everything she has done.

I must also recognize Dana Hines, Membership Consultants, and Patricia E. Rich, ACFRE, EMD Consulting Group. Dana and Pat are the authors of *Membership Development: An Action Plan for Results*. They gave me the opportunity to taste what it is like to write chapters for a book. I thank them for allowing me to participate in their book project. If I had not had the benefit of that experience, this project would have been an even greater challenge.

Stephen F. Schatz, CFRE, author of *Effective Telephone Fundraising*, co-founded The Development Center with me. As direct-response fundraising pioneers, we experimented for years to develop many of the donor-centered techniques that are commonplace today in direct-response fundraising. I thank Steve for being my fellow warrior in the trenches long before "donor-centered" became fashionable and for extending to me the honor of writing the foreword for his own book.

I must also express my thanks to all of the clients I have ever served, the people I have worked for, the people who have worked for me, my teachers, my mentors, and my professional and personal friends. These people have helped shape who I am in ways that I cannot even identify. As a result, they have had a profound impact on this book.

I also want to thank Judy Howarth, Adrianna Johnson, Melissa Lopez, Susan McDermott, and the rest of the superb team at John Wiley & Sons. Their patience with a new author was nothing short of amazing and inspiring. The many dozens of magazine and journal articles I have written over the years only barely prepared me for this arduous and exhilarating process. I thank them all for their trust and great assistance.

I must also thank my parents, Evelyn and Bernard, who taught me much about philanthropy though we often had very little ourselves. They showed me that no matter how little one has, there is always someone else worse off that we can help, and that we have an obligation to do so. In addition to being philanthropic in the traditional sense, they also opened our home and their hearts to numerous children in need by serving as foster parents. Others may be able to donate more money, but my parents exemplified a true philanthropic spirit. They are the greatest philanthropists I have ever known.

I also want to thank the many philanthropists whose voices are heard at various points throughout this volume. They remind us what is important. I take particular inspiration from H.F. (Gerry) Lenfest, who was gracious enough to lend his endorsement of this book's donor-centered approach to pro-active planned giving advocacy. His contribution of the Foreword lends a balanced perspective from one of the leading philanthropists of our time. Gerry's personal blend of passion and humility is very compelling. I thank him for his leadership and vision.

Bruce Melgary, Executive Director of The Lenfest Foundation, was the first person to read my manuscript besides my wife and the staff at Wiley. I am grateful that he took the time to read the material. His kind feedback was quite a welcome relief. After working so many months on this project, it was wonderful to learn from him that I had hit my target.

I must also thank the most important person in my life, my wife Lisa. She is a terrific fundraiser and a brilliant wordsmith. She has helped edit my manuscript, shared her wisdom with me during this project, and has remained patient despite unbelievable tests. She is my best friend. She is an inspiration. Without her, this book quite simply would have been impossible.

Finally, I want to thank you, the reader, for investing the time to study this book and for your desire to start or enhance your planned gift marketing program. I wish you the very best.

Donor-Centered
Planned Gift Marketing

CHAPTER 1

Introduction to Donor-Centered Marketing

Get wild with planned giving: Think of it as fundraising!

—*Philip J. Murphy, Zimmerman Lehman*

 After reading this chapter, you will be able to:

- Understand that all nonprofit organizations can secure planned gifts.
- Define "donor-centered marketing."
- Describe the potential for planned gift growth for the nonprofit sector.
- Debunk five common myths about gift planning.
- Explain the fundamental marketing steps of a successful gift planning program.

Donors and prospective donors are not geese. However, one can learn something about how to treat these individuals from Aesop's well-known fable "The Goose That Laid the Golden Eggs." In this tale, a man owns a perfectly ordinary looking goose that happens to lay eggs of gold. However, the man becomes impatient with the goose. He wants all of the gold the goose has to offer immediately. So, imagining that the goose must be made of gold inside, the man kills the bird to get the entire store of gold all at once. Unfortunately, the man discovers too late that his goose is really just like any other.

In Aesop's fable, the man succumbs to greed. He focuses on his own needs and desires. In the process, his inward focus results in the death of the goose and the loss of a vast treasure of gold. If the man had simply taken care of the goose, seeing to its needs, and if he had remained patient, waiting for the goose to lay her eggs on her schedule, he would have become fabulously well off.

Take Care of Donors: A Lesson from Aesop

Development professionals can learn from this tale. While a nonprofit organization's mission is of critical importance, one must not let it overwhelm consideration of donors. Development professionals must take care of the needs of donors and prospects while respecting their individual lifecycles and personal decision-making schedules.

"We have all heard of the Golden Rule—and many people aspire to live by it," writes President of Assessment Business Center, Tony Allesandra. He continues:

> The Golden Rule is not a panacea. Think about it: "Do unto others as you would have them do unto you." The Golden Rule implies the basic assumption that other people would like to be treated the way that you would like to be treated. That is patently false. In fact, it could be argued that the Golden Rule is a self-centered rule—and not unlike a traditional salesman who assumes his product is right for his prospect and approaches the sale without considering the prospect's needs. In sales—and relationships—one size (yours) does not fit all. With the Golden Rule, you run a greater risk of creating conflict than chemistry. After all, people have different needs, wants, and ways of doing things. The alternative to the Golden Rule is much more productive. I call it the Platinum Rule: "Treat others the way *they* want to be treated." Ah-hah! Quite a difference. The Platinum Rule accommodates the feelings of others. The focus of relationships shifts from "this is what I want, so I'll give everyone the same thing" to "let me first understand what they want and then I'll give it to them." Building rapport with people based on the Platinum Rule requires some thought and effort, but it is the most insightful, rewarding, and productive way to interact with people.[1]

By shifting the focus from the organization to donors and prospects, development professionals will achieve greater success and organizations will receive far greater benefit. By helping donors and prospects discover their philanthropic passion and by showing them how gift planning can help them realize their philanthropic aspirations while taking care of their loved ones, development professionals can perform a great service for these individuals while serving and benefiting the nonprofit organizations that employ them.

This process is the core of *donor-centered* planned gift marketing. Penelope Burk, in her book *Donor-Centered Fundraising*, describes what she means by the term,

> Donor-centered fundraising is an approach to raising money and interacting with donors that acknowledges what donors really need and puts those needs first. Donor-centered fundraising impacts fundraising success in three ways. First, it retains more donors longer, giving them time to develop their own philanthropic resiliency; second, it causes more donors to offer increasingly generous gifts; and third, it raises the performance of even the most active and loyal donors to a new standard. Donor-centered fundraising aims its sights at our two worst enemies in fundraising: attrition and stagnation.[2]

By contrast, traditional, organization-focused fundraising has often concentrated on:

- Tools including philanthropic instruments like wills, trusts, life insurance, and so on.
- Techniques including direct mail, face-to-face visits, telephone appeals, and so on.
- The needs of the charitable organization.
- The community.
- The cause.

While tools, techniques, organization need, community benefit, and the cause itself are all important, the fact is that it is donors and prospective donors that are most important in the philanthropic process. So, while this book will

KEY CONCEPT

Always treat donors and prospective donors how *they* want to be treated. Keeping the focus on them will lead to greater benefit for the organization.

certainly address these other items, it will do so while recognizing the fundamental importance of maintaining a donor-centered perspective.

Planned Gift Marketing for All Organizations

Virtually all nonprofit organizations can ask for, receive, and benefit from planned gifts. Many already are. For the most part, those organizations that currently do not ask for planned gifts probably should, yet may not be doing so out of a misplaced sense of fear rather than any legitimate reason. For example, one misguided fear is that a bequest donor will give less to the annual fund. However, the Center on Philanthropy at Indiana University has found that bequest donors actually give more than twice as much annually as people who have not named a charity in their will.[3] Among those nonprofits that are already seeking planned gifts, most can be doing a much more effective job of it. Regardless of one's experience or the size of one's organization, this book will help development professionals either create or enhance philanthropic planning programs while helping others better understand the marketing challenges faced by nonprofit organizations. While this book will not explore the technical side of philanthropic planning, it will provide detailed information about the marketing of planned gifts.

If one works for a small to mid-sized nonprofit organization, it is easy to think that the organization is too small to worry about marketing planned gifts with the expense of doing so incurred now while the return is garnered at some point in the future. If one works for a mid-sized to large nonprofit organization, it is easy to think that the organization has already mastered the art of planned gift marketing. However, both perspectives are incorrect.

While small to mid-sized organizations might not be prepared to speak with donors about a wide array of planned giving instruments, such organizations can certainly accept gifts of stock. In addition, they can also easily encourage donors to demonstrate their support through a charitable bequest. "Charities with mature planned giving programs estimate that deferred gifts, consisting primarily of bequests, make up 70 percent to 80 percent of all planned gifts,"[4] writes Kathryn W. Miree, President of Kathryn W. Miree & Associates. So, if an organization does nothing else in the area of planned gift marketing other than promote bequest giving, it will have accomplished a great deal. Even large organizations can benefit from doing more to educate individuals about the value of bequest giving.

More complex gift opportunities can be established easily by working with a community foundation that offers a charitable gift annuity (CGA) program. Even for the smallest organizations, a CGA program may provide virtually no risk and limited expense. (A glossary of gift planning terms can be found at the end of the book.) Many community foundations around the country allow nonprofit organizations to market CGAs. A donor makes the gift to the community foundation and receives regular income from the community foundation. Upon the donor's death, a fund is established and the income from the community foundation is given to the nonprofit organization.

While mid-sized to large organizations might already have sophisticated marketing efforts in place, learning about the donor-centered approach described in this book may help achieve even greater outcomes. One can discover a new idea or a new perspective in an old idea in this book. Or, current strategies and tactics might be validated by the text, which could prove enormously useful when budgeting and when trying to bring along others within the organization.

Percentage of Americans with a Planned Gift

It is difficult to estimate the percentage of Americans who have made a planned gift or planned gift commitment. For starters, there is some debate about what is and is not a planned gift. For example, some organizations consider a gift of appreciated stock to be a planned gift. After all, a gift of stock often avoids capital gains tax, may involve a financial advisor, and always involves an element of planning. Fortunately, a number of research projects over the past several years have helped the nonprofit community come closer to understanding how many individuals have made planned gift commitments and what the potential is for growth.

While most Americans have the ability to make a planned gift, the research reveals that relatively few have actually done so and that vastly more are willing to consider such gifts. This means two things. First, there is a significant gap in what traditional planned-gift marketing is achieving and what people are willing to consider. Second, traditional planned-gift marketing is just scratching the surface of planned giving potential.

By better understanding what the sector has achieved, development professionals will be poised to understand the overall potential for planned giving. Individual organizations will be able to do some very basic benchmarking while setting appropriate goals that take into account both what the sector is doing and what the potential for growth is.

Dr. Russell N. James, III, then of the University of Georgia Institute for Nonprofit Organizations, looked at the rate of planned giving among older Americans. Specifically, James studied charitable bequest giving since that is, by far, the most popular type of planned gift instrument. James found that among Americans over the age of 50, only 5.3 percent had made a charitable bequest upon death.[5] This figure comes from data collected by the University of Michigan "Health and Retirement Study," a longitudinal study from 1995–2006 sponsored by the National Institute on Aging that tracked the deaths of over 6,000 study participants. The 5.3 percent figure is one-third lower than the rate of bequest commitment cited in "Planned Giving in the United States 2000: A Survey of Donors" (NCPG). The 2000 survey reported that 8 percent of Americans surveyed had made a charitable bequest commitment. However, the figure—identified in the "Health and Retirement Study" and cited within *Giving USA 2009*—is within the margin of error cited in the NCPG survey report. For these reasons, this book will use the 5.3 percent figure when describing the percentage of Americans making a charitable bequest while recognizing that the figure might be somewhat lower if Americans under the age of 50 were included.

Looking at a less popular form of planned giving, the NCPG Survey found that 1 percent of those responding said that they have established a charitable remainder trust (CRT).[6]

Compellingly, the Center on Philanthropy at Indiana University found that 33 percent of respondents would be willing to consider a charitable bequest.[7] The NCPG Survey found that 5 percent were considering a CRT. Figure 1.1 illustrates the difference between the percentage of donors with a bequest or trust commitment and the percentage of people willing to consider making such gifts.

The Stelter Company conducted a survey that found that once individuals know at least a little bit about various gift planning instruments or techniques,

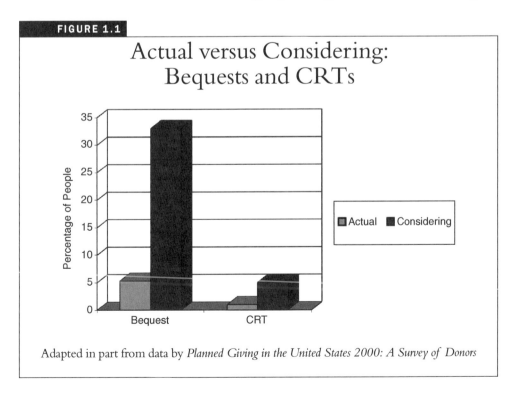

FIGURE 1.1

Actual versus Considering: Bequests and CRTs

Adapted in part from data by *Planned Giving in the United States 2000: A Survey of Donors*

half of the individuals would be willing to consider making at least some type of planned gift or had already done so.[8] During the 11-minute survey call, the interviewer quickly described six different gift planning options without going into great detail about any single option. While information clearly has an impact on what individuals are willing to consider, relatively little information is required in order to inspire a fairly significant increase in interest. However, Stelter also discovered that as the age of respondents increased, the receptivity to planned giving decreased. Among those age 70 and over, only 33 percent would be willing to consider a planned gift.[9] So, nonprofit organizations need to do a more effective job educating prospects, and they need to do so while prospects are younger.

Among older Americans, CGAs can help donors make significant gifts while offering a measure of financial security by providing them with a regular income. However, based on extrapolation from the last survey of the American Council on Gift Annuities, there might only be as many as 400,000 gift annuities in force, according to Frank Minton, Senior Advisor at PG Calc and former ACGA board chair. That number, however, does not represent the number of donors who have elected this form of planned gift vehicle; many donors have established more than one annuity. Enormous potential for increasing the number of CGA donors exists as those figures represent only a small percentage of the senior population. The market of older Americans continues to grow, thereby increasing the potential for more CGAs. In 2004, there were 36.3 million Americans age 65 or older. By 2050, that number will increase by 147 percent to 86.7 million, 21 percent of the U.S. population.[10]

For 2008, the Center on Philanthropy estimated that Americans contributed $22.66 billion through charitable bequests.[11] Even if the sector would have convinced 6.3 percent of Americans rather than 5.3 percent to make a charitable bequest, an additional $4.53 billion might have been raised. With relatively incremental changes in marketing effectiveness, nonprofit organizations can realize significant increases in revenue. In 2008, bequest revenue accounted for 7 percent of all contributed dollars.[12]

If incremental changes in marketing had increased the percentage of Americans making a bequest commitment from 5.3 percent to 6.3 percent, bequest giving might have accounted for 9 percent of all giving. Now, imagine if the nonprofit sector significantly enhanced its marketing effectiveness. Imagine if the percentage of Americans engaging in bequest giving increased by one-third. This is not an idle fantasy. In the United Kingdom, the Remember a Charity consortium states that 7 percent of the public there has named a charity in their will.[13] Even with that rate of success, the British are not content and are engaged in a national campaign that seeks to boost the bequest giving rate still further.

With a donor-centered marketing approach, nonprofit organizations can encourage more individuals to consider a planned gift and more effectively close gifts from those considering action. This could, for example, shrink the gap between the 5.3 percent who make a charitable bequest and the 33 percent considering it or the 1 percent with a CRT and the 5 percent willing to consider it as more individuals pondering planned gifts actually make them.

Five Common Myths about Planned Giving

While there is enormous potential for the nonprofit sector to significantly grow the amount of revenue developed from planned gifts, the sector continues to limit itself. A number of myths surround the professional practice of philanthropic planning. These myths can lead organizations to take no action or to take the wrong action where planned giving is concerned. The following five common myths are rebutted.

Myth 1: Planned giving is very difficult. The best kept secret about planned giving is that it is just not that difficult. Admittedly, for a wide variety of reasons, there are plenty of people who like to *think* that planned giving is daunting. From time to time, planned giving can even pose a real challenge that can lead people to believe it is always very complicated. However, for the most part, planned giving is simple. If one knows how to generate current gifts, she is well on her way to being able to secure planned gifts. After all, planned giving is just like every other type of fundraising: one has to identify prospects, cultivate them, and ask for the gift. Most large nonprofit organizations may employ an entire, well-staffed gift planning department to handle all types of planned gifts, while most smaller organizations simply add planned giving to the director of development or major gift officer portfolio of responsibilities. Too many small, and even mid-sized organizations, simply ignore planned giving altogether. However, with the vast majority of planned gifts falling into one of three simple categories—bequests, CGAs, and gifts of stock—there is no reason why all organizations cannot be engaged in some form of planned giving program. While some organizations may never move beyond simply promoting bequest giving and other organizations may grow their program over time to include more sophisticated giving options, virtually all organizations can do something to encourage some type of planned giving.

Myth 2: One needs to be a planned giving expert to be involved in gift planning. One does not need to be an expert. However, one does need to be knowledgeable. Fortunately, of all planned gifts, the vast majority are simple bequests. Charitable gift annuities and stock gifts are also popular forms of planned giving. The more complex forms of planned giving (i.e., charitable lead trusts, charitable remainder annuity trusts, real estate gifts, etc.) make up only a small fraction of all planned gifts. For the more complex transactions, one simply needs to be aware of them and know who to call for assistance when the need arises. The Partnership for Philanthropic Planning (formerly the National Committee on Planned Giving) has found that since 2000, there are fewer planned giving specialists employed by nonprofit organizations and more development professionals now doing gift planning along with their other responsibilities.[14] Increasingly, organizations are taking a more holistic approach to fundraising and development professionals are expected to know just enough to know when to suggest an appropriate planned gift instead of a current gift option. For technical advice, donors are more often seeking input from professional advisors other than development professionals. The Partnership has found that even with the simple bequest, 4 percent of such donors reported hearing of this option from a legal or financial advisor in 1992 compared with 28 percent in 2000. Among CRT donors, 70 percent learned of this giving option from a legal or financial advisor. So, a development professional does not need to be the technical expert for the donor. However, development professionals must be knowledgeable enough to earn a seat at the table with the donor and his trusted advisors in order to assist the donor in fulfilling his philanthropic aspirations while taking care of other needs.

Myth 3: All planned gifts are deferred gifts. Many organizations are reluctant to commit the necessary resources to planned giving because they incorrectly believe that all planned gifts are deferred gifts that will take decades to be realized. While it is certainly true that bequest expectancies represent deferred gifts, they are not necessarily deferred for decades. Depending on the size and age of the pool of bequest expectancies, some gifts will be realized within three to five years of commitment based on basic actuarial forecasts, and sometimes sooner. Other types of planned gifts such as CGAs represent an immediately bookable asset for nonprofit organizations. Gifts of stock also represent an immediately bookable contribution. So, organizations that commit resources to planned gift marketing, can see a return on investment in a very reasonable time frame.

Myth 4: Good marketing focuses on organizational needs. While it is essential for an organization to have a compelling case for support, a great marketing effort will focus on the donor. Understanding what motivates a donor and knowing what a donor's interests are, then matching the organization's needs to the donor's motivations and interests is part of the core of donor-centered marketing. There are plenty of good causes out there. Show a donor how an organization can help realize his philanthropic aspirations while ensuring that the needs of loved ones are met, and one will be more likely to secure the gift. By focusing exclusively on the organization's needs, one will be less likely to secure a gift. By treating a donor file as a homogenous group, one will be less likely to secure a gift. Donor-centered marketing, and not just marketing, will help build stronger relationships and secure more gifts.

IN THE REAL WORLD

Marketing versus Donor–Centered Marketing in Practice

An elderly woman in Philadelphia contributed a $25,000 charitable gift annuity to a well-known hospital in New York City. In addition to sending an acknowledgment letter, the development officer contacted the donor by telephone to thank her for her generous gift and to arrange a meeting when he was due to be in Philadelphia. So far in this story, the development officer has behaved in a donor-centered way. He has personally thanked the donor, learned a bit about why she made the gift, and has arranged to meet with the donor to learn more about her and her philanthropic interests. To recognize her generous support, the development officer invited the donor to lunch which she accepted.

When they got together, the development officer picked up the donor at her home and drove her to the Four Seasons Hotel for lunch in the very lavish Fountain Room. The donor was appalled. She refused to be seated and told the development officer that lunch in the more casual, and less expensive, Swan Lounge would be more appropriate.

When relating the story to a friend, the donor expressed her outrage that the hospital would waste her money by taking her out to such a fancy restaurant. She even thought the more informal Swan Lounge was too much. When asked if she would be making another gift to the hospital, she said, "Absolutely not! They waste too much money."

While lunch at an exclusive restaurant might be something that donors in New York might appreciate, this frugal Philadelphian most certainly did not. Unfortunately, the development officer, while trying to do the right thing, made a simple mistake. He assumed something about the donor that he did not know. A more donor-centered approach would have been for the development officer to simply have asked the following in the initial telephone contact, "I'll be in Philadelphia next Wednesday and would love to talk with you more over lunch. Would you be available? . . . Great! *Where would you like to go?*" With that one simple question, the development officer would have remained donor centered, would have enhanced the relationship, and would likely have secured another gift. Sometimes donor-centered marketing really is that easy.

Myth 5: Planned gift marketing should be passive. Except when working with major donors, many organizations believe that planned gift marketing should be relatively passive. In other words, planned gift donors should self-identify their interest before they are asked for a gift. Organizations that would never think twice of picking up the telephone and soliciting annual fund gifts would never use the telephone to solicit CGAs. After all, if someone is interested in a CGA, she would respond to the advertisement in the newsletter. The reality is that those organizations that are proactive in their marketing are enjoying greater success than would otherwise be possible. Planned giving is fundraising. The same fundamental principles apply.

There Has Never Been a Better Time

There has never been a better time to engage in a planned giving program. The population is aging, donors are more aware of their gift planning options, more individuals have wills, and generations beyond the Boomer have demonstrated they possess philanthropic values. Organizations that have recognized the opportunity and have worked to effectively cultivate and ask for planned gifts have experienced dramatic philanthropic growth in recent decades.

As the population gets older and passes on, vast sums of assets will be passed from one generation to the next. The Center on Wealth and Philanthropy at Boston College projects that at least $41 trillion (in 1998 dollars) will transfer to the next generation by 2052. Of that transfer, at least $6 trillion could go to nonprofit organizations, according to researchers John J. Havens and Paul G. Schervish (see Table 1.1). The numbers could be much greater.

The Center on Philanthropy provides some evidence that the nonprofit sector is, in fact, beginning to benefit from the leading edge of the wealth transfer. The report reveals that bequest giving, when adjusted for inflation, has almost doubled from 2004–2008 ($116.88 billion) compared with the period 1968–1972 ($60.22 billion).

TABLE 1.1

Projections for Intergenerational Wealth Transfer, 1998–2052			
	Low Estimate	**Middle Estimate**	**High Estimate**
	Total (2% secular real growth in wealth)	Total (3% secular real growth in wealth)	Total (4% secular real growth in wealth)
Number of estates	87,839,311	87,839,311	87,839,311
Value of estates	$40.6	$72.9	$136.2
Estate fees	$1.6	$2.9	$5.5
Estate taxes	$8.5	$18.0	$40.6
Bequest to charity	$6.0	$11.6	$24.8
Bequest to heirs	$24.6	$40.4	$65.3

In 1998 dollars. Dollars are in trillions.
Source: John J. Havens and Paul G. Schervish, "Why the $41 Trillion Wealth Transfer Estimate Is Still Valid," Center on Wealth and Philanthropy at Boston College, 2003.

In addition to the positive impact of the wealth transfer on planned giving results, a number of the more recent research studies provide a greater understanding of donor behavior and how donors view planned giving. The nonprofit sector has also gained a greater appreciation for the role of sound marketing in the planned giving process; the creation of the National Committee on Planned Giving (now the Partnership for Philanthropic Planning) in 1988 offers some evidence of this as gift planning professionals came together to share ideas, provide training programs, and offer other services.

A number of factors have come together at this time to make this the best time ever to engage in a planned giving effort: (1) the largest intergenerational wealth transfer in history, (2) a greater understanding of donor attitudes through recent research, and (3) an enhanced appreciation for the role of marketing within the nonprofit sector. However, while the environment has never been better for planned giving programs, it remains up to nonprofit organizations to actually capitalize on the opportunity.

Executive Insight

For those who think the generational transfer will automatically flood their organizations with resources, it's time to think again. Without putting in the hard work of generating these planned gifts, 90% of donor mortality will simply result in lost current giving.

—Russell N. James, III, Director of Graduate Studies in Charitable Planning, Texas Tech University

An Illustration of Donor-Centered Fundraising

Thanks to the minds at Wordle (www.wordle.net), one can illustrate the difference between a donor-centered fundraising approach and one that is not, both using word clouds. In Figure 1.2, a fictional hospital foundation is the major focus. The needs of the hospital are prominent as are the various fundraising

FIGURE 1.2

Organization–Focused Language

Source: www.wordle.net

FIGURE 1.3

Donor-Centered Language

Source: www.wordle.net

tools at its disposal. The emphasis is on securing donations for the hospital by the end of the year. Little if any emphasis is put on the donors. The words are largely focused on the hospital with the words most emphasized being those most focused on the hospital and its needs.

By contrast, Figure 1.3 emphasizes collaboration between the hospital and the community. The words and the emphasis are much more focused on the donor. For example, instead of emphasizing words such as *Give* and *Pledge*, this illustration emphasizes the words *Together, Thank-You*, and *health care*.

In the donor–center illustration, one sees that the hospital has less prominence than in the previous illustration. Obviously, the hospital is a key component, but the focus has been shifted to the community and to the donor's philanthropic desires, need for appropriate information and recognition, and hope for positive impact. It is a view of the world more from the donor's perspective.

When designing any marketing, communications, or solicitation program, it is important to create and maintain a donor-centered focus. For example, does *year-end* describe the end of the organization's fiscal year or the end of the donor's year? Donors care far less about the end of the organization's year than they do their own year-end. So, a year-end appeal should be sent in October, November, or December rather than in April, May, or June.

Proactive versus Reactive Planned Giving

A great number of planned giving efforts involve primarily passive and reactive marketing. Organizations may have a planned giving button on their web site home page (though it is very often buried deeper in the web site if it exists at all), or may include an advertisement about CGAs in a newsletter, or tell a story about a planned gift donor in the annual report. While each of these marketing examples represents valid promotional approaches, they are at best reactive and at worst passive marketing methods. An article in the annual report may simply inform and contain no call to action. An advertisement in a newsletter may contain a call to action, but it relies on the donor coming forward. As background marketing, these are important awareness-raising techniques. However, much more needs to be done to have an effective planned giving program.

A truly effective planned giving program will contain a mix of reactive marketing methods and proactive techniques. The most effective proactive technique is to talk with donors and prospective donors, preferably face-to-face. If one's organization has a planned giving officer, this individual should spend less time at his desk and more time in front of donors and prospects. If the organization employs major gift officers, these individuals should take a holistic approach to their conversations with donors and prospects to help them with their philanthropic planning. This means they should be prepared to discuss gift planning options. To ensure that this is done, nonprofit organizations must maintain a culture that supports and, indeed, encourages such a donor-centered approach. Unfortunately, while many organizations pay lip-service to a holistic approach, they only evaluate and reward major gift officers for the large current gifts that they secure.

KEY CONCEPT

You usually will not get the gift unless you ask. So: Ask!

Proactive fundraising is nothing new in the development profession. One would never be satisfied with a capital campaign that personally requested gifts from the top 150 donors while simply sharing a newsletter article with everyone else asking them to contact the development office in response if they feel like talking about giving. However, as Philip J. Murphy from Zimmerman Lehman observes, this is how most planned giving programs are run. He writes, "But there is a lot you can do on your own. Applying basic fundraising principles to planned giving is a good place to start."[15]

IN THE REAL WORLD

Get Out from Behind Your Desk!

During a seminar at an Association of Fundraising Professionals chapter conference, the director of development for a regional theater company asked a question: "Could I have some of our repertory actors cultivate our major donors?" The presenter initially thought this was a terrific idea. Theater donors often like to think of themselves as true patrons of the arts. The opportunity to interact with the actual performers would be meaningful to many of the theater's major donors. The presenter mentioned this and asked, "How many major donor prospects do you have?" The answer was 50. The presenter then suggested that the director of development schedule appointments with the major donors and plan on bringing one of the actors with her. At this suggestion, the director of development exclaimed, "I don't have time for that! I was hoping that the actors could go out on their own." The presenter patiently responded, "If *you* visit with only two major donors per week, you will have seen them all within six months. And, not only will they have been cultivated by having the chance to interact with one of the actors, *you* will have developed a relationship and, in the process, learned more about the donor's interests and philanthropic abilities. You will be well positioned to renew and upgrade their current support while being able to begin a conversation about planned giving. What could possibly be a better use of time?''

While the development director was not pleased with the response, the reality is that the most effective fundraising happens at a coffee table not at a desk. Being proactive and actually talking with donors and prospects, understanding their needs, cultivating them, and asking for the gift is always the most effective development strategy.

Stepping Stones to a Successful Planned Giving Program

A planned giving program cannot be developed in a vacuum. At the foundation of all development efforts is the organization's mission. A development professional must know and understand this so that she can explain it to prospective donors and inspire them to give. One way to begin the process of inspiring donors is to develop a comprehensive case for support, based on the organization's mission, that identifies the organization's various programs and services, explores the organization's plans for the future including a review of how the organization provides benefit to those served, examines why prospects might want to support the organization, and outlines how prospects can contribute.

The development of an internal case for support will help engage the organization's leadership and will help garner their support. Without the support of the organization's volunteer and staff leaders, no planned giving program will realize its full potential. From the comprehensive case for support, and based on the internal case, the organization should develop the external case for planned giving support. Prospects must understand why planned gifts are important to the well-being of the organization. More important, prospects must understand the effect that planned gifts will have on the beneficiaries of the organization. As many planned gifts will not be fully realized for decades, donors must understand the impact they will have at some distant point in the future.

Once an organization has refined its mission, developed the case for support—including internal, comprehensive, and planned giving specific—and secured the endorsement for a planned giving program from the organization's leaders, the organization is then ready to create its planned giving program. For some organizations, the planned giving program will be relatively simple and involve existing staff and the marketing of bequests. At the other end of the spectrum, the launch of a new planned giving program might include the addition of staff, the engagement of outside professionals, and the creation of a broad array of gift planning instruments.

To begin building the planned gift marketing program, regardless of the size of the effort, staff will want to focus on five fundamental steps:

1. Identify prospects.

2. Educate.

3. Cultivate.

4. Ask.

5. Steward.[16]

While everyone who has had contact with a nonprofit organization is a viable planned giving prospect, no organization has the budget and staff resources to treat every prospect as a high-priority opportunity. Therefore, development professionals need to segment their database and establish who the priority prospects are. While there are some sophisticated things that one can do to rate and prioritize prospects, the best prospects are often fairly easy to spot. The highest-priority prospects are those with the closest relationship with the organization such as consistent annual fund donors, long-term members, board members, volunteers, and others with well-established bonds to the organization.

Educating donors and prospective donors about planned giving is a fundamental component of any gift planning program. Relatively few individuals have even heard of the term *planned giving*. One cannot expect others to engage in an activity that they are not even aware of. While development professionals can have face-to-face meetings with a modest number of prospects to discuss gift planning, an organization's message must be delivered far more broadly to better prepare prospects for face-to-face meetings and to reach people that may not be reached through visits but who may, nevertheless, be willing to make a planned gift commitment.

An organization can educate its target market through its existing media such as newsletters, web site, e-publications, annual report, and special events. Additional, affordable media can be added to the mix as well. For example, an organization can add an informational brochure to a receipt mailer, host educational seminars related to tax and estate planning, or use display advertising. The key is to understand that the best prospect identification process will not uncover all of the truly viable prospects, and it will not educate the prospects it does identify. So, an effective educational strategy is essential.

For prospects that have been identified, a sound cultivation program will help further educate the prospects, warm them to the idea of gift planning, help the development professional learn more about the prospect, and help both better understand how gift planning can help the prospect fulfill his philanthropic aspirations while meeting the needs of loved ones. One of the easiest and most powerful ways to cultivate prospects is to actually speak with them, preferably during a face-to-face visit.

The next step in the marketing process is to ask for the gift. While virtually all organizations would not think twice about asking for annual fund support, with many doing so several times throughout the year, many of those same organizations are uncomfortable asking for a planned gift. However, good fund-raising requires an actual ask, even for planned giving. For upper and mid-level prospects, the ask should be done in person. For lower priority prospects, the ask might be done by mail or even telephone. By carefully identifying and prioritizing prospects, organizations will be well positioned to know who to ask in what way. While in-person solicitation will always be the most effective, it is not always the most practical. It is, therefore, far better to ask through the mail or a telephone call than to not ask at all.

The final step in the marketing process is consistent and effective stewardship. Because many planned gifts are revocable, it is essential that donors continue to feel engaged and appreciated. Furthermore, a fully engaged and
appreciated planned gift donor is more likely to enhance the value of his gift,
more likely to make an additional planned gift commitment, and more
likely to support the annual fund. Excellent stewardship may also lead to gifts
from family members. So, the marketing of planned gifts does not end with
the ask or even the signed gift agreement. The marketing process, really the
relationship-building process, continues with strong stewardship.

While this book will not provide technical planned giving advice or
comprehensive information about how to structure a planned giving program, it will guide readers through the planned gift marketing process and
offer donor-centered suggestions. By implementing a donor-centered
planned gift-marketing program, organizations will be able to secure more
gifts than ever before.

Summary

Planned giving is fairly simple. The vast majority of all planned gifts are simple
bequests, charitable gift annuities, or gifts of stock. While it is important to be
aware of the other gift planning vehicles that exist, it is not necessary to be an
expert. One simply needs to know who to call for assistance when the need
arises—be it a local estate planning attorney, certified public account, financial
planner, banker, or community foundation official. Because planned giving is
simple at its core, any organization can have a planned giving program. Not all
programs will be sophisticated and offer all giving options. However, even the
smallest nonprofit organization can encourage donors to include the organization in their wills.

There has never been a better time to engage in planned giving. As the
population ages, we will continue to experience, over the coming decades,
the largest intergenerational wealth transfer in human history. Whether in
economic boom times or recession periods, planned gifts remain an excellent

way for donors to realize their philanthropic aspirations with minimal or no pain and, depending on the gift vehicle, significant personal or estate benefit.

To successfully generate planned gifts, development professionals must be proactive with their marketing. Yes, passive background marketing is an important component of a comprehensive marketing plan. But, for one to be truly effective, she will need to actually ask for support.

This book is an attempt to define the key elements of a successful, well-rounded planned gift marketing program that is proactive and donor centered. Whether read from cover-to-cover or used as a handy desk reference, readers will find practical information, helpful tips, and illustrative stories from some of the profession's greatest practitioners. By putting even a few of these ideas to work, your donors will be more inspired, and your planned giving program will be more effective. Along the way, you will also find yourself having more fun energized by the momentum your program will take on.

Exercises

- It is essential that you know your organization's mission because all of your activity should be devoted to achieving that mission. Does your organization even have a mission statement? If it does, learn it, memorize it, and share it. Consider if your donors and prospective donors know the organization's mission.

- You must know what your donors and prospective donors have seen and heard from your organization. It is helpful for you to experience your organization as your donors and prospects do. So, gather one year's worth of communications to your planned giving donors and prospective donors. Be sure to include all communications and not just those concerned with gift planning. These materials will be used in future Exercises and will help you better position future communications.

- Once all of the organization's various communications are assembled, take time to review them and then ask yourself:

- Are all materials brand consistent? Among other things, is only one logo used consistently, are the correct institutional colors always used, is the same font style used?

- Do both words and images make it clear what your organization's mission is?

- Determine if your gift planning communications are donor centered. One way you can test your communications is to visit www.wordle.net. Then copy and paste the text of your letter, e-mail, web copy, or brochure into Wordle to create a word cloud. The words that appear largest are those used most often. Are those words institution focused or donor centered?

- On an ongoing basis, it is important for you to see what your donors and prospective donors see. So, add your name and contact information to your organization's database so that you will be included in all communications sent to your planned giving donors and prospective donors.

CHAPTER 2

Identify Who Makes Planned Gifts

Are there not thousands in the world . . .
Who love their fellows even to the death,
Who feel the giant agony of the world,
And more, like slaves to poor humanity,
Labour for mortal good?

—*John Keats*

After reading this chapter, you will be able to:

- Explain the formula for identifying ideal prospects.
- Describe the 10 broad characteristics of planned gift donors.
- Identify some easily accessible ways to gauge a prospect's ability and propensity to give.
- Reference common sources of prospect information.
- Understand what prospect information is important.

Because virtually everyone is capable of making a planned gift, everyone is a planned gift prospect. While most individuals will not be interested in or qualify for more complex planned gifts such as trusts or real estate donations, virtually anyone can make a charitable bequest commitment and many can contribute through a charitable gift annuity. This represents an enormous opportunity for nonprofit organizations, but it also poses some serious challenges.

Everyone Is a Planned Gift Prospect

Charitable bequests comprise the vast majority of what are most commonly thought of as planned gifts. Anyone who is going to have any assets remaining in his name at the time of his death is able to make a charitable bequest commitment, as just one type of planned gift. This describes the majority of Americans. A survey by The Stelter Company found that 69 percent of respondents over age 30 expect to leave an inheritance.[1] Even among the lowest income segment of survey respondents, those with annual income less than $50,000, 57 percent expect to leave an inheritance of some value. During the *Planned Giving Course*, it was noted:

> The Bequest is the major gift of the middle class. As people live longer, they are concerned about having enough to live on in an extended retirement. Also, parents are living longer often without having saved sufficiently for their longer retirement. And, the cost of a college education for children is more expensive than ever with children often returning home rather than living independently after college. It's Generation Squeeze! While people might be reticent to make a major gift of current assets while they are alive given their economic uncertainty about the future, many are willing to make a large gift when they know they will definitely no longer need the money, in other words: a charitable Bequest."[2]

Another common planned giving instrument is a charitable gift annuity (CGA). Such a gift requires the donor to irrevocably contribute cash or other liquid asset in exchange for a tax deduction and income for life. Depending on the nonprofit organization and state regulations, a donor can establish a CGA for as little as $1,000. So, with a relatively moderate donation, one can even make a life-income gift.

For nonprofit organizations, the opportunity is the challenge. Virtually every American has the ability to make a planned gift of some type. While few have actually done so, many have indicated that they are willing to consider it. That is the opportunity. The challenge is that, with limited budget and staff resources, most organizations acknowledge they must prioritize who their best planned giving prospects are. Donor-centered marketing recognizes the broadest possible prospect universe while further recognizing the need to

KEY CONCEPT

A multifaceted marketing effort will ensure that the general population of planned giving prospects receives a certain base level of care and attention while staff focuses additional effort on high-priority prospects.

focus solicitation efforts where they will yield the greatest, most immediate return on investment.

General Characteristics of Planned Givers

Enormous potential exists for increasing planned giving. However, one of the major challenges for development professionals is determining how to figure out who are the highest-potential planned giving prospects. The more limited an organization's staff and budget resources, the more important it is to prioritize prospects.

Laura Fredricks, fundraising consultant and internationally recognized author and speaker, describes the ten major characteristics of planned gift donors[3]:

1. *They know about the organization and its mission, priorities, and direction.* Planned gift donors actually care about the organization's mission and long-term priorities. In cases where the planned gift will not be realized until some point in the future, this is particularly true. For an annual fund, when a proper appeal is made, donors know exactly what immediate need will be met by their gift. The same is true with current planned gifts, such as gifts of stock. However, with a deferred planned gift, such as a bequest commitment, it is often impossible to know exactly what the need will be since the gift might not be realized for years or decades to come. So, what donors support is the mission and not necessarily a specific need. This means that the development professional must know the mission in order to passionately share it with and explain it to prospects.

2. *They have confidence in the leadership.* Prospects who trust an organization's leadership, both staff and volunteer, are more likely to give. The more trust a donor has, the more likely they are to increase giving and to make a planned gift. Because a planned gift is often an investment of sorts in the future of the organization, the donor must have confidence that the organization will be there in the future and will still be effectively fulfilling its mission. The development professional must work within the organization to help key staff and volunteers understand their roles in the development process and the importance of adhering to the highest ethical standards. (The *AFP Code of Ethical Principles and Standards, The Donor Bill of Rights,* and the PPP *Model Standards of Practice for the Charitable Gift Planner* are included as supplemental material in this book.)

3. *They are satisfied with the organization's fiscal management.* Donors want their precious, hard-earned dollars to make a difference. If they feel that their funds will be wasted, they will take their money elsewhere. The development professional should help the organization adopt policies and procedures that will inspire donor confidence. For example, organizations should have procedures in place to acknowledge gifts quickly, accurately, and personally. Additionally, organizations should make sure that their Federal Form 990s are filled out completely, accurately, and tell the correct story, as filed 990s are posted for public access at www.guidestar.org. These are two important, fundamental steps to inspiring donor confidence.

4. *They believe their gift will be perpetuated well into the future and that they will have a long and lasting legacy through the organization.* Donors want to know that their planned gifts will have an impact. Depending on the type of gift, donors will want to know that they are securing some measure of immortality through the organization's continued good works. By practicing strong stewardship, development professionals can give donors confidence in this.

5. *They give when the time is right for them economically.* Donors' schedules are dictated by their own lifecycles and economic situations. For example, they care much more about the end of their calendar year than they

do about an organization's fiscal year close. They are also more likely to include a nonprofit organization in their will when they first write or update their will. So, development professionals must make sure that planned giving messages are delivered regularly.

6. *They may have supported the organization in the past with smaller gifts, but a number of them will have no giving history with the organization.* Planned gift donors can appear from anywhere in an organization's donor file, general database, or from the community at large. So, while development professionals will maintain a portfolio of priority prospects, marketing messages must consistently educate and cultivate the broadest possible audience. For example, an individual who volunteers regularly at a community hospital but does not contribute to the annual giving campaign may nevertheless be a very good planned giving candidate.

7. *They possess the assets to give without compromising their economic comfort level.* A common expression in nonprofit circles is that donors should "give until it hurts." While nonprofit executives might feel that way, donors seldom do. Most people do not enjoy pain. Instead, donors will give as long as it feels good. Development professionals must strive to understand what motivates prospects and what their asset situation is before they can provide advice that will help donors maintain or enhance their financial comfort. Regardless of income or asset level, it is the prospect's perception of his financial security that will impact his willingness to make a gift and that will, in part, also affect the size of that gift.

8. *They want to ensure that their loved ones are taken care of in conjunction with the planned gift.* Part of what will make a donor feel good about making a gift is knowing that her loved ones will benefit in some way from the gift or, at the very least, not be harmed by it. Development professionals need to know who the prospect's loved ones are and what their needs are. This will give prospects greater comfort in making a gift and will allow the development professional to recommend the right gift. This combination will make it more likely that a prospect is converted into a planned gift donor.

FIGURE 2.1

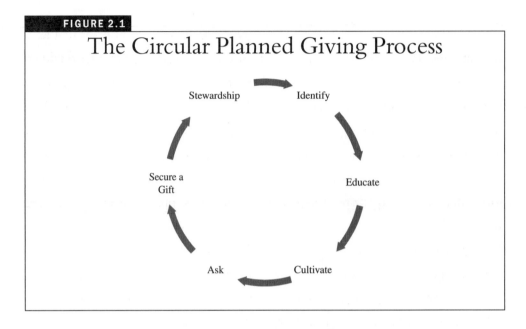

The Circular Planned Giving Process

9. *They tend to make several planned gifts over their lifetime.* While donors may make several planned gifts, they may not be to the same organization. Development professionals should strive to identify and steward planned gift donors to ensure that revocable commitments are maintained, that gift values are increased when possible, and that multiple gifts can be secured when appropriate. Securing a planned gift is not the end of a linear process. The process is circular as illustrated in Figure 2.1. For example, a donor who establishes a CGA may, with proper acknowledgment and additional cultivation, establish yet another CGA with the organization or may also decide to remember the organization in his will, if asked.

10. *They usually consult tax advisors, financial planners, attorneys, colleagues, and family members before making the gift.* Donors will often want to consult advisors. In all cases, they should be encouraged to do so. Development professionals should focus on closing for a seat at the table and not necessarily simply closing for the gift. When a development professional identifies, acknowledges, and works with the individuals who are key advisors to a prospect, the prospect will feel more comfortable and will ultimately develop a better philanthropic plan that meets her needs while fulfilling her philanthropic aspirations.

While the previous list of characteristics does not mention race, it is nevertheless important to note that there are presently some distinctions. For instance, African Americans and Hispanics in the general population are less likely to make charitable bequests because they are also less likely to have wills. However, when looking at African Americans, Hispanics, and whites who do have estate plans, bequest giving rates are essentially the same. "This may suggest that the primary barrier for minority estate gifts was not donative preference but the planning process itself," according to James.[4]

By better understanding who planned gift donors are, development professionals will be able to identify more effectively these traits in prospects and, therefore, will be better able to identify those more likely to become planned gift donors themselves. In addition, by understanding donors, development professionals will be better positioned to help prospects become donors.

The Priority-Prospect Equation

While virtually everyone might be a planned giving prospect, a number of details will help determine who is a *priority* prospect or which groups of prospects should be given greater priority over other groups. Simply put, virtually everyone has the means to make a planned gift. However, most nonprofit organizations do not have the resources—financial or staff—to treat all prospective planned gift donors equally. The fact is that not all prospective donors are equal. Ability is an important characteristic. Not all prospects are able to make large planned gifts. By understanding a prospect's ability to make a planned gift, fundraising professionals will be better able to evaluate what gift planning instruments might best serve the prospect, if any, and what the potential size of that gift might be. Furthermore, development professionals will be better able to help a prospect understand his ability to make a planned gift. For example, David might not feel financially able to make a planned gift because he requires a certain income in retirement. The development professional can show David that he can earn a regular income through a gift to establish a CGA. If the CGA income is sufficient, David might very well make the gift that he previously had not known enough about to even consider.

Unfortunately, merely having the ability to make a planned gift does not mean that a prospect will make such a contribution, and it certainly does not mean that a prospect will make a contribution to a particular institution. A number of factors determine whether an individual has a strong propensity to make a planned gift, and additional factors help determine whether a prospect is likely to give to a particular organization. Some propensity factors include age, giving history, relationship with the organization, the financial independence or absence of children, and education level.

For example, Jane might have sufficient means to make a planned gift, but the gift might be a $5,000 CGA at best. By contrast, Bob may have sufficient means to make a planned gift of far greater potential value, perhaps a $1 million charitable remainder trust (CRT). In this example, it is easy to see how the planned giving officer will set his priorities. Jane will receive mailings, newsletters, invitations to events, and perhaps a telephone call. However, if the planned giving officer only has time for one additional face-to-face visit with a prospect before the end of the year, that visit is going to be with Bob assuming all other factors besides ability are in common between the two prospects.

This example, of course, is a gross simplification designed only to demonstrate the importance of ability in the fundraising equation. However, ability is one thing; propensity to give is a completely different matter that is also a critical element of the philanthropic equation. Building on the example, what if Jane loves her alma mater but Bob has been angry with it ever since the school rejected his son's application? Bob may have stronger means for giving, but his propensity for giving to that particular institution is much lower than Jane's. In that case, the planned giving officer might choose to visit with Jane. When judging both ability and propensity, a large variety of factors must be considered.

Social capital is another factor that must be considered, both in general and as it relates to a specific organization, because it also drives propensity. For example, a social service agency might have a regular donor who also volunteers and attends various cultivation events. That person will likely be a better planned giving prospect than someone who only donates occasionally to the agency and does not volunteer or attend events. In addition, the person who is more engaged in community life—attending church, belonging to Rotary, coaching Little League—is more likely to support nonprofit organizations, in general. The more an individual is engaged within the community and the more points of contact between the specific organization and the prospect, the better.

If one were to develop an equation to broadly describe the prospect factors that can lead to a planned gift, it might look something like this:

$$\textbf{Ability} + \textbf{Propensity} + \textbf{Social Capital} = \textbf{GIFT}$$

The greater the component parts of the equation, the more likely the organization is to secure a gift and have that gift be a sizable major or planned gift. The lower the component factors, the less likely it is for the organization to close a gift or, if it does, to have that gift be sizable. The challenge for development professionals is to evaluate prospects for ability, propensity, and social capital in order to set priorities while ensuring that all prospects receive a certain base level of education and cultivation with higher priority prospects receiving more attention.

Factors That Impact Ability

While nearly all Americans have the ability to make some type of planned gift, the size of that gift might be somewhat modest even if meaningful to the donor. James, in his analyses of the "Health and Retirement Study," finds that the estate gifts from those with estates valued at less than $100,000 do not even equal the donor's total annual giving.[5] However, as estate values grow, so too does the size of estate gifts and the ratio of estate giving to annual giving. For example, among those with estates valued at $500,000 to $999,999, estate giving was 1.89 times greater than the annual giving total for these individuals. Those with estates valued at over $5 million have estate giving totals that are more than

TABLE 2.1		
Estate Giving to Annual Giving Comparison		
Total Estate Value	**Giving Multiple**	**Estimated Estate Percent to Private Foundation**
< $100,000	0.15	0.0
$100,000– < $500,000	1.89	0.0
$500,000– < $1,000,000	3.73	4.2
$1,000,000– < $5,000,000	8.12	11.7
$5,000,000 +	11.65	43.7
TOTAL	5.07	23.6

Source: Russell N. James III, "The Presence and Timing of Charitable Estate Planning: New Research Findings." AFP International Conference, March 2009.

11 times greater than their annual giving total (see Table 2.1). These figures represent total estate values, total annual giving, and total estate gift value rather than figures related to giving to a particular organization. Since donors tend to support far fewer organizations with a planned gift compared to their annual fund donations, the multiple of planned gift to annual donation to a particular organization might be many times greater than the study has revealed.

The downside of targeting those individuals who have estates greater than $5 million is that they are often less likely to support existing nonprofit organizations and more likely to establish a private foundation with their estate gift. While this might be a perfectly fine development for the nonprofit sector as a whole, it is not particularly helpful to the development professional attempting to secure an estate gift for a particular, existing organization.[6]

When looking at donor ability, measured by estate size, the best prospects will often be those with larger estates. Those with larger estates tend to have the ability to make larger estate gifts. Those gifts will be even more meaningful relative to annual gift size for these donors. However, those with the largest estates will be more likely than those with smaller estates to establish a private foundation or donor-advised fund with their estate gift.

For many, the largest single investment they make in their lifetime will be their home. In our culture, we have been trained to think that senior citizens are financially needy. For example, a great many businesses offer senior citizen discounts. Seniors can receive discounted fares on public transportation, discounts at movie theaters, discounted museum memberships, and so on. While some of our seniors are indeed facing financial difficulty, a great many are doing quite well, certainly well enough to make a planned gift particularly when considering their home value. Consider just five simple economic facts:

1. People over the age of 50 control 70 percent of all privately held financial assets in the United States.

2. Of those 65 years or older, 81 percent own their own home, according to the U.S. Census Bureau in 2005.

3. Of those 55 to 64 years of age, 79.8 percent own their own home.

4. The average home value in 2000 was $96,442.

5. The median household net worth for those age 65 and older was $108,885 in 2000.[7]

While these figures will fluctuate with changes in the economy, one fact is consistent. The vast majority of older Americans have sufficient assets with which to make a charitable planned gift should they choose to do so.

A gift of appreciated stock would be another way for an individual to give. Because a gift of appreciated stock avoids the expense of capital gains tax and involves an element of planning on the part of the donor and often his advisors, many organizations would consider this a type of planned gift. A 2005 study found that 50.3 percent of U.S. households owned equities in some form with 34.7 percent owning equities outside of employer-sponsored retirement plans.[8] So, many Americans have the ability to make a gift of appreciated stock, particularly when the market is doing well but often even when it is not.

While various prospect rating and screening tools can provide information about wealth, they cannot provide information about a prospect's *perception* of her financial security and the needs of her family. It is important for development professionals to understand this distinction. It is one of the major shortcomings of prospect rating and screening technologies.

There are a variety of ways to gather wealth information. In the Information Age, it is relatively easy to gather information about major stock transactions, probable income levels, and other wealth indicators. One can research information about a single prospect or invest in a prospect screening that will append information to files on the complete database and then rate the prospects on a variety of factors. Some screening services also attempt to evaluate prospect loyalty in an effort to gauge propensity as well as ability.

Regardless of the prospect screening system used, organizations will need to do additional work to validate the information and further refine the results. For example, a university might screen 100,000 alumni and find it has 10,000 highly rated prospects, according to David Moore, Director of Planned Giving, Chapman University.[9] However, not all of those prospects will be accurately rated. Moore notes that many younger alumni still reside at home and that it is really their parents' residence that has been factored into the rating algorithm providing a misleading result. Ultimately, the screening will only be as good as the information in the organization's database. The more complete and accurate the information maintained, the more valid the results of a prospect screening.

Other information sources are completely free. An organization's own database may contain valuable information about a prospect's ability. For example, the prospect's data record might include employment history; a corporate attorney may have greater means than a teacher, for example. Another free source of information involves a simple search on the Internet that can reveal a great deal of information about a prospect including professional information, family members, and even real estate value. For example, if one knows a prospect's home address, it can be entered into

KEY CONCEPT

The value of prospect screening will be in direct proportion to the completeness and accuracy of the information in an organization's database.

the search field at www.zillow.com to produce a fact sheet about the home, report of current and historical real estate value, and photographs of the home and the surrounding neighborhood.

However, when gathering information about individuals, one must always remember that data sources have their limitations. *The Millionaire Next Door* was a book published in 1996 that revealed that many of the nation's millionaires do not look or live like stereotypical millionaires. Many might not be rated very highly by prospect screening services but might nevertheless possess great wealth. So, in addition to doing research, it is important to speak with people. Prospect screening groups can help answer questions about a prospect's ability to give. A *prospect screening group* is a volunteer committee assembled by an organization to help evaluate prospects and identify connections. While such groups can be very useful, it is important that, despite their volunteer status, they operate within the confines of professional fundraising ethical standards.

Ultimately, the best source for information about a prospect is the prospect himself. Talking directly with prospects will reveal a great deal of valuable information because the prospect will be talking about her favorite subject: herself and her family. If that conversation is face-to-face and takes place in the prospect's home, the development professional will be surrounded by useful clues.

While estate size is one critical measure of ability, other factors impact an individual's real or perceived capability to make an estate gift. One's perception of family need will impact estate giving. For example, a woman with an estate valued at just under $1 million decided that her children did not need an inheritance from her estate. So, she made arrangements for virtually her entire estate to be donated to a scholarship foundation through a charitable bequest. Another person, with a similar estate size, might have reached a different conclusion about the needs of her family and, therefore, might have given a much smaller amount or might have structured the gift differently. To understand a prospect's perceptions and family needs, one must talk with the prospect.

IN THE REAL WORLD

Best Source for Prospect Information: The Prospect

One story of trust and relationship building comes to mind as it relates to planned giving. Often, we look far and wide for opportunities to develop financial support for our organization, but sometimes the best donors are right under our noses or, in this case, right next door. It is important to share what we do with those that we work with and to develop internal relationships so that they might be comfortable in referring us to those that they know.

Several years ago, at another organization, a colleague told me of her neighbor who was an older man who had helped her while her husband was away. She repaid his generosity of time and assistance with a batch of chocolate chip cookies. They became good friends so much so that when she moved away, she continued to keep in touch and would visit with him from time to time. He would occasionally talk about his rental properties and would confide in her that as he was getting older (he was in his 70s), the maintenance and rental process were starting to be cumbersome.

She told me about her former neighbor and asked if I would like to speak with him. I called him and we discussed his situation and what bothered him about his current arrangement which included a C corporation. He also shared information about his other assets that included many more properties worth more than $20 million. He also talked about how his wife had died and how he had raised his two sons. We decided to meet, which led to several additional meetings and an eventual seven-figure gift.

In the end, the donor's trust for his neighbor, and her warm introduction and the opportunity to build on her relationship led to a planned gift. It was also a case of a millionaire living next door since they both lived in modest homes, and my colleague had no idea about her neighbor's wealth.

Source: Robert E. Wahlers, CFRE, Senior Director of Development and Gift Planning, Meridian Health Affiliated Foundations, 2009.

Factors That Impact Propensity

Just as there are many factors that impact an individual's ability to make a planned gift, there are also many factors that impact an individual's propensity to make such a gift. Some of these factors have to do with the individual's relationship with a particular nonprofit organization while other factors have nothing whatsoever to do with a particular organization or the nonprofit sector at-large. While someone might develop an interest in making a planned gift in general based on personal factors, the individual will almost always be influenced by his relationship with a particular nonprofit organization when making the decision where to give.

James has reported, "The most dominant factor in predicting charitable estate planning was not wealth, income, education, or even current giving or volunteering. By far, the dominant predictor of charitable estate planning was the absence of children. Among current donors over age 50 who had already completed a will or trust, only 9.8 percent of those with grandchildren included a charitable component. For similar donors without any offspring, 50 percent had a charitable estate plan."[10] Table 2.2 details the impact of offspring on gift planning.

James' findings speak to whether an individual will be likely to make a charitable estate plan in general. His findings do not address the likelihood of a particular donor making a planned gift to a particular organization. However, if one has identified a large prospect pool based on other factors such as giving history and other loyalty indicators, James' findings can help one refine that prospect pool based on additional personal factors related to the prospect.

TABLE 2.2

Share of Americans over age 50 with a Charitable Testamentary Provision			
Family Status	**All**	**Current Donors**	**All with Will/Trust**	**Current Donors with Will/Trust**
No offspring	19.1%	32.7%	36.4%	50.0%
Children only	7.3%	10.9%	13.0%	17.1%
Grandchildren	4.1%	6.8%	7.2%	9.8%

Source: Russell N. James III, "Causes and Correlates of Charitable Giving in Estate Planning: A Cross-Sectional and Longitudinal Examination of Older Adults," Association of Fundraising Professionals, July 2008, 2.

While the existence of children or grandchildren is the greatest indicator of overall propensity, other prospect characteristics will have an impact just as other prospect characteristics are meaningless in terms of propensity to make a bequest or trust commitment. Understanding which characteristics are important and the degree to which they are important will help one better refine the prospect pool. Table 2.3 looks at the impact on propensity of a number of individual characteristics.

While the absence of children is the most important characteristic determining propensity to make a charitable bequest or establish a charitable trust, a donor-centered approach may be able to help mitigate the impact of this factor as the gift-planning process shows prospects how a planned gift can protect the interests of children or grandchildren. A prospect's education level is another important personal trait. Those with a graduate degree have a greater propensity than those with only a high school diploma. The Center on Philanthropy

---

TABLE 2.3

Impact of Demographic and Financial Characteristics

Considering two otherwise demographically and financially identical senior adults, how does the likelihood of one of them having a charitable estate plan change if he or she:

Has a graduate degree (versus high school)	+4.2 percentage points
Gives at least $500 per year to charity	+3.1 percentage points
Volunteers regularly	+2.0 percentage points
Has a college degree (versus high school)	+1.7 percentage points
Has been diagnosed with a stroke	+1.7 percentage points
Is ten years older	+1.2 percentage points
Has been diagnosed with cancer	+0.8 percentage points
Is married (versus unmarried)	+0.7 percentage points
Has been diagnosed with a heart condition	+0.4 percentage points
Attends church at least once per month	+0.2 percentage points
Has $1 million more in assets	+0.1 percentage points
Has $100,000 per year more income	not significant
Is male (versus female)	not significant
Has only children (versus no offspring)	−2.8 percentage points
Has grandchildren (versus no offspring)	−10.5 percentage points

Source: Russell N. James III, "Causes and Correlates of Charitable Giving in Estate Planning: A Cross-Sectional and Longitudinal Examination of Older Adults," Association of Fundraising Professionals, July 2008, 3.

found that those with at least a bachelor's degree were more likely to have already made a charitable bequest commitment (9 percent) and, if they have not done so, are more likely to consider such a gift (39 percent).

If a prospect has a positive feeling toward the nonprofit sector as demonstrated by donating more than $500 a year or by volunteering, he or she will have a greater propensity to make a planned gift. Two factors that have little or no impact on propensity are an estate value over $1 million or an annual income over $100,000 (refer back to Table 2.3).

While an estate valued at $1 million or more, or an annual income of more than $100,000 may not impact propensity, such factors may have a substantial impact on ability. Furthermore, estate value will have an impact on which planned gift vehicle a donor may choose. Therefore, estate value and income remain important parts of the planned giving equation.[11]

Another propensity factor is age of the prospect. The Center on Philanthropy at Indiana University has discovered that "people with a charity named in their will tended to be between 40 and 50 years of age."[12] Those most likely to consider a charitable bequest are between the ages of 40 and 60. The NCPG Donor Survey found the average age when an individual names a charity in his or her will to be 49. One reason that bequest donors may be younger than many have previously thought is that this is the age when many individuals first draft a will. While this means that those as young as their 40s should be considered planned giving prospects, they may not necessarily qualify as priority prospects. An older prospect may have a lower propensity to give, but a commitment made by a much older individual is far more likely to be realized much sooner than a similar commitment from a much younger donor.

Some development professionals are reluctant to approach younger prospects for a revocable planned gift for fear that, over the following decades, the individual will change his mind. This fear is unfounded. By far the most common revocable type of planned gift is the bequest. The Stelter Company discovered that once a donor puts a charity in his or her will, the charity is almost never removed. Stelter reports:

KEY CONCEPT

Appeal to prospects on *their* schedules. When a prospect chooses to draft his or her first will or when a prospect chooses to update a will, that is when an organization really wants the prospect to think about a charitable bequest.

We cannot over-emphasize the importance of the data about the staying power of Bequests. Very few—less than one in 10—who have bequests in their wills say they have ever removed a nonprofit from their plans. This reinforces the urgency of working with younger givers to put a plan in place. At a younger age, they probably have fewer nonprofits they would want to honor with a legacy gift; the competition is likely greater later in life. So, getting in the door early makes logical sense.[13]

Age is also an important factor for CGAs. Most nonprofit organizations target prospects as young as ages 60 to 65 while some will go a bit younger to offer deferred CGAs. The minimum age targeting for CGAs is more a function of tax issues and organizational policy than actual motivation of the donor. This is a gift for older individuals who are interested in receiving a regular income – for themselves, a spouse, or other loved one – as a result of their contribution.

For charitable remainder uni-trusts (CRUT), the best prospects are people with an optimistic view of future asset growth and enough time to benefit from it. A CRUT is generally a gift planning vehicle chosen by those with a 15-year life expectancy or more. Based on actuarial tables, that would mean prospects 72 years of age or younger. However, people operate on their own life expectancy estimates and, therefore, an older prospect might still be interested, suggests Scott R.P. Janney, President of PlannedGiving.com and Director of Planned Giving at Main Line Health[14].

For charitable lead annuity trusts (CLAT), the age of the donor is somewhat less relevant than is the age of the prospect's children. The unique tax implications associated with a CLAT make it of particular interest to those with children 35 to 55 years of age, Janney recommends.

Other gift-planning vehicles are less age dependent. When age is a factor, in addition to impacting propensity to give, it will also impact donor motivation as people of various generations have different inspirations for giving.

British playwright David Hare observed the cultural changes resulting from enhancements in life expectancy. Commenting on his play "The Breath of Life," he wrote:

> One of my immediate impulses was to express how vital the lives of older people have become. Thanks to modern medicine and all that milk we drank after the Second World War, there's almost a new category of life in the West. You can no longer call it middle age, and you certainly can't call it old age. It's something in between—a period when men and women can look back and see the transit of what used to be a whole lifetime . . . and yet that backward view is from the advantage of an actuarial hope of another 20 years to come.[15]

As individuals live longer, bequest, CGA, and trust philanthropic options help donors overcome their own economic concerns and allow these individuals to become major donors when they might not be able to or feel comfortable enough to do so with current dollars.

Gender can sometimes be a propensity factor. In general, men and women are just as likely to make a charitable bequest, according to James.[16] However, men and women do have preferences when it comes to the types of nonprofit organizations they choose to support. Table 2.4 illustrates this point based on an examination of estate tax returns filed for people who died in 2001.

Another consideration that might lead one to prioritize female prospects over male is the fact that women live longer and, therefore, are more likely to be the surviving spouse; however, this gap is beginning to close. According to research at Harvard Medical School by Thomas T. Perls, and Ruth C. Fretts, "It is primarily the reduction in male mortality, as opposed to the increase in female mortality, that is narrowing this gender gap. In general, the higher a nation's level of social and economic development, the greater the life expectancy for both men and women and the greater the convergence in the two figures."[17] At the very least, when working with a married

TABLE 2.4			
Gender Preferences in Bequest Giving (2001)			
Type of Charity	**Preferred by Women**	**Preferred by Men**	**Preferred Equally by Women and Men**
Environment	X		
Health	X		
Human services	X		
Religion	X		
Art			X
International affairs			X
Other			X
Education		X	
Public/Society benefit		X	
Source: The Center on Philanthropy at Indiana University. *Giving USA 2006*			

couple, the development professional will want to take this issue into account when discussing the options for structuring the gift.

The development professional will also want to include both parties in all discussions pertaining to bequest giving. Margaret May Damen, co-author of *Women, Wealth and Giving* and President and Founder of The Institute For Women and Wealth, states that "women make 84 percent of all philanthropic decisions."[18] This is especially relevant for Boom Generation women, many of whom are business owners who earn and invest a significant amount of the family's net worth.

A study by the Fidelity Charitable Gift Fund offers another reason to involve women in gift planning discussions and to perhaps even prioritize female prospects, "High-income women (those with an annual household income of $150,000 or more) demonstrate a high level of sophistication in their giving by seeking expert advice and then making use of innovative giving vehicles such as donor-advised funds and charitable remainder trusts."[19] In 2008, 7 percent of high-income women made charitable gifts using securities while only 3 percent of high-income men did so. Among high-income women, 16 percent have or use a donor-advised fund, charitable remainder trust, or private foundation while only 10 percent of high-income men do so.

Factors That Impact Social Capital

"The core idea of social capital theory is that social networks have value . . . social capital refers to connections among individuals—social networks and the norms of reciprocity and trustworthiness that arise from them,"[20] according to Robert Putnam, a professor at Harvard University. The more engaged an individual is with his community, the more likely he is to volunteer and contribute money to nonprofit organizations. The more points of connection there are between an individual and a particular nonprofit organization, the more likely that individual is to give, give often, and give generously to that organization. Furthermore, the very act of giving builds additional social capital.

One group of supporters for an organization that have obviously high levels of social capital are the members of an organization's governing board. There are other common points of contact including volunteers, staff, former board members, former staff, beneficiaries of service, family members of those who have received services, long-standing members, and frequent annual fund donors. Development professionals should look at these and other factors to help evaluate the level of social capital a prospect has. One word of caution: While event attendees who are engaged with an organization in many other ways may be good planned giving prospects, those whose only point of contact with an organization is that they have attended an event are generally not very good prospects for planned giving. However, they are good prospects for further cultivation and involvement, possibly someday resulting in their transition into viable planned giving prospects.

"More important than wealth, education, community size, age, family status, and employment, however, by far the most consistent predictor of giving time and money is involvement in community life," Putnam finds.[21] The challenge for development professionals is to identify the ways in which prospects engage with the community at-large as well as the organization in-particular. It also means that development professionals must keep meticulous records about each donor and prospect. Such detailed notes will help prioritize prospects and will help the development professional build rapport with prospects.

Good fundraising often means good friend-raising. Get to know your prospects and what interests them.

Collecting information about the various ways in which a prospect is engaged in the community is difficult. News sources, including the local newspaper's "society page," can supply some information. Visiting other nonprofit organizations in the community to read their donor wall, or honor roll of contributors in their printed program is another way to gather information. Collecting and reviewing annual reports from other nonprofit organizations will provide information about board service and individuals donating. Reviewing an organization's Federal Form 990 at www.guidestar.org will provide free information about a nonprofit organization's major donors and board members. Publicly held companies often include biographies of their corporate board members in their annual reports or post the information at their web sites. Visiting the prospect is another way to learn more. Donors and prospects will generally be more than happy to discuss their various interests. If visiting in someone's home, one can look for awards, books, and other items on display that can provide clues to how the individual engages with the community and what other organizations they might support. In addition, clues will be found that will help gauge the individual's ability. When such information is discovered, one should make sure it becomes part of the individual's record back at the office. One should be sure to take good notes and then enter the information immediately upon returning to the office while the information is still fresh and easier to recall. While it might be awkward to take notes during a meeting, one should write down notations about the meeting as soon after the meeting as possible. For example, after visiting with a prospect, one can drive down the road, pull into a parking lot or go into a coffee shop, and write down everything that is relevant or enter the information into a laptop computer.

KEY CONCEPT

When meeting with a prospective donor, try to visit him in his home rather than at a restaurant or at your office. The prospect will feel more comfortable and you will have access to more personal insights.

Whenever a donor or prospect engages with one's organization, the organization should note that in the individual's record. When staff outside of the development office engage a donor or prospect, they should let the development office know (i.e., when inviting prospects to a lecture, the development office should be notified who will be attending). The volunteer coordinator for an organization should share the list of volunteers with the development office. The more points of contact the organization has with prospects, the more likely they will be to give and give generously. Involvement builds the social capital that leads to philanthropy. When attempting to prioritize prospects, evaluating social capital is important. However, that evaluation will only be as good as the information that has been gathered.

Beyond gathering information about how donors and prospects engage with the community and one's organization, it is essential that the development office find ways to proactively involve these individuals in ways that are meaningful to the donors and prospects. By enhancing the quantity and quality of contact, social capital will be enhanced.

To build social capital, to cultivate support, donors and prospects should be given opportunities to become involved. Depending on the organization, points of engagement might include volunteer opportunities, invitations to nonfundraising events like lectures, tours of the facility, special reports about mission fulfillment, speaking opportunities, a meet-and-greet with performers, and so forth.

The more social capital that is developed, the more likely an individual is to support a given organization and to do so generously. The more a prospect learns about the organization, how it fulfills its mission, how efficiently it is

IN THE REAL WORLD

A Tour That's Worth a Thousand Acres

A hospital in the rural Pacific Northwest held an event to thank individuals who had made a planned gift commitment as well as to express appreciation to those seriously considering such support. The event involved a tour of the facilities, including the pediatric services wing, followed by lunch. During the lunch, an elderly gentleman stood up and said that he was very impressed. He was familiar with the hospital, the only one in town. But, neither he nor his wife was familiar with the pediatric services wing. The gentleman told those gathered that he and his wife have no children themselves. However, during the tour of the pediatric services wing, they realized that the community's children were their children. He went on to announce that he and his wife would be leaving their entire estate, consisting of a rather large farm (even if not a thousand acres), to the hospital for the benefit of the pediatric services wing. If the couple had not been given the opportunity to meet staff, see those benefiting from the services, and better understand how the hospital is fulfilling its mission, they may very well have made a much less generous commitment.

run, who staffs it, who is served by it, the more she will care. Also, more trust will be established.

Trust is vital to the philanthropic process. When people trust an organization, they are more likely to give to it and, with even greater trust, they are more likely to give more. A study conducted by researchers at the Henley Management College in the United Kingdom found that "there would appear to be a relationship between trust and a propensity to donate."[22] Furthermore, "there is some indication here that a relationship does exist between trust and amount donated, comparatively little increases in the former having a marked impact on the latter."[23] Independent Sector conducted a study in 2001 and found that individuals who have a high confidence in charities and believe in their honesty and ethics gave about 50 percent more to charity than those not holding either opinion.[24] Trust allows an organization to acquire more donors, secure larger gifts, and maintain those commitments. The ability to maintain commitments is critical in the planned giving process as many types of such gifts are revocable.

Just as a high level of trust can lead to greater philanthropy, a crisis in trust can have a severely negative effect on philanthropy. In Scotland in May 2003, *The Sunday Mail* newspaper published a report highly critical of a professional fundraising company working with a breast cancer research charity. The report sent a shockwave through Scotland, even impacting organizations that had never contracted the fundraising company at the center of the controversy. Some unrelated cancer charities saw contributions drop as much as 30 percent in the months following the controversy.[25]

To build trust and enhance social capital, nonprofit organizations must embrace the highest ethical standards in all facets of work. Furthermore, organizations should let donors and prospects know about these standards. Making *The Donor Bill of Rights* available to donors, creating and promoting a privacy policy, and exercising strong stewardship of gifts are just a few of the things that organizations can do to secure generous support for their own organizations and inspire greater confidence in the nonprofit sector as a whole.

Pros and Cons of Information

Information is critical for the success of any development effort. For the philanthropic planning process, information will help one effectively identify and prioritize prospects. Good information will help the planned giving professional develop roadmaps for conversations with prospects. Having good database software will help store important information in a retrievable, useable fashion. Embracing a privacy policy and adhering to prospect research and fundraising ethics codes will help protect that information and give donors and prospects greater comfort.

One will also want to develop policies to govern what types of information will be collected and recorded. Prospects have the right to inspect their file. A prospect should never be horrified by what they find in their file. For example, if a prospect screening group reveals that a prospect is in the middle of a messy divorce, such information is probably relevant but the information should be noted in neutral terms and only with the minimal relevant information recorded and the more personal details left out.

Good information is particularly important to have in preparation for a face-to-face meeting with a prospect. With traditional planned gift marketing, much of the information emphasis is on the organization, its mission, needs, planned giving products, and giving instruments. With donor-centered marketing, gift planning officers are certainly expected to know about mission, needs, products and instruments, but they are also expected to know a great deal more about prospects beyond the basics in order to better understand the prospect. With access to solid information about prospects, volunteers and staff will be much more comfortable when meeting with prospects. They will have greater confidence and, therefore, be even more likely to actually arrange the meeting. At the meeting, they will be much better equipped to meet the needs of the prospect and help him develop a meaningful philanthropic plan.

While one must gather valuable facts about a prospect, one should avoid information pollution, a situation where so much worthless data is gathered that it becomes difficult to recognize the important details. The other pitfall to avoid is information paralysis, a situation where one delays and delays visits with prospects for fear of not having some mythical, elusive piece of data. The keys to successfully using information are to gather what will be useful, store it so it can be easily retrieved, protect it, add to it but, above all else, actually use it.

Basic Prospect Data

When preparing for a meeting with a prospective donor, one would ideally have a wealth of information about the prospect. At an absolute minimum, one should be prepared with the following information:

- Accurate and complete contact information.
- Age.
- Gender.

- Affiliation with the organization including activities.

- Donor history.

- Marital status.

- Offspring status.

- Basic financial information such as real estate value.

During meetings with a prospect, one will want to maximize the opportunity to gather additional information about the prospect including:

- Employment status.

- Work history.

- Additional financial information.

- Why does the individual support the organization?

- What other organizations does the individual support and why?

- Who are the prospect's key influencers?

- What are the prospect's financial goals?

- What are the needs of other beneficiaries, if any?

- What are the prospect's philanthropic aspirations?

- What assets are most logical to use for a gift?

- When is the gift most likely to be made?

With the additional information in hand, one can more accurately rate the prospect, better determine the appropriate next steps with the prospect, and develop a philanthropic plan with the prospect and her advisors that will meet the needs of the prospect while meeting a need for the organization.

KEY CONCEPT

If there is something you need to know when speaking with prospects, ask them. The more they trust you, the more they will reveal.

Prospect Rating

While prospect screening and rating services can supply useful insights, no single system is perfect. Electronic screenings are ultimately only as good as the information an organization has in its database or can append to it. A number of pieces of information are publicly available and can be electronically appended to a database with varying degrees of accuracy (i.e., addresses, telephone numbers, and age). By surveying prospects—by mail, e-mail, or telephone—a virtually unlimited amount of information can be gathered.

Unfortunately, even when screening a database full of facts, electronic screening systems cannot provide information about how an individual perceives her financial security, or how an individual feels about the needs of his loved ones. Another limitation is that electronic screening services either do not take into account offspring status or cannot take this into account when such data is absent from the database. As noted earlier, the number one determinant factor for bequest and trust giving is the absence of offspring. An electronic screening cannot effectively measure social capital in general or loyalty to a particular organization though some services do make an attempt at the latter. Evaluating propensity is an art form that has yet to rise to the level of science.

Roger Ellison, Vice President for Planned Giving at West Texas Rehabilitation Center Foundation, has developed a simple chart that takes into account the relationship between generosity (total giving) and passion (number of gifts) (rogerellison.com). While other forms of "generosity" can be incorporated into an evaluation of a prospect (i.e., volunteer hours), Ellison provides an acceptable, basic unit of measure. Likewise, there are other factors that could indicate "passion," but Ellison again provides an acceptable basic measure (see Table 2.5). Ellison notes:

> The theory behind this chart and its process is that those who give the most gifts are more likely to be planned giving prospects, and that the numbered squares create a priority ranking of which donors should be "worked" first. As an example, those

TABLE 2.5				
Passion–Generosity Index				
Generosity—				
Total Giving	$10,000 or more	9	5	1
	$5,000–$9,999	10	6	2
	$1,000–$4,999	11	7	3
	$1–$999	12	8	4
		1–24 gifts	25–49 gifts	50 or more gifts
		Passion—Total Number of Gifts		

donors who fall in the square numbered 4, having given 50 or more gifts with only a total value between $1 and $999 during the period reviewed, are generally a greater priority than those in square 9 who have given a smaller number of gifts (somewhere between 1 and 24 gifts) though for a greater total value (over $10,000) during that same time period. Every gift is an act of passion; the greater the number of gifts given, the greater the acts of passion toward that charity. Passion trumps generosity. . . . Obviously, the numbers on either axis can be altered to fit a particular charity's donor characteristics. Although rudimentary, this simple analysis can be very helpful to a planned giving program with limited resources, to a larger charity with a higher degree of analytical data available on a large number of donors, as well as in other circumstances. And while the numbering from 1 through 12 suggests a rather linear process of cultivation, reality probably suggests this is merely a good guide rather than a requirement.[26]

The key for nonprofit organizations is to gather useful data and to use it, with the benefit of electronic screening information or not, to prioritize prospects. Higher priority prospects will receive greater attention. However, all prospects should be part of an education, cultivation, and ask process in one form or another.

When Brian Sagrestano, President of Gift Planning Development, works with charities, he recommends that they consider their prospects as being part of one of four broad groups.[27] By identifying which group a prospect is a member of, the development professional will know how to best work with that prospect. The first group is comprised of principal gift donors. For this group, it is important to integrate gift planning into all conversations, since these individuals will benefit the most from complex, structured current gifts and future gifts. Representatives from the charity should already be talking face-to-face with all of these donors and prospects, so gift planning can simply be incorporated as one of the talking points.

The second group is made up of major gift donors. Like the people in the first group, these individuals should also be having face-to-face contact with a development professional. Gift planning should be part of the conversation. At a minimum, this should involve a conversation about bequests or retirement plan designations. In organizations that have both major gift officers and planned giving officers, Sagrestano suggests encouraging or, when possible, requiring major gift officers to ask a percentage of their assigned prospects to consider a planned gift each year. Over a period of five to seven years, that percentage should equal 100 percent of the prospects in a major gift officer's pool.

The third prospect group includes regular, consistent annual fund donors, and those who have already set up planned gifts. These are the best "gift planning" prospects. This is where prospect screening can make a particularly positive difference, either internally or utilizing a screening service. Most charities cannot afford to mail to everyone on their database even though everyone is a viable prospect for planned giving. Organizations need to focus limited resources where they will do the most good, targeting those most likely to respond. Creating this general priority list does two things: (1) it creates a group of people to send gift planning information to on a regular basis as part of an education and cultivation effort, and (2) it gives gift planning officers and major gift officers a list of prospects to go see as "filler" when they are out seeing their identified special prospects.

The fourth group of prospects is "everyone else." Again, since everyone is a viable gift planning prospect, messages must be ubiquitous, though delivered cost effectively. Planned gift messaging should be integrated into virtually all communications from an organization. For example, in an organization's general newsletter, an article might describe services provided by the organization; the article can include a line or two about how a bequest gift provided funding for the endeavor. The key is to, at very little or no cost, find ways to deliver the gift planning message to everyone so that those not touched with planned giving mailings or personal visits may still learn about and have the opportunity to express their interest in gift planning.

Summary

Everyone is a planned giving prospect. However, most organizations lack the staff and budget resources to involve all constituents in the gift planning process. So, while providing information to as many people as possible, development professionals will want to prioritize their planned gift prospects to determine where the focus should be placed.

There is no simple way to identify quality planned gift prospects. While there are a number of prospect rating and research services in the marketplace, none of them can identify all of an organization's potential planned gift donors. However, many of these services can provide useful information that can help development professionals segment and prioritize prospects.

With information provided by outside services, internal resources, and the prospects themselves, development professionals will be able to consider a prospect's ability, propensity to give, and level of social capital. By understanding these three broad factors, development professionals will be able to determine which prospects have the greatest potential of making a planned gift and what type of planned gift might be most appropriate.

In the process of gathering information about prospects, organizations must take care to collect only the data that is necessary, store the material in a usable and efficient fashion, and ensure that all information is protected to guarantee the privacy of the prospect. Good information will help the organization prioritize prospects and then more effectively engage individual prospects in meaningful conversations.

Exercises

- Nationally, 5.3 percent of Americans over the age of 50 have made a charitable bequest commitment. By examining your own database, you can determine how well your organization is doing compared with the national figure. What percentage of *all individuals* in your database have made a bequest commitment to your organization? What percentage of your *donors* have made a bequest commitment?

- Once you have a sense of the percentage of individuals in your database who have made a bequest commitment to your organization, you are ready to look at the average bequest value (ABV) for those commitments. Take the total known dollar value for all bequest commitments and divide that by the total number of bequest commitments with an expressed value. This will give you the average bequest value. To arrive at a more accurate number, you may want to eliminate the lowest and highest bequest values from the calculation of the average or you may want to consider the median figure rather than the average.

- After you have calculated your organization's ABV, you are ready to use the Planned Gift Program Potential Worksheet in Appendix A to calculate your organization's potential. While this calculation will not provide you with information concerning overall gift planning potential, it will give you valuable insight about the potential for the most popular form of planned giving for your organization.

- You cannot analyze information you do not have. Examine your organization's database to determine what types of information are available. Look elsewhere within your organization to see what information has been collected and whether it can and should supplement your development records. For instance, incorporate your organization's event attendee and volunteer information into your development database. Look for those critical other points of contact.

- To begin to understand how many planned giving prospects you might have, you will want to run a series of queries to your database: How many individuals have given five times or more in the past seven years? How many individuals have given seven or more times in the past 10 years?

- Those most likely to make a planned gift to your organization are those closest to the organization. How many of your board members have made a planned gift commitment? If few have done so, you have some potential and some work to do. If many have, then you have a good group of committed individuals who can help you spread the word and who are good prospects for another gift.

CHAPTER 3

Identify What Motivates Planned Gift Donors

Motivation is the art of getting people to do what you want them to do because they want to do it.

—*Dwight D. Eisenhower*

After reading this chapter, you will be able to:

- Distinguish between manipulation, motivation, and inspiration.
- Recognize what motivates or inspires donors to give generally.
- Describe the key motivators for a donor to make a planned gift.
- Understand what demotivates prospects and donors.

To inspire a prospective donor to make a planned gift contribution, development professionals must understand what motivates donors in general as well as what drives specific individuals. Furthermore, development professionals must understand what demotivates people so that those stimuli can be avoided. Donor-centered planned gift marketing involves showing prospective donors how their wishes and aspirations can be fulfilled through the philanthropic support of an organization they care about.

Manipulation versus Motivation versus Inspiration

Important differences exist among manipulation, motivation, and inspiration. Manipulation is the art of using insidious and sometimes unfair means to serve one's own purposes. This is antithetical to donor-centered marketing. Ethically run nonprofit organizations do not rely on manipulation to trick people into giving. Instead, well-run organizations develop long-term relationships with supporters based on integrity and respect. When the conversation turns to gift planning, these organizations judiciously learn what might inspire their prospects, and work to encourage giving, while also keeping the donor's best interests at the forefront of discussions; furthermore, these ethical organizations recommend that prospects and donors seek third-party financial and legal counsel.

Motives are needs or desires that cause people to act. The motives that move one to act are deeply personal and developed over a lifetime. Development professionals cannot truly motivate prospects. And, if they could, it might result in manipulation not motivation. Motives reside deep within the mind and heart of the individual. While development professionals should strive to understand the motives of donors and prospects as a group, as well as those of individual prospects and donors, this should be done so that these professionals can help meet the needs of donors and prospects and help them to fulfill their philanthropic aspirations. By understanding donors and prospects, an organization will be better able to inspire support.

Inspiring donors and prospects means encouraging them to take a desired action, ultimately supporting the organization in a variety of ways that also meet the donor's needs and fulfill his own philanthropic goals. Organizations inspire individuals when they treat donors and prospects the way these people want to be treated, and share information with them that is meaningful and relevant to them on a timely basis.

Manipulation is cheating. Motivation is something that exists within the donor and prospect. By contrast, inspiration involves understanding the donor's motivations and making a clear and compelling case for how one's organization can best help the donor achieve his philanthropic objectives.

What People Want

To understand what people want is to begin to understand what motivates them. With this knowledge, development professionals can more effectively inspire prospects to give and give more than they otherwise would. Jay Conrad Levinson, author of *Guerrilla Marketing Excellence*, developed a list for the business world of what customers really want from those with whom they do business.[1] Much of that list, in no particular order, can easily be adapted to the nonprofit sector where it is extremely relevant and helpful in understanding the motivations that impact giving:

Donors give if the organization is credible and will not give if it is not. Annual fund donors can evaluate trustworthiness, both the development professional's and the organization's, on an annual basis. Bequest donors, for example, do not have that luxury at the point the gift is realized. Those who make a substantial irrevocable, life-income gift cannot change their minds if the organization disappoints them down the road. Before a prospect makes a long-term investment in an organization, they will need to trust it and its representatives.

Donors give because of the promises the development professional makes. One should always under-promise and over-deliver. Donors and prospects are listening. One should never make promises lightly. Donors will hold development professionals to their promises and make them pay dearly if they break them.

Donors give to the development professional, her colleagues, employees, and stewardship team. Organizations are nothing more than an assembly of people. People give to people. If they like and respect the staff and volunteers they encounter, they will be more likely to give, keep giving, and give more. This means that everyone in the organization is part of the development effort. For example, an organization's receptionist is often the first personal contact a donor or prospect will have with the organization. If the receptionist actually answers the call, responds professionally and courteously, and effectively assists the caller, that person will have a positive impression of the organization. If the caller has a terrible experience, the actual development professional will have quite a hole to dig out of.

Donors give to neatness. If the development professional or his offices are messy, prospects will fear that the organization is unstable or unprofessional. Sloppiness erodes trust. Neatness counts.

Donors give to honesty. Lie once to a donor or prospect and the relationship is destroyed. Honesty is the cornerstone of trustworthiness. Relationships cannot develop and flourish without it. If a certain gift vehicle is not right for the prospect, the planned giving professional should tell her and suggest a more appropriate option even if it means securing a smaller gift. It should be considered an investment in the relationship and one's reputation.

Donors give to success and security. If one begs for money to keep the lights on, prospects will likely think the organization does not have much of a future. People do not want to throw money into a black hole. People give to successful organizations that can effectively fulfill their missions. Planned giving donors want to know that the organization will be able to fulfill its obligations regarding the gift and that the gift will be well invested and utilized in the future.

Donors give because of one's guarantees, one's reputation, and the organization's good name. This is related to, but goes beyond, trustworthiness and keeping promises. Prospects will consider their own direct experience with the development professional and the organization. An organization's reputation must be carefully cultivated through professional behavior and appropriate assurances. Prospects will also consider what others say about the organization. A good reputation must be carefully developed and fiercely defended. In the Information Age, reputations are made over time but can be destroyed quickly.

Donors give when they see others accepting and giving to an organization. Most donors do not want to feel they are blazing a new trail. If others are seen giving to an organization, thereby endorsing it, prospects will be more likely to jump on the bandwagon.

Donors give for the tangible and intangible benefits they receive. A planned gift donor cares much less about the features associated with giving and much more about the benefits they or their loved ones will receive. For example, someone who gives a charitable gift annuity (CGA) is less concerned about the technical and legal particulars of the gift vehicle and are much more interested in the income this will provide in order to meet retirement needs. Sometimes, the primary benefit a donor will care about will simply be the good feeling she will receive by being able to make a major gift commitment that would not otherwise have been possible with current dollars.

Donors give when the risk is minimal or nonexistent. Prospects hate risk. During the great recession of 2009-10, people have seen some of the world's largest, most solid companies and financial institutions collapse. It is well known that many nonprofit organizations were invested heavily in what turned out to be risky investments, and that they incurred great losses during this time. Some institutions even entrusted and lost virtually all their investments with a shady investment manager whose multibillion dollar empire of lies came crashing down very publicly. This served to erode the public's confidence in institutions. If someone is being asked to make a life-income gift, the organization will have to provide the prospect with evidence of the organization's sound fiscal management and ability to deliver on its commitments. Individuals do not want to risk their own financial futures, or those of their loved ones, nor see their philanthropic goals subverted when they make a donation.

Donors give because the development professional offers solutions to their problems. Solve a prospect's problem, and they will be much more willing to help solve the organization's problem. If a donor holds appreciated stock and faces a significant capital gains tax burden, one can show the donor how making a gift of appreciated stock instead of a cash gift can avoid the tax expense. The donor can then make a larger gift that "costs" the same as the smaller cash gift or make a stock gift at a lower cost than a cash donation.

Donors give to create hope for themselves and their loved ones. People want to help secure a better future for themselves and those they love. Show people how their gift can help achieve a brighter future. For example, Susan G. Komen for the Cure markets hope. There is still no cure for breast cancer, but Komen has given millions of women hope. When Komen was founded in 1982, the five-year survival rate, when caught early before the cancer spread beyond the breast, was 74 percent; it is now 98 percent. The annual government funding for breast cancer research, treatment, and prevention totaled just $30 million in

IN THE REAL WORLD

Avoid the Tax Collector

A member of the board of a scholarship foundation was approached at a cultivation event by a modest donor who wanted to give a $5,000 cash gift. The board member thanked the donor but asked, "Do you own any appreciated stock?" The donor was a bit puzzled by the question, but replied, "Yes, I do. Why do you ask?" The board member then explained that if the donor contributed appreciated stock valued at $5,000, rather than cash, she could avoid the capital gains tax, thereby resulting in a savings. The donor replied, "I can avoid giving my money to the government, by giving the foundation stock? That's a great idea! And, since I really don't need the money, why don't I just increase my gift by the amount I'll save in taxes?" She did exactly that. However, her generosity did not end there. She was so moved by the work of the foundation and the good advice she had received that allowed her to avoid some capital gains tax that she consulted with her family and her advisors eventually giving over $15,000 to create a namesake scholarship fund.

1982 and has now increased to $900 million. Komen has helped women live longer with this terrible disease and, through research funding and advocacy, is giving women legitimate hope that a cure will be found sooner rather than later.

Donors give based on the organization's marketing. Prospects will not give unless they understand what the organization does, who it serves, and how well it delivers its services. Prospects also need to know that the planned giving professional can help them with their gift planning, and they need to understand how a planned gift can help them and their loved ones. Marketing is the way organizations deliver those messages. It is the way organizations educate, cultivate, ask for support, and steward supporters.

Donors give to an organization's identity as conveyed by its marketing. An organization is its marketing. Perception is reality. Use marketing to educate prospects. Work with colleagues throughout the organization to make sure that the organization's overall marketing message is effective and that the development messages are consistent with the overall marketing impression.

Donors give to brand name organizations over unknown groups. When it comes to planned giving, people will certainly be more willing to support a solid, brand name organization rather than a new, nearly unheard of charity. This links back to trustworthiness. Planned gift donors are long-term supporters. They give to organizations they trust.

Donors give to believable claims, not just honest ones. It is essential for organizations to be honest. But, honesty is not enough. An organization's claims must be believable. For example, in its marketing, a hospital might rightfully claim to have the region's greatest recovery rate for stroke cases. However, prospects may or may not actually believe the extreme claim. If the hospital quotes from an independent rating service as part of its claim or includes individual testimonials, the claim will be more believable.

Donors give when it is convenient for them to do so. People enjoy convenience in all aspects of their lives. Show prospects respect by making it easy for them to support the organization. If someone is interested in learning more about planned giving, how many buttons do they need to click from the organization's home page before he finds the gift planning page? If they do not feel like reading, can they easily find a telephone number to call for more information? Is the telephone number for an office or a person? Think of all the possible obstacles to giving and then work systematically to get rid of those in your power to eliminate.

Donors give to clarity. Keep all messages clear and simple. Prospects who are confused will seldom take the time to do the research for answers. Instead, their attention will be captured by another organization. The average newspaper is written on a sixth-grade reading level. It is not that the average newspaper reader has poor reading skills. Instead, newspapers make it easy for readers to quickly and easily get information with minimal effort. Do not make prospects work hard to figure out what the organization is trying to communicate. If one does make it difficult, prospects will either not take the time to figure it out, will not figure it out, or will be unfairly made to feel unintelligent.

Donors give to the consistency they have seen the organization exhibit. Consistency is a key element of trust. If an organization keeps changing its mission, communicates sporadically, is friendly then cold, a prospect's confidence in the organization will be shaken. If an organization is seen to be consistent over time, donors will develop the belief that this behavior will continue into the future after they are no longer able to monitor the organization. Consistency leads to predictability which leads to trust.

Donors give to certainty. Like consistency, donors seek certainty. They do not like wishy-washy, noncommittal responses to inquiries. They do not like vagueness. They want to know what they can expect today and tomorrow.

Donors give when their own ideas, personality, and values are respected. Never argue with a donor. Even if the development professional proves he is in the right, the donor will feel challenged and diminished. One does not always need to agree with donors and prospects, but one must show them respect. If you are open to them, they will reciprocate and be open to you and the organization's ideas.

IN THE REAL WORLD

Listen to Prospects, They Will Tell You What Matters

When I first arrived at the small liberal arts college in New England, I was introduced to an alumni couple by the very capable Director of Major Gifts. We were in the quiet phase of a major campaign and various staff had been working with this couple for a couple of years trying to convince them of the benefits of a charitable remainder trust (CRT) in making a magnificent gift to the college. They had shown them the PG Calc illustrations of the tax, income, and estate benefits, and were at a loss as to how to reach them. Beyond the illustration, the focus had been on the needs of the college.

I was very fortunate to hit it off with both of them right away. It helped that I shared their rather conservative political leanings. Over the next several years, I visited them regularly, building an honest relationship with them. I would keep them up to date about happenings on campus and plans for the future but, more important, I listened to them. I would correct their perceptions, supporting the position of the college when I felt they were off base, but I would also agree with them when I thought they had a point. While they were thrilled with the steady and rapid improvement in the quality of the education provided by their school as well as the improved quality of the student body, they were upset by what they saw as the steady leftward lean of the institution.

I invited them to events on campus and off where they could meet and talk with both faculty and senior administrators. As our relationship developed, we never lost sight of my role with the college. And, during this time, it became clear that what they wanted to do was make a gift that in some small way they could feel was helping to balance what they saw as the liberal leanings on campus.

I spoke to my Vice President and to the President about this (the potential gift was large enough), and we identified two possibilities. The first was that they endow a chair in constitutional law and a second chair in history. These would be filled by incumbents.

The last time I met with them before they made their commitment to the campaign, we cracked open a very good bottle of single malt whisky that I had brought as a thank-you for the dinner on their boat. Because of the relationship we had developed, I was able to speak frankly and finally said, "You know, we've been dancing around the idea of your gift for a few years now. I think it's time to fish or cut bait. I have a couple of ideas that I think would accomplish your goals, and I'd like you to think seriously about them." I proceeded to tell them about the two options and invite them to campus to meet these two faculty members. The ideas intrigued them and they agreed to come to campus.

After meeting alone with both faculty members, I asked them what they thought. They had been very impressed with both faculty members. In the end, they endowed the first chair for a junior faculty member in constitutional law with an outright gift of around $350,000 and the remainder of the $1.25 million gift for the chair was contributed through a charitable remainder uni-trust (CRUT). In addition, they were so taken with the history professor that they contributed an additional $200,000 to establish an endowed research fund for her.

I believe this gift happened because we at the college put the focus on the needs of the donors and were sensitive to the issue that was most important to them in addition to their tax and estate planning concerns. The CRUT was merely a means to an end, not an end in itself and that, I believe, is as it should be. By the way, this turned out to be the final gift of the campaign, coming mere days before the official celebration event that the couple attended and at which, you can be sure, they were appropriately recognized.

—Steven C. Greaves, Director of Planned Giving, Quinnipiac University (not the college in the above story)

Donors give to what enables their own lifestyle. Be a lifestyle enabler and people will be more likely to support the organization. For example, if a prospect feels uncomfortable giving because she is financially uncertain about her upcoming retirement years, a life-income gift could enable her to have a more comfortable, secure retirement while having the satisfaction of giving now. Show prospects how they can enhance their lives by giving. Many middle-class annual donors would very much like to see themselves as major gift donors but know they cannot part with the funds necessary to achieve such status. Through careful gift planning, you may be able to show these individuals a pathway to become the supporter they have dreamt of becoming.

Donors give to what fits within their comfort zone. Some donors like complex gift vehicles. Such vehicles make some people feel smart and creative and like they are successfully beating the system. For others, complex giving vehicles simply cause confusion, distrust, and anxiety. When helping a prospect with his gift planning, it is important to learn what makes him comfortable and uncomfortable. Endeavor to stay in his comfort zone.

Donors give to good taste. Prospects know the difference between good and bad taste. When the American Cancer Society produced its famous antismoking television commercial in 1985, it did not show images of an emaciated, sickly Yul Brynner hooked up to tubes and wires as he wasted away from lung cancer. Instead, the commercial opened with a simple black screen with the famous actor's name, date of birth, and date of death.[2] This gave way to a filmed image of Brynner, looking reasonably healthy, gazing into the camera urging people not to smoke. Tasteful does not necessarily mean low impact. More than 25 years later, the commercial is still having an impact with over 408,507 views on YouTube.com alone.

Assuming that an organization has been completely sensitive to all of the previously listed wants that prospects and donors have, there is still another important want. *Prospects and donors want to associate with organizations that care.* They want to know that the organization and everyone who works there cares about those served and cares about them. Also, donors want to be recognized for caring and not just for giving.

Prospects and donors also want organizations to address what is of interest to them. People are most interested in:

- Themselves.
- How an organization benefits them, their loved ones, and the community (both tangibly and intangibly).
- The importance of those benefits to them.
- Not being cheated.
- Why they should act now.

Peter Benoliel, Chairman-Emeritus of Quaker Chemical, is a generous philanthropist and recipient of the Partnership for Philanthropic Planning of Greater Philadelphia's Legacy Award for Planned Giving Philanthropist. Benoliel offered additional insight when he provided five suggestions regarding the actions of development professionals:

- Development professionals, senior staff, and volunteer leadership should be passionate about the organization and its mission.
- Staff and volunteer fundraisers should be morally armed by making their own donation first.
- Development professionals should send personal, handwritten notes.
- Development professionals should recognize gifts in unexpected ways.
- Development professionals should avoid silly mistakes like sending multiple copies of the same appeal, sending a form appeal to a donor who has just made a gift, or ignoring a donor who is in the middle of a multiyear gift commitment.[3]

By focusing on what a prospect or donor wants and by communicating with them about what is of most interest to them, organizations will be more likely to capture their focus and interest. It is always easier to secure a gift if one has the prospect's attention and the prospect has an interest in what the development professional has to say.

Executive Insight

[C]harity unleashes enormous benefits not only to the givers themselves but also to their families, communities, and the nation. Everyone understands that charitable organizations create value by providing for the needy. What many organizations misunderstand is who the 'needy' truly are. In addition to those in need of food, shelter, education, the needy are also those who *need* to give to attain their full potential in happiness, health, and material prosperity—which is every one of us.

—Arthur C. Brooks, author, *Who Really Cares*

Demographic Factors Impacting Motivation

To better understand donor motivation, one must recognize that planned giving donors and prospects are not part of one homogeneous group. They can be grouped in a variety of ways including income level, religious attendance, geographic region, and gender. For example, individuals also fall into a number of different generational cohorts:

- Great, born before 1929.

- Silent, born 1929 to 1945.

- Boomer, born 1946 to 1963.

- X, born 1964 to 1981.

- Millennial, born since 1981.

Interestingly, few differences exist between the generations when it comes to philanthropy in general. According to a 2008 study by the Center on Philanthropy at Indiana University, other factors such as educational attainment, frequency of religious attendance, and income have a greater impact on philanthropy than do generational differences.[4] Nevertheless, some generational differences do indeed exist, including:

- The Silent and Great generations are significantly more likely to give to religious purposes than members of younger generations.
- Millennial, Gen X, and Boomer generations have similar propensity to give to religious causes, yet they are less likely than the Silent and Great generations to give to religious causes.
- Millennial, Gen X, Boomer, and Great generations are each similarly likely to support secular causes.
- The Millennial generation is more likely to give to make the world a better place.
- The Silent generation is more likely to give to nonprofit organizations to provide funding where the government does not.

Other generational differences, according to Brian Sagrestano, President of Gift Planning Development, include:

- The Silent and Great generations both trust charities. While members of the Great generation want simply to see their gifts put good ideas to work, the Silent generation has a preference for giving that has a local impact.
- The Boomer generation has a distrust of nonprofit organizations that is more pronounced among younger Boomers. All Boomers want their gifts to have a verifiable impact.
- The members of Generation X have a significant mistrust of nonprofit organizations. They want to be involved in the charities they support. They give and volunteer. They are mission driven rather than brand loyal.
- The Millennial generation is just as likely to think a nonprofit organization is an obstacle as much as they are to think it is part of the solution. Members of this generation want to make a difference, and their thinking is global. They are very active in the community and will give the most to organizations with which they are actively engaged and where they think they can make a real difference, or they may even start their own.[5]

When marketing to Baby Boomers, it is better to focus on the impact of a gift rather than specific gift vehicles, according to Judith E. Nichols.[6] Baby Boomers often aspire to be major givers though they may lack the resources to do this with a current gift. Planned giving can be the route for this generation to realize their philanthropic desire and have the type of impact they would like to have. Therefore, when communicating with this generational cohort, it is important to describe benefits of planned giving rather than the mechanisms. For example, rather than describing in great detail how a CGA functions, it is more important to explain how such a gift can provide the donor funds for retirement, financing for a child's or grandchild's education, or even needed revenue to help support an aging parent, all while helping a cause he or she cares about passionately.

The Center on Philanthropy found five motivations for general charitable giving that are the most important for donors in all generational cohorts:

- Providing for the basic needs of the very poor.
- Desire to make one's community a better place to live.
- Giving the poor a way to help themselves.
- Desire to make the world a better place.
- Those with more have a responsibility to help those with less.

Motivations for overall philanthropy vary by income, race, education, region of the country and religious attendance, according to the Center. Those individuals who earn less than $49,999 are more likely than those who earn more to support causes that help the poor help themselves. Those in households earning more than $125,000 are motivated to give by a sense of responsibility to help others who have less.

All racial groups are philanthropically inclined. However, some differences in motivation do exist with African American and Hispanic donors more likely than non-Hispanic white donors to say that they gave to help meet people's basic needs. Hispanic donors were more likely than non–Hispanic white donors to say that they gave to help the poor help themselves, according to the Center on Philanthropy.

IN THE REAL WORLD

"I Like This Philanthropy Stuff!"

The African American community has always been a generous one. Though it was typically focused on helping neighbors in need and supporting the church, philanthropy has always been alive and well for black folks. We just never called it that. I recently interviewed my 75-year-old mother about her own giving history. As she told story after story, it dawned on her that while growing up in Cincinnati, Ohio, so much of what they did in the community was about helping those in need. From dance recitals to thrift shops, it was all about raising money for families that needed help with buying food, clothing, and going to college.

Planned giving on the other hand has not been something that was talked about let alone practiced much in the African American community over the years. However, I have had the honor of seeing a sea change happening in the work that I do at The Philadelphia Foundation. Having been an open, welcoming community foundation for much of our 92-year history, we have been the place where "anyone can be a philanthropist," and I have been fortunate to see ordinary people doing extraordinary things.

For example, Shirley is an African American woman who decided that in honor of her seventieth birthday, she would create a CGA that would fund an endowed fund at TPF to benefit her sorority and her alma matter. The day she came in to sign the paperwork, she brought along with her two young grandsons to witness the occasion. Shirley made sure to tell them how important this was to their family. She has since created a second CGA and her daughter, who is in her 50s, wanted to support her mother's efforts. She, too, created a CGA to benefit her mother's fund. I remember the day Shirley came in for a visit and plopped down in a boardroom chair and said with a big smile, "I like this philanthropy stuff!"

—Heather Gee, Vice President for Development Services, The Philadelphia Foundation

As educational level positively impacts propensity to give, it also impacts what motivates individuals to give. The Center on Philanthropy found, among those with a college degree compared to those with just a high school diploma, a greater likelihood of citing the responsibility to help others, a lower likelihood of giving to help meet the basic needs of the very poor, and a lower likelihood of giving from a desire to control where one's money goes instead of having the government decide.

The Center also found that some regional differences exist when it comes to donor motivation. For example, when compared with those living in the northeastern United States, donors living in the Southern states are more likely to say they donate to help the poor help themselves while those living in either the South or the Midwest were less likely to say they had a desire to make the world a better place to live.

Religion is a powerful motivator for charitable giving to both religious and secular causes. "Religious people are far more charitable than secularists, no matter what their politics," writes Arthur C. Brooks in *Who Really Cares*.[7] The Center on Philanthropy found that people who attend a religious service at least once a week "are more likely than non-attenders to say they give to help meet the needs of the poor, to help the poor help themselves, or because those with more have a responsibility to help those with less."[8]

In Chapter 2, we discovered that while gender does not impact bequest giving propensity in general, it does have some influence over the type of nonprofit organization that one might be more or less inclined to support. Patrick Rooney of the Center on Philanthropy, has also reported that some slight gender differences exist in motivation for becoming a bequest donor. For example, women are particularly interested in the impact that a bequest gift can have. Men under age 65 who attend religious services frequently and women, regardless of religious attendance, have an interest in helping those with less. Among older men with incomes above $100,000 a year, there is a strong belief that nonprofit organizations deliver services better than the government does.[9]

Just as there are subtle motivational differences among men and women, Rooney also reported slight motivational differences between rural and nonrural residents. Among rural donors who are not yet bequest donors, a message demonstrating the efficiency of the nonprofit organization will resonate. Among nonrural residents who are not yet bequest donors, the emphasis is better placed on the impact that the bequest gift can have.

General Individual Motives

While understanding the overall motivations for philanthropy in general can be useful, it is also important for one to understand what motivates donors to make a planned gift, particularly bequest commitments since they are such a popular vehicle for planned giving. Adrian Sargeant and Jen Shang of the Center on Philanthropy found three broad motivational categories for bequest giving:

- General Individual Motives.
- Organizational Factors.
- Bequest-specific Motives.[10]

General individual motives are the motives that have to do with the individuals themselves and their personal philanthropic beliefs in general. These are motives that can impact both current and planned giving behavior. For example, in its 2000 survey of planned gift donors, the Partnership for Philanthropic Planning found that "a desire to support the charity" was the leading reason cited by planned gift donors for making a commitment (see Table 3.1). The second most cited reason was "the ultimate use of the gift by the charity."[11] These are also reasons why individuals make current gifts.

A number of factors that motivate major gift donors, identified by Schervish and Havens, of the Boston College Center on Wealth and Philanthropy, likely have some role in planned giving behavior, as well. When individuals recognize that they have sufficient financial means to meet their needs and the needs of their loved ones, they are able to think about helping others in ways that bring deep personal satisfaction. These donors give because it makes them feel good or happy to do so. However, it must be noted that financial security

TABLE 3.1	
Reasons Donors Make Planned Gifts	
Reason	**Percentage Responding**
Desire to support the charity	97%
Ultimate use of the gift by the charity	82%
Desire to reduce taxes	35%
Long-range estate and financial planning issues	35%
Create a lasting memorial for self or loved one(s)	33%
Relationship with representative of a charity	21%
Encouragement of family and friends	13%
Encouragement of legal or financial advisors	12%

Source: National Committee on Planned Giving (now Partnership for Philanthropic Planning. *Planned Giving in the United States 2000: A Survey of Donors* (Indianapolis: 2001).

is in the eyes of the beholder. One person with $1 million in assets may feel secure while another may not. The more financially secure one feels, the more likely he or she is to make a major gift.[12]

A number of other factors also prove important to the major gift process. People tend to help others who are perceived as being like themselves. For example, a college in the northeastern United States found that its older alumnae had difficulty identifying with the school as it now is. The older alumnae attended a women's college populated by many children of immigrants. Today, the school has a relatively new campus, is coeducational, and is attended by many first-generation college students from the inner city. Giving from the older alumnae was initially modest with many stating, "It's just not my school anymore." The college launched a comprehensive marketing campaign to deal with this issue. At the core of the campaign, the college demonstrated that today's inner-city student may look different than yester-year's pupil, but that the core values and work ethic remains the same. As a result, the older alumnae were better able to identify with today's student body and giving increased.

Gratitude is also a powerful motivator. Gratitude manifests itself in two particular ways. Donors may desire to give back because they received certain meaningful benefits from the organization. Donors may also want to more generally give back by sharing their good fortune with others. Some donors, particularly those of wealth, will be motivated by entrepreneurial impulses. These

Sense of Community Inspires Planned Gifts

In the African American community, fraternities and sororities are a very important part of social and civic life. They help provide a sense of community. These organizations were important to men and women when they attended college. For many people, these organizations continue to play a relevant role in their lives.

Several years ago, a member of an African American sorority passed away and left a $25,000 bequest as a challenge to the sorority members to raise another $25,000 for scholarships. The members were so in awe of such a gesture, they decided that they would not only meet her challenge but, with hard work, ended up raising $250,000 for the scholarship endowment.

Years later, a member of the sorority, at age 92, decided that she would like to create a CGA to benefit the sorority's scholarship fund. We went to her home with one of her sorority members to complete the paperwork. Although she was thrilled to be able to make such a gift, she lit up like a Christmas tree when her sorority sister told her that she was the first one of her sorority to make such a gift, that she was blazing a new trail! I felt like I was witnessing a change of the face of philanthropy right before my eyes.

—Heather Gee, Vice President for Development Services, The Philadelphia Foundation

donors give to make something happen that might not otherwise happen. Some donors make significant gifts out of a sense of morality and a desire to teach philanthropic values to their children. Finally, Schervish and Havens recognize that some donors need to discover for themselves "the point of convergence where what needs to be done coincides with what they want to do."[13]

Match what a donor wants to do with what the organization needs done. When interests merge, a gift will be more forthcoming.

Sargeant and Shang found that two generic giving motives stood out as bequest motives as well.[14] The most common motivator is the notion of reciprocity, or giving back for the services or benefits one received themselves or someone close received. Many donors express an interest in giving back to a nonprofit organization for benefits they received from the organization or for benefits they received from a prior generation of donors. For example, a donor might want to "give back" to a college because of a scholarship she received from a fund established with alumni contributions.

The George Washington University commissioned a series of focus groups to learn more about what motivated its alumni to give. One of the comments from an alumnus nicely illustrates the importance of reciprocity and making a difference as motivators, "[Universities] are growing the next generation of leaders. Look what they did for us. It's investing in the future. If the alma mater treated you well and is still delivering on their mission, you'd want that to continue."[15]

Prestige is also an important motivator. An organization that structures a gift agreement in a way that allows the donor to see the impact of his or her gift and receive recognition while he or she is still alive might be more likely to receive a gift. A donor who desires to have the prestige associated with being a major donor, but who cannot afford to become one with a current gift, might become a planned gift donor if status is conferred or perceived. One of the donors who participated in the Sargeant and Shang focus groups recited, "There was a certain deference to people who care enough about the institution and have the means to do this sort of thing."[16]

Conversations with donors and prospects seldom focus exclusively on planned giving. Many factors that play a role in motivating current giving also motivate planned giving behavior. So, development professionals will want to understand these factors. As the conversation with a donor tilts toward gift planning, the development professional will want to pay particular attention to the motivating factors most closely identified with planned giving.

Organizational Factors

Organizational factors are the unique characteristics or behaviors of an organization that, when handled well, can inspire donors or, when handled poorly, can lead them to give elsewhere or not at all.

Not surprisingly, donors have concerns about the performance of the organizations they support. Bequest donors want to know that an organization is efficiently run and that it effectively achieves its mission. Both organizational efficiency and effectiveness are key issues for donors because they want to know that their support will make a difference. This concern is greater among bequest donors than annual fund donors. This could be because annual fund donors can evaluate the organization each year to determine if it is worthy of continued support. However, a bequest donor will not have that luxury at the point the gift is realized and, therefore, they require a greater level of confidence in the organization before they will support it for the long term. The same would hold true for someone making a substantial irrevocable gift commitment.

One of the Sargeant and Shang focus group participants stressed the importance of sound fiscal performance when saying, "Cut the overhead, cut the overhead . . . some organizations have high indices for what money goes to the causes and what money goes in order to be able to administer the causes and so that's one of the things that I look at and get value if it's in the right direction."[17]

One way that organizations can build a strong relationship with prospective planned gift donors is to exhibit a high degree of professionalism and responsiveness. This means adhering to the highest ethical standards, providing exemplary service, and dealing with prospective planned gift donors in a professional fashion. Prospects and donors alike know that a planned gift is a significant, special gift. They want to be assured that the organizations they give to recognize this fact as well. How responsive an organization is says a great deal about how efficient they are, how much they care, and how professional they are. For example, if a prospect requests sample language for his or her will, staff should

KEY CONCEPT

Everyone employed by a nonprofit organization is part of the development process. Every encounter that an individual has had with an organization will factor in to the prospect's determination of whether to give. Organizations should work hard to make sure those encounters, at every level, are warm and professional.

provide that information immediately and in a way most useful to the prospect. A long delay or a hard-to-read fax will send the message that the organization does not care.

One of the Sargeant and Shang focus group participants summed up the importance of an organization's professionalism in this way, "[A planned gift] is such a big thing. It's not something you would consider doing lightly, and oftentimes the only clue you have about how good the organization really is, is how you are handled by its people. It's a kind of surrogate measure. I mean I know it's not the same people handling [the service provision] but what else can you look at?"[18]

The quality of communications inspires prospects to make gifts and planned gift donors to maintain or increase their commitments. Donors want information about how their gifts are or will be used, they want to know the impact they are or will have, and they want to understand how effectively the organization is fulfilling its mission. Be sure to provide prospects with information they can actually read since many planned gift donors have eyes that are over age 40, and they may gloss over or ignore text that is too small. Also, by properly thanking them, by recognizing their importance, by engaging them, organizations will inspire support. Communications needs to be regular, delivered in the way the donor wants, and provide meaningful information or opportunities to engage.

An alumnus participating in The George Washington University focus group study stated the importance of good communications quite simply, "If they explain to me what they're doing, they're more likely to get my support."[19]

KEY CONCEPT

Communication involves a two-way exchange. Do not just talk at donors. Give them the chance to talk with you and provide their feedback.

Donors are also concerned about the quality of service provided by the organization to them. While this certainly ties into how efficiently and effectively the organization fulfills its mission in a general sense, it also refers to the quality of service received directly by the donor and his or her loved ones. A participant in a Sargeant and Shang focus group discovered the value of a National Public Radio station when it was temporarily no longer available, "I will tell you how it [NPR] changed life down in Bethany Beach, Delaware. I bought a place about eight years ago and, honest to God, that drive, once you got close to the bay bridge you lost the station. It was really a sacrifice. I didn't realize how much I missed the radio and thoughtful conversation . . . it got me thinking."[20]

Bequest-specific Motives

Bequest-specific motives are those that move individuals to include a charitable bequest provision in their will. While these motives are specific to bequest behavior, they may also have an influence on other planned giving behaviors as well.

One of the key issues for prospective donors identified by Sargeant and Shang, and other researchers, is the perception of the need of loved ones, both family and close friends. Many people believe in the old aphorism, "Charity begins at home." People will only consider a charitable bequest if they feel that their loved ones have either been sufficiently provided for already, if a gift can actually help their loved ones, or if their loved ones do not have a need. The charity sector in the United Kingdom has launched a series of television commercials that encourage people to draft a will to take care of their loved ones and *then* "remember a charity." By recognizing this dynamic, the charity sector in the UK has seen significant growth in the number of charitable bequests since the campaign began.[21]

IN THE REAL WORLD

Take Care of the Family and the Donor Will Take Care of the Organization

When I first arrived at the Smithsonian Institution as Director of Planned Giving, a colleague recommended that I contact Cliff, a person who had responded to a CGA advertisement in *Smithsonian* magazine a few months before. Cliff wanted to make sure the Smithsonian was strong financially. At age 96, he was still incredibly alert mentally, and he wanted to provide a lifetime income for his wife, who was nearly 20 years younger. He appreciated the Smithsonian, but frankly was more concerned about the safety of her guaranteed payments than supporting a particular charitable purpose.

A consultant to the Smithsonian had traded more than 20 e-mails with Cliff, who originally inquired about a $10,000 CGA. As he became convinced of the Smithsonian's financial strength, he quickly increased his inquiry to a CGA for $1 million. But no one had ever called him—they had simply been trading e-mails! I telephoned Cliff, and the discussion quickly progressed; within another two months he sent in stock certificates to establish a $500,000 CGA for his wife. Over the next year, he created two additional $500,000 CGAs for his wife—for a total of $1.5 million.

But that's not the end of the story. He had a son who was not strong with money management. Cliff still actively managed his own finances and made periodic distributions to his son. I suggested setting up a CGA or CRT now for the son, but Cliff insisted that he wanted to manage his money outright for as long as possible. We agreed, however, that a testamentary CGA for his son would meet his desires. I provided sample language, and Cliff's lawyer modified his estate plan to include a $2 million testamentary CGA.

From a $10,000 inquiry, we received $3.5 million in gifts because we took the time to show Cliff how we could help him take care of his family.

—John B. Kendrick, Executive Director of Development–Planned Giving, The George Washington University

Tax consequences, specifically the desire to reduce the amount of money that goes to the government, influences many people to engage in estate planning including the use of a variety of planned gift mechanisms. However, while a desire to minimize taxes drives many individuals to engage in estate planning that includes charitable giving, it does not necessarily lead them to make a planned gift to a particular organization. The reason for this is quite simple. Donors can receive the same tax benefits regardless of which specific nonprofit organization they give to. One Sargeant and Shang focus group participant illustrated the lesser importance of tax benefits saying, "Tax was definitely an issue, but more in terms of structuring things properly. We wanted to make our money work for them, not the government."[22]

Some donors are motivated by a need for immortality. They believe that they can live on through their bequest gift. For some, the desire to live on is grounded in their own ego and the need to leave something of themselves behind. For example, a Sargeant and Shang focus group participant said, "Sure, I want to see [the charity] continue and, when it does, a little bit of me will, too." For others, the need is slightly different as they want to leave something behind so that their loved ones can remember them in a positive light and so that their favorite cause will continue to benefit others. Another focus group participant summed it up this way, "It's been really important to me in my lifetime and I want to think that it will continue to touch the lives of other folks when I'm gone."[23]

Another motivator of bequest giving is spite or concern for loved ones. For example, some donors do not believe that their children deserve to be

KEY CONCEPT

Discussing tax avoidance can encourage prospects to engage in estate planning. However, there are more effective ways to inspire prospects to make a planned gift to a particular organization.

handed a cash windfall by winning the genetic lottery. Other donors are concerned that giving their children a large sum of money might demotivate them and, therefore, actually be bad for the children. In those two cases, donors may leave a certain portion of their estate to family while giving the rest to charity. However, other donors simply have a contentious relationship with their families and will give all or most of their estates away out of a pure sense of spite.

One Sargeant and Shang focus group participant illustrated the issue of spite in this way, "When [my mother] died she gave the money to the five of us kids, and I watched two of my siblings just rip through the money. It was just an unbelievable waste and I thought, I don't have any kids, and I had originally had my will going to my siblings and then I thought—why? They'd do the same thing with my hard-earned money."

Another focus group participant did not want to spoil the children. The participant said, "My fiancé is very aligned with me in the sense of not wanting . . . [that is] wanting to give a gift to family, but not wanting to give them everything and make it too easy."[24]

Bequest donors want to make a difference. While many individuals might want to be a major donor to their favorite charities, many cannot afford to do so in their own lifetime. However, they recognize that a bequest gift can be significant and, therefore, allow them to ultimately have the kind of impact they desire to have. In addition, many donors who feel that their current giving has made a difference desire to keep making that difference when they are no longer here to keep writing the checks. One Sargeant and Shang focus group participant noted, "[W]e feel this strong sense of wanting to make a difference."[25]

Demotivating Factors

While it is important to understand what motivates people to donate money and, more specifically, to make planned gifts, it is also necessary to recognize how individuals can become demotivated. While an organization's being self-centered and running afoul of the factors that motivate people will certainly

The Gift That Keeps Giving

During a conversation about estate planning, an elderly, childless woman was asked by her nephew if she had included any charities in her will. She asked, "Why would anyone ever give money to a charity after they're dead?" Knowing the answer, he asked, "Do you support any charities now?" The aunt replied with a list of organizations she supported including an animal welfare organization. When the nephew probed, the aunt said, "I give them money because I want to help protect the unwanted cats and dogs." The nephew then asked, "Okay, I understand. But tell me, who is going to take care of the little kittens and puppies when you're no longer here to write out the checks to help them?" The aunt's eyes grew wide. In that moment, the nephew may have reduced or eliminated his inheritance, but many kittens and puppies will likely be better off as his aunt realized she could endow her annual gift and continue to make a difference long into the future.

demotivate prospective donors, there are two particular factors that are noteworthy as The George Washington University discovered in a focus group study they commissioned involving university alumni.

One of the biggest deterrents to making bequest commitments is the universally held belief that family comes first, before any nonprofit organization. The priority for individuals is to take care of their families. This often means keeping wealth within the family. To overcome this concern, organizations need to show prospects how a meaningful gift can be made, at a minimum, without asking loved ones to suffer. When possible, prospects should be shown

Executive Insight

It's not my job to motivate players. They bring extraordinary motivation to our program. It's my job not to de-motivate them.

—Lou Holtz, NCAA Hall of Fame coach

how a planned gift can actually benefit loved ones, as with the Smithsonian example given earlier.

The other major demotivator discovered by The George Washington University is the mistaken belief that bequests involve very large financial commitments from those who are very wealthy. Three problems arise. First, prospects believe that bequest giving is simply not for them, but rather the wealthy—many who are truly wealthy do not perceive themselves as such and, instead, think of themselves as merely "comfortable." Second, while some prospects might be willing to give through a bequest, they might not actually do so because they feel their gift would be too insignificant to matter. Third, some prospects expressed embarrassment over the notion of giving a modest bequest gift while the perceived norm is much larger. For example, one focus group participant said, "When you see bequests given to universities they are substantial. You really feel embarrassed that you don't have that money."[26]

These findings were similar to what was discovered by the organizers of the "Remember a Charity" campaign in the United Kingdom. There, many prospects either did not know what the term *legacy* means or thought it something that only wealthy people and celebrities do. To overcome this demotivator, organizations must speak the prospect's language. In the U.K. campaign, prospects are not asked to make *a bequest commitment* or *leave a legacy*. Instead, they are simply asked to *remember a charity* in their will. By using less formal language and by educating prospects about the importance of all planned gifts, organizations can help prospects feel more comfortable with the idea of gift planning and recognize its appropriateness for them.[27]

To promote the point that bequest giving is for everyone, the Arizona State University School of Nursing and Health Innovation did an article in its alumni magazine that focused on an average nurse, an alumna who made a generous but not particularly dramatic bequest commitment. The message was a simple one: All bequest gifts are greatly appreciated, and people just like you are making such gifts.

Summary

Ethical nonprofit organizations avoid any attempt to manipulate prospective donors into giving. Even for a good cause, the ends do not justify the means thereby making manipulation out of the question. Donors come to the table with their own set of personal motives. By understanding what motivates donors in general, and the individual prospect specifically, the development professional will be better positioned to inspire the prospect to take action.

Most planned gift donors will be primarily motivated by a sense of reciprocity, or desire to give back. They will want their gift to make a difference. Others are also motivated by the sense of prestige, either conferred or perceived, that can come from making a major gift, even in the form of a planned gift.

Because donors have choices when making philanthropic commitments, many consider an organization's efficiency, professionalism, frequency and quality of communications, and responsiveness when deciding which organization they will support. Others will be motivated to support those organizations that provide them or their loved ones with quality service and, sometimes, even financial security. Still others are concerned about their ability to, in effect, live on forever. In nearly all cases, there will be more than one motivator in play.

While tax avoidance might lead some to consider a planned gift in general, it is not a particularly powerful motivator when a prospect considers which specific charity to contribute to. The reason is simple. A donor can receive the same tax benefits regardless of which nonprofit organization he supports, provided that organization is equipped to handle a planned gift.

While understanding donor motivation is important, it is also essential to understand why prospects do not take philanthropic action. Most donor prospects will want to ensure that their families are well taken care of before they consider a charitable gift. If a planned gift can be shown to have little negative impact on the donor's family or, better yet, can have a positive impact on their financial position, the prospect will be more likely to give. Prospects also need to understand that whatever they are able to do will be valued and appreciated.

A great variety of planned gift options are open to everyone, not just the wealthy or celebrities.

By focusing on the prospective donor's needs and interests, the development professional will be able to better satisfy those needs and match those interests with the organization's own programmatic needs. When this happens, a gift can be closed.

Exercises

- People give more often and more generously to organizations that "care." Take a few moments to list the ways in which your organization shows donors and prospects that it truly cares. List 10 things your organization can do to show it cares, but that it is not yet doing.

- Examine your communications file. Do the materials use words like *bequest* and *legacy*, or do the materials use simpler, less off-putting language?

- Talk to a few planned gift donors and ask them to tell you why they made the gift. You could commission a full-blown focus group study of your prospects and donors, but a few conversations will give you enormous insight at a fraction of the cost.

CHAPTER 4

Educate and Cultivate Planned Gift Prospects

We have two ears and one mouth so that we can listen twice as much as we speak.

—*Epictetus*

After reading this chapter, you will be able to:

- Understand the need for educating and cultivating people.
- Identify key points to consider when branding the planned giving program.
- Follow a strategic approach for building marketing communications.
- Recognize the elements of effective messaging.
- Utilize various marketing channels in an effective way.

Donors know many things. They know what nonprofit organizations they like. They know their own financial situation. They know what is important to them. One thing most donors do not know, however, is what nonprofit organizations mean by the term *planned giving*. Among U.S. residents over the age of 30, only 37 percent are familiar with the term (see Figure 4.1).[1]

Among U.S. residents over age 30, only 22 percent say they have been approached by a nonprofit organization to consider a planned gift. Even among

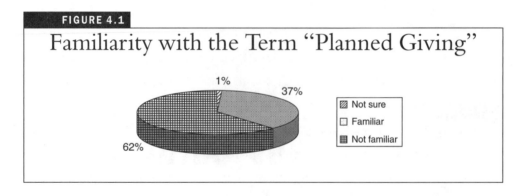

FIGURE 4.1

Familiarity with the Term "Planned Giving"

those who know what planned giving is, only 42 percent report being asked for such a gift (see Figure 4.2).[2]

The Need for Education and Cultivation

At best, prospective donors and nonprofit organizations do not always speak the same language. At worst, they are not even having a conversation. Planned gifts do not just happen. To be successful or to attain greater levels of success requires sound marketing. It also requires asking for the gift. Nonprofit organizations must do a more effective job of educating and cultivating prospective donors. Prospects need to understand an organization's mission, how effectively it is fulfilling its mission, how the donor can make a difference, what planned giving is, and how planned giving can help the donor achieve her philanthropic and financial aspirations.

There are a variety of marketing channels that an organization can use to deploy its messages. Which combination of these channels should be utilized,

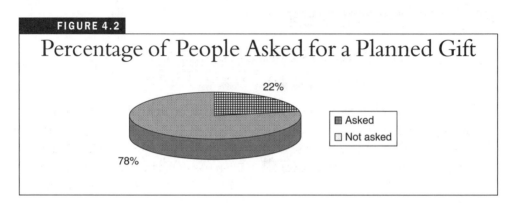

FIGURE 4.2

Percentage of People Asked for a Planned Gift

however, will depend on many factors including the size of the organization, the scope of the planned giving program, the number of development staff, the number of prospects, the geographic dispersion of prospects, and program budget among other factors.

Educational efforts regarding gift planning should be broadly available since even the best prospect screening process will leave many viable prospective donors unidentified. Even the smallest organizations with the most limited planned giving programs can cost-effectively piggyback planned gift marketing onto existing marketing materials. The educational effort targeting prospects should include information about the organization, the planned giving program and, most important, what gift planning can do for the donor. Generally, education occurs at arm's length and involves printed material, web site, advertisements, and so on.

Cultivation may involve some arm's-length techniques to more targeted prospects, but the best cultivation will involve face-to-face time. Cultivating with face-to-face time can involve one-on-one visits or may involve face time at a group setting such as at an estate planning seminar. The more time one can spend in front of prospects listening to them, the better. All other marketing techniques and media will get one just so far. To be truly effective requires some personal contact. The cultivation period is the period during which the development officer learns what gift opportunity might be most appropriate to propose while the prospective donor at this time is building trust in the development officer and the organization while learning about how he can make a difference or give back.

IN THE REAL WORLD

Build Relationships with Service and Face Time

I convinced Alicia, the head of our Senior Resource Services (SRS), to accompany me on my occasional lunches with our Legacy Society donor, Ellen, who was absolutely resolute in her loneliness. SRS is a significant beneficiary of Ellen's estate. Over time, Ellen has come to accept Alicia as a

(continued)

friend and resource. In addition, Glenda, our Foundation secretary, has given Ellen rides to our recognition events. Jackie, a volunteer with SRS, has taken Ellen for her annual flu shot at our auxiliary's Thrift Korral. Alicia is now very accomplished in what she calls my "schmoozing." Glenda knows how to help our Ellen—within acceptable limits. Good things happen when the circle of attachment broadens.

—Jim Brozo, Senior Gift Planning Advisor, Grossmont Hospital Foundation

Create a Planned Giving Brand Identity

Branding a planned giving program will help it stand out as something important, which of course it is. It will help differentiate the gift planning program from other fundraising or membership activities. It will signal that planned giving is about special gifts that can have a lasting impact.

Some organizations cobrand their planned giving program with their planned giving recognition society. Just as some organizations create a unique brand identity for their capital campaigns to distinguish them from annual fund appeals, so too do wise organizations uniquely brand their planned giving program. However, when branding the planned giving program, it is important to remain somewhat consistent with the organization's overall brand identity. The planned giving brand identity should be an identity within an identity. For example, while the planned giving recognition society logo might be used, the colors could still be those of the organization.

Good branding will also give prospects and donors a sense of the values and culture of the organization. So, the planned giving brand must be consistent with the organization's overall brand identity. Effective branding will say a great deal about an organization to an individual before they even have a chance to absorb a particular message. Solid branding will also continually reinforce the organization's core values in every communication regardless of what the particular message is.

To ensure that the brand identity achieves what is hoped for, development professionals should test it through formal focus groups or, at a minimum, by getting reactions from selected individuals.

Create an Appropriate,
Recognizable Brand Identity

Gift planning is a serious business. Donors make choices that affect their financial future and the future of our agencies. That does not mean, however, that your marketing has to be serious too. The purpose of marketing is to create the initial inquiries that can then lead to serious discussions with our donors.

Five years ago, when I started at Catholic Charities, I sat down with our marketing manager to discuss developing a marketing plan. She asked who my audience was and I told her that, for charitable gift annuities (CGAs), it was donors who are primarily 70 years of age or older. As we talked, she suggested the idea of an ad that would appeal to nostalgia, such as, "Remember when a loaf of bread was 50 cents." I said, "That's it, 'Rebecca's Recipes for Planning Gifts©.'"

I dragged out my grandmother's old cooking supplies—mix-master, aprons, utensils, and dishes—and had photographs of myself taken stuffing a turkey, making soup and cookies, counting eggs, kneading dough, slicing bread and so forth. Thus began the ads and postcards I continue to use to this day. Headlines have included:

- You don't have to be upper crust to have a trust.
- You don't have to be rolling in dough to make a gift that will last forever.
- You can have your cake and eat it too—you can make a gift and receive payments for life.
- You can count your chickens before they hatch—you can make a gift and count on receiving payments for life.
- Don't let taxes knock the stuffing out of your IRA.
- You can use your stock to make more than soup, you can use it to make a charitable gift.
- Too much on your plate to plan your estate?

Catholic Charities' best-known and most popular program is our soup kitchen. Our older donors tend to be primarily housewives whose primary identity was as homemakers, even if they worked. Their family lives

(continued)

centered on the evening meal. My ads and postcards match Catholic Charities' mission to our donor culture. Rather than position myself as an "expert" in a suit, I want to be viewed as the woman you'd sit and chat with across your kitchen table.

Donors have responded, making inquiries and completing gifts. I have had donors come to meet me with my postcard in hand, "I wanted to be sure I'd recognize you." Others have told me they look for my monthly ads in the *Catholic Review*.

My brand has had another, unexpected side-effect, though. It was a huge hit with our executive management. It made people laugh and generated many jokes such as, "What's really in those recipes?" It made me approachable and increased the comfort level with our planned giving program significantly.

I believe it is possible to brand most planned giving programs. Over the years, I have seen some wonderful ideas including:

- Our local SPCA used a picture of a basset hound with a headline, "Stock market got you down? Consider a Charitable Gift Annuity."
- The local art museum uses its artwork in its planned giving postcards.
- A private school had a picture of a student going down a slide reading *The Wall Street Journal* with an ad about CGAs as the alternative to the declining market.
- And, most famously, for years the planned giving program at Johns Hopkins University under Ron Sapp used cartoons to market its program.

There is something unique about what each of our organizations do. Your brand may not be able to be as playful as mine, but it can still capture the essence of your mission and position you and your planned giving program within your agency's overall fundraising spectrum. There are vendors who do a wonderful job helping to create these brands. However, before you pick up that phone, I encourage you to take some time yourself, or with your colleagues, to brainstorm about finding your image. After all, you know your mission and your donors the best. And, you never know what you might cook up!

—Rebecca Rothey, Director of Planned and Principal Gifts, Catholic Charities

When creating a brand identity for planned giving, one should keep the following points in mind:

- Exercise creativity.
- Remain consistent with the organization's overall brand identity.
- Make certain that the values conveyed are true core values.
- Ensure cultural sensitivity and appropriateness.
- Test the brand identity to ensure it has the desired impact.

Fundamental Strategic Approach

To effectively educate and cultivate prospective planned gift donors requires adherence to a fundamental strategic marketing approach involving a number of key steps:

1. *Define the objective.* Before one can achieve something, one must know what one wants to achieve. Is the objective to educate a group of people about planned giving options? Is it to inspire a group with what the organization is achieving? Is it to enhance a relationship with a particular individual? Does one want to generate general or specific inquiries? All marketing should begin with a clear understanding of what one is attempting to achieve.

2. *Identify the appropriate audience.* Once one knows the objective, one can identify the appropriate audience. For example, information about CGAs might be targeted to individuals over age 60 rather than those under age 50.

3. *Ensure that the contact will have value to the prospect or donor.* To maintain a donor-centered focus, one should always ask, "How will the prospect or donor benefit from this?"

4. *Select the appropriate medium for delivering the message and achieving the objective.* Depending on the objective or the audience, the medium could be a direct mail letter, telephone call, e-mail, special event, or personal visit. Or, it could involve multichannel communication.

5. *Develop an effective message.* Regardless of the medium, the development professional must carefully craft the message to ensure it is focused and helps achieve the objective. Generally, the more focus, the better. Trying to accomplish too many things at a single moment of contact often results in accomplishing nothing.

6. *Determine the best time to deliver the message.* For example, hosting a seminar for senior citizens might best be offered in the afternoon since many do not like to drive at night. On the other hand, hosting a similar seminar for working adults might work best in the evening after business hours.

7. *Create a follow-up plan that takes into account all possible outcomes.* Ideally, every point of contact will set the stage for the next. If hosting a seminar, for example, one should plan on sending a letter or note of thanks to all who attended as a follow-up communication. Another follow-up step might be to e-mail seminar handouts to those who expressed regret at not being able to attend. The important thing is to have an appropriate action plan in place.

Words Matter

Regardless of the communication channel used (i.e., direct mail, e-mail, web site, telephone, advertisements, etc.), the words one uses are of critical importance. The message one conveys is nothing more than a collection of words and images. Carefully selecting the words that are most meaningful to the intended audience will ensure that one's messages are correctly understood and have the desired impact.

Executive Insight

[T]he power of poignant language is immense, but the destructive power of an ill-thought sound bite is unending and unforgiving. Successful, effective messages—words and language that have been presented in the proper context—all have something in common. They stick in our brains and never leave, like riding a bicycle or tying our shoelaces. Not only do they communicate and educate, not only do they allow us to share ideas—they also move people to action. Words that work are catalysts. They spur us to get up off the couch, to leave the house, to *do something*. When communicators pay attention to what people hear rather than to what they are trying to say, they manage not merely to catch people's attention, but to hold it.[3]

—Frank Luntz, international pollster and author of *Words That Work*: *It's Not What You Say, It's What People Hear*

Frank Luntz, an international pollster and author of *Words That Work: It's Not What You Say, It's What People Hear*, has invested literally a million hours to interview individuals and conduct focus group studies to identify a list of the most important words for superior communication now and through at least 2020. While his list was developed with commercial and political purposes in mind, much of it can be easily applied to the fundraising world. The following are some of the power words that appear on his list.

Imagine. When one asks prospective donors to *imagine*, one is engaging the prospects and getting them to willingly take action. This is, of course, one small step. However, to close a gift requires the prospect to take many small steps. When one asks a prospect to imagine, one does not simply engage the prospect, one engages the prospect on his or her terms. If a college asks a prospect to imagine a future where no student is turned away for financial reasons, different prospects will imagine quite different benefits of that scenario. For some, the scenario will lead to lower unemployment and a stronger economy. Others will see a future full of innovation from an increased number of college graduates. The future that is imagined will vary from prospect to prospect. The result is that the message will be effectively personalized to each individual by each individual. If the college were simply to state that "alumni gifts will provide scholarships to all students in need thereby ensuring fuller employment in the future," the college might lose the interest of those who do not see fuller employment as the real benefit. Instead, asking alumni to imagine, engages the prospect, gets them thinking of the impact most meaningful to them and, therefore, allows the appeal to be personalized to the interests of the prospect rather than the institution. Nevertheless, it promotes the institution's mission.

Hassle-free. No one wants to be hassled, about anything. If organizations can show prospects how the gift planning process can be *hassle-free*, prospects will be more willing to pay attention to the idea. When it comes to product sales, Luntz has found that this is so important that people would rather have an item that is hassle-free (62 percent) than less expensive (38 percent). For development professionals, this means making the planned giving process as easy as possible for prospective donors to navigate at every stage and, then, conveying that message.

Lifestyle. This word is unique to each individual. Each prospective donor knows the *lifestyle* he aspires to. While the word has meaning for everyone, it is particularly powerful among younger people. Using the word puts the focus on the prospective donor and can be used when showing prospects how a gift can be meaningful for them. For example, a museum might market CGAs by speaking of how such gifts can help donors secure the lifestyle they want in retirement by providing a regular income. The development officer does not necessarily know what lifestyle the prospect wants in retirement, but chances are the prospect does. Getting the prospect to think about this is one way to engage her.

Results. Donors want to make a difference. They want to see evidence of how their gifts will impact the organization; this is particularly true among the Baby Boom generation and those younger. One can speak of *results* in three ways. One can show what has been accomplished thanks to prior planned gift support, and one can illustrate what can be accomplished with future planned gift support. Donors want to give to outcomes and not just ideas. The third way one can speak of results has to do with the impact the gift will have on the donor, his estate, and his loved ones.

Innovation. "New and improved" is a phrase that once created excitement. Today, it is a tired, worn-out, old-fashioned collection of words seen as gimmicky and probably not very true. By contrast, *innovation* is a word that is fresh, future focused, active, and desirable. Organizations can talk about innovative gift planning solutions, though this will appeal to younger prospects instead of older prospects who will want what is tried and true. Innovation can also be applied to what the organization is attempting to accomplish, particularly if it involves technology. For example, a hospital might speak to donors about how planned gifts will be used to acquire innovative technology that can save lives. By associating with a cause that is innovative, donors will see themselves as being innovative, a characteristic many see as desirable.

Renew. Actually, there are a number of *re-* words including *revitalize*, *rejuvenate*, *restore*, *rekindle*, and *reinvent* that one could use. Each of these words is rooted in tradition, but conjures forward-thinking thoughts. An organization can use these words to describe how gifts will be put to use. Among older prospects, the words can have a similar impact as innovation does on younger audiences. One can think of *re-* words as innovation with a history. For example, an historic house museum might talk to prospects about the need to restore the mansion to its historic condition. The use is forward thinking, but harkens back to the past, to tradition.

Efficient. Donors want to know that the organizations they support will efficiently use their hard-earned dollars. Donors know that an *efficient* organization will have more of a positive impact than an inefficient one. If efficiency is combined with innovation, an organization can deliver a high-impact message. For example, planned gifts might allow a hospital to acquire new, innovative, minimally invasive surgical technology that will enhance patient outcomes and shorten hospital stays thereby improving efficiency and lowering health care costs.

The Right To. Americans highly value their rights. A *right* is an entitlement that cannot be easily taken away. A person enjoys a right whether they choose to exercise it. For nonprofit organizations, some benefits could be described in this way to heighten their importance and stress the institution's commitment to the benefit. For example, an organization might give a donor's heirs the right to continue receiving the annual report and attend the annual donor recognition event.

Patient-Centered. This book advocates for a donor-centered approach to development because, from the donor's perspective, he really is the center of the universe. Increasingly, the commercial sector is reinforcing this image. Hospitals should not provide managed care and, instead, should provide *patient-centered* care. Colleges might provide student-centered services and facilities. Just as there are many *re-* words, there are many *-centered* words that can be used. By using such a phrase, an organization stresses that it desires to provide quality services that are meaningful to those receiving them. Donors want to make an impact that is meaningful for those receiving services. Assuming that the organization shares this view, it should remind prospects that this is what the charity aspires to do.

Investment. This is a word with two meanings in the gift planning context. While prospects should make a planned gift based on philanthropic intent, some gifts do have an *investment* component. While a CGA may not pay as well as a commercial annuity, it still provides an income and, therefore, has an investment feature. Depending on the individual donor's needs, development professionals should not be shy about discussing the investment benefit to the donor. The other application of investment is as a synonym for *spending*. Simply put, organizations should not "spend" money. Spending implies waste. It implies handing money out that will never be seen again. By contrast, *investing* implies wise stewardship and a return or benefit. For example, instead of spending money on new appliances, a soup kitchen might invest in an upgrade to its kitchen facilities in order to serve more homeless individuals.

Prosperity. This is a word that means more than wealth or financial well-being. *Prosperity* implies financial well-being and success acquired through hard work. Generally, people want to prosper, and they would like their children to prosper even more. Prospects should be shown how philanthropic planning can help them preserve their estate value while allowing them to realize their philanthropic aspirations. For example, an organization can show a prospect how a trust can be used to make a contribution while minimizing estate tax exposure for heirs thereby helping to ensure their prosperity.

Financial Security. Given the great recession of 2009-10 and the bursting of the dot-com bubble before that, Americans want *financial security*. They want to make sure that they and their loved ones are protected. A planned gift might help a donor in this regard. For example, a CGA might provide the donor, as well as a surviving spouse, with a retirement income. Knowing that a gift will continue to provide an income stream to a spouse, thereby providing financial security, could help inspire a prospect to make such a gift.

Peace of Mind. Most people want to feel a sense of security. However, today, *security* has a more militant context given the scourge of international terrorism. When thought of outside of the militant context, the word *security* has a fairly narrow application, usually financial. By contrast, *peace of mind* has a broader application that ties into one's desire for a hassle-free life. A nonprofit organization might educate prospects about the importance of having a will in order to gain the peace of mind that comes from knowing that one's loved ones have been taken care of. Prospects can also be encouraged to remember their favorite charity when writing that will.

Spirituality. The United States remains a very religious nation. There is an enormous amount of religious and *spiritual* diversity in the United States, and faith has relevance for an overwhelming number of Americans, even those who do not attend religious services regularly. This has obvious implications for charities that have a religious history or that continue to have a religious or spiritual connection. Those organizations should embrace and promote their own spiritual values. However, depending on the community, even secular organizations can embrace appropriate spiritual values whether or not the actual word is used. For example, a social service agency involved in providing medical care to expectant mothers who are economically disadvantaged might talk to prospects about the need to support strong family values with a planned gift to fund such medical services in the future.

Independent. Independence is an important, American core value. This is not surprising considering the country itself was established with a Declaration of Independence. When an organization is *independent,* it is seen as free from conflicts of interest, constraining ties, and outside influences. For example, a preparatory school might talk about how planned gifts will help build the endowment to ensure the school's independent future where faculty and parents will continue to design the curriculum rather than politicians. Or, a message might mention how a CGA can provide the donor with financial independence during retirement years.

Certified. Professional *certification* is one way development professionals can earn a bit of a prospect's trust. There are a number of relevant certification programs: Certified Fund Raising Executive, Certified Advisor in Philanthropy, and Certified Financial Planner to name just a few. Development professionals should earn at least one professional certification to give themselves more credibility when working with the public.[4]

KEY CONCEPT

When crafting messages, use power words that are appropriate to the organization and meaningful to the target audience.

Keep Messages Meaningful and Memorable

Effective marketing messages are simple, meaningful, consistent, and memorable. Coca-Cola billboards serve as a great reminder of this fundamental marketing principle. Many of the Coke billboards have simply shown the word *drink* above the famous, easily recognizable red and white Coca-Cola logo. It does not get simpler than that. The message is meaningful because everyone knows what Coke is. The billboards are familiar because they are common and are consistent with Coke's other advertising. The billboards will not necessarily cause people to leave the highway at the next exit in search of the bubbly beverage, but it will keep the product in people's minds when they are thirsty and ready to reach for a soft drink. That is good marketing.

Chip Heath and David Heath, authors of *Made to Stick: Why Some Ideas Survive and Others Die*, outlined six principles of effective messaging:

- Simplicity.
- Unexpectedness.
- Concreteness.
- Credibility.
- Emotion.
- Stories.[5]

A basic axiom of marketing is KISS—Keep It Simple and Stupid. Regardless of the medium being used, it is essential to know what your objectives are. This will help keep the message focused. Margaret Holman, principle at Holman Consulting, suggests that there are two primary questions one must ask of any message: (1) What do you want to gain? and (2) What do you want your audience to gain? [6] When looking at what the organization hopes to gain from the communication, it is necessary to keep the list short. Trying to accomplish too many things will dilute the message and ensure that nothing is accomplished. When considering what the audience might gain from the communication, consider how they will actually benefit from hearing or receiving the message. The more value there is for the prospect or donor, the more interest there will be in the message. The objective is not necessarily to be brief, but to be focused and meaningful.

When the content of a message is unexpected, it will capture attention. For example, an advertisement promoting a CGA might say something like, "Don't just give your money away; earn an income, too." Prospects expect to be asked for money. They do not expect to be told not to just give their money away. Many do not even know they can earn a lifetime income when they make a gift. So, this would be a message with two surprises. Even where bequest giving is concerned, many prospects have not considered what types of assets can be given and would be surprised to learn that their estates are as large as they are. The key to successfully delivering the unexpected is to do so it in a truthful *and* believable way.

By expressing ideas in concrete terms, development professionals will ensure that everyone receiving a message interprets it the same. Using simple language, illustrations, and examples can help ensure that the message is clearly understood. Testing a message with a small audience before deploying it more broadly will help the development professional refine it for maximum impact. However, planned giving officers need to be careful to speak in the correct concrete terms. When donors decide to make an annual fund contribution or current planned gift (i.e., stock), they are thinking about the here and now. For example, an animal shelter might talk about how many puppies can be fed with a gift of $50. However, as Sargeant and Shang have learned, since many planned gifts (i.e., bequests) will not be realized until some point in the future, it is often more useful for organizations to speak more abstractly about the preservation of institutional values.[7] For example, a rural hospital might talk about the need to ensure quality care close to home.

There are a number of ways to establish strong credibility in messaging. One can have the message delivered from someone with impeccable credentials relative to the message itself. For example, an environmental group might send information to a prospect in response to an inquiry. The package might contain a letter from the gift planning officer, a brochure, and a lift-note from a well-respected scientist at the organization speaking about the

Asking people instead of telling them, particularly when one knows the answer, is a powerful way to communicate.

impact of the group's work. A "lift-note" is simply a small, brief note inserted into the mailing package. The third-party endorsement of a concept is another way to help establish credibility. For example, a web page encouraging a prospect to consider a charitable bequest commitment might contain a story about an individual who has already made such a commitment. Another way to deliver a message with credibility is to get the audience to arrive at an idea themselves. Often times, if we tell someone something, they will not believe it. If they tell themselves, they are more likely to accept it. For example, a hospital could send former patients a letter noting the results of its patient satisfaction surveys and tell readers that 98 percent of patients had a favorable experience. Many patients might be suspicious of a claim promoting such a high number. However, if the hospital asks former patients to reflect back on the care they received, 98 percent (based on the patient satisfaction surveys) will have a positive feeling.

To really get people interested in a message, one must engage their emotions. For different causes, different messages will engage different emotions. Which emotions to engage will also depend on the audience. Save the Children engages emotions in a variety of ways. The organization's web site,[8] in the spring of 2010, showed dozens of smiling Haitian children. Save the Children did not exploit suffering children following the tragic earthquake to manipulate the feelings of web site visitors. Instead, the organization showed the results of its work in Haiti by highlighting the children who have benefited from its services. Rather than evoking pity, Save the Children stimulated a sense of hope. The positive images also encouraged visitors to dig deeper into the web site to learn how these children who have suffered so much can still smile so broadly.

When engaging the emotions of prospective planned gift donors, there are slightly different approaches that one can take depending on whether one is seeking a current planned gift (i.e., stock) or a deferred gift (i.e., bequest). Sargeant and Shang found that it is a matter of the subordinate versus the superordinate.[9] For example, for current gifts, a university might talk about the nuts-and-bolts needs of students, faculty, and facilities. In the context of deferred gifts, the bigger outcomes are more important. Donors want to know the broader impact of their gifts. So, a university might talk about the impact it will have on the community, how it will open up the lives of students, or how faculty research will save lives.

Another issue, identified by Sargeant and Shang, is that of context, contextualized versus decontextualized.[10] Appeals for a current planned gift might focus on meeting needs that exist today. For example, a homeless shelter might talk about the current economy and the need to provide meals for 100 people a night. When speaking about deferred giving, the shelter will want to speak more broadly. For example, the shelter might talk about how no one deserves to die on the street or how society has an obligation to help the less fortunate. By speaking more broadly, the organization reveals how a planned gift will preserve institutional values. It is important to speak of institutional values that are in alignment with the prospect's own long-term goals and sense of self. Show prospects how giving can help them be more the person they aspire to be.

For current planned gifts, a somewhat unstructured appeal can be effective since the focus is on the here and now. However, Sargeant and Shang found that a more structured message, one that focuses on a carefully conceived broader and longer-term vision will be more likely to move prospects to make a deferred gift commitment.[11] Vision matters.

Telling stories is a compelling way to get a message across and ensure it is remembered. Stories help anchor messages in the audience's mind. Stories allow the audience to imagine the situation and could even allow audience members to imagine themselves in the situation. Going back to the example of Save the Children, the web site contains numerous video and audio clips showing how Save the Children has positively impacted the lives of real children. The stories are sometimes horrifying but almost always hopeful. They allow prospects to imagine that they can help achieve the same tangible outcomes, that they can put a smile on a child's face.

Consistency in messaging is also of vital importance. One isolated advertisement about planned giving is easily forgotten or, worse yet, simply overlooked. Getting messages about gift planning out on a regular basis and through a variety of channels will eventually capture the attention of the desired audience and will increase the likelihood that a message will hit when it will be most meaningful to the recipient. This is the combination of multichannel marketing and the cumulative effect of advertising.

In *The Stanford Social Innovation Review*, Robert Cialdini outlined four rules for influence[12] that can be applied by the nonprofit sector. When followed individually in messaging, each can be useful. When messages follow all four of the rules together, messaging will be powerful. The four principles are:

1. *Reciprocity*, people want to repay what another has done for them.
2. *Scarcity*, people value that which is uncommon.
3. *Authority*, people defer to legitimate authorities as a decision-making shortcut.
4. *Consistency*, people want to behave consistently with the choices they have already made.

There are a number of ways nonprofit organizations can leverage *reciprocity*. Organizations can remind prospective donors of the services they or loved ones received or the services provided to the community that are cherished by the prospect. Organizations can also cultivate reciprocity by providing prospects and donors with special communications, small recognition gifts, free seminars, behind-the-scenes tours, and other amenities that are not available to the general public and further engage the individual. Far too many people do not even have a simple will. Showing people how they can protect their loved ones with basic estate planning will earn their appreciation. The challenge for the organization is to provide value to prospects and donors on an ongoing basis. For example, university alumni may be grateful for their education. However, if the last time the university did anything of value for them happened 40 years ago at graduation, the spirit of reciprocity will have faded, at least somewhat. The university needs to find a way of continuing to be relevant to each alumnus. This might involve reunion events, homecoming celebrations, invitations to lectures, sporting events, alumni magazine, just to name a few.

To leverage the principle of *scarcity*, organizations need to identify what makes them unique. In the commercial world, this would be called the "unique selling proposition." Organizations should describe and reinforce the features, benefits, characteristics, and services that make them unique. People generally value uniqueness.

Leveraging the principle of *authority* means identifying for people what the organization's area of expertise is. It also means securing relevant third-party expert endorsements of claims the organization makes or services it provides.

The fourth principle of influence is *consistency*. People want the organizations they support to be consistent. However, people also feel internal pressure to behave consistently themselves. This means the more engaged an individual is with an organization, the more likely they are to continue to engage. So, organizations will want to strive to remain relevant to the lives of prospects and donors.

When managing the relationship between prospects or donors and the organization, it is essential to keep these four principles of influence in mind. When messaging, the more of the principles that are leveraged, the more compelling the message will be.

Organizations can disseminate a variety of gift planning messages. Messaging can involve:

- Education of prospects and donors about planned giving, in general.
- Instruction about the various planned giving vehicles.
- Information about the specific impact that a planned gift can have. The more specific an organization can be the better.
- Asking for the gift (addressed later).
- Recognition of planned gift donors (addressed later).

Organizations can also distribute a variety of messages that support the planned giving effort, but that do not directly have anything to do with gift planning. For example, organizations should communicate with prospects and donors about the good work the organization is doing. Organizations can also distribute information that speaks generally of the importance of having a will.

In all cases, content should be developed with the focus on donors and prospects. To keep messages relevant and productive, organizations should identify each of their target audiences. Then, organizations should determine what messages must go to each audience to further educate and cultivate them. Then, organizations need to identify the tactics that will be most useful in disseminating the message. Tactics include timing, media, and selection of an appropriate messenger.

Existing Materials

One of the most effective and least expensive ways to market planned giving is to leverage existing communication materials. With little or no cost, an organization can deliver powerful and consistent messages about gift planning. For example, an organization can simply include the following line on all letterhead, business cards, and e-mail signatures: "Please remember us in your will and trusts." This simple reminder can yield results because it keeps the message in front of a very broad audience over time.

Most organizations already have a hardcopy or electronic newsletter. A gift planning message can appear in a variety of ways. The organization can devote a page or portion of a page to a planned giving advertisement. Or, the development professional can write an article featuring a planned gift donor. The article can describe what motivated the donor to make the gift, the impact the gift will have, and how the donor feels after having made the commitment. An article about something the organization is accomplishing can include a tag that says, "This work was made possible through a bequest gift that endowed the project."

KEY CONCEPT

Before telling donor stories, get their permission. Also, make sure the target audience can identify with the donors in the stories by highlighting a variety of different donors over time.

Virtually every nonprofit organization has a web site. While having a full-blown planned giving section can offer many benefits, even a simple one- or two-page section on the web site can educate prospects about the value of gift planning for both them and the organization.

Some organizations sponsor a lecture series. Perhaps, one of the lectures can be about estate planning. Or, perhaps there can be a simple "meet the speaker" planned gift donor recognition event following a regular lecture.

Every development professional has a business card. One should consider using the flipside for a message that supports philanthropic planning. For example, Rebecca Rothey, Director of Planned and Principal Gifts at Catholic Charities, has her organization's bequest language printed on her card. Dan H. Murrell, Director of Planned Giving at the University of Memphis, prints a short message on the back of his business card explaining what the Columns Society (the university's planned giving society) is and that the support of its members is critical to the future of the university. David B. Moore, Director of Planned Giving at Chapman University, has the university's mission statement printed on the back of his card. Roger Ellison, Vice President for Planned Giving at West Texas Rehabilitation Center Foundation, places his card in a holder made of cardstock that contains a list of benefits for the donor when making a planned gift: (1) increase your income, (2) bypass capital gains taxes, (3) reduce your income taxes, (4) increase what your heirs receive, and (5) reduce gift and estate taxes and probate costs. Ellison's card holder also outlines five promises that he makes to everyone he meets: "(1) careful listening, (2) attention to your best interests, (3) solutions which reflect your values and priorities, (4) professional expertise, (5) absolute integrity and confidentiality."

Nonprofit organizations already communicate regularly with prospects and donors in a variety of ways. By piggybacking on these existing communication channels, the planned giving message can be disseminated very economically.

Direct Mail

Even in the electronic age, direct mail remains a potent communications tool for nonprofit organizations, particularly those targeting older audiences. Direct mail can be used to educate prospects about gift planning, cultivate prospect interest, solicit inquiries, and even ask for gifts. Just like all other applications of direct mail, when using direct mail for planned gift marketing, the most important component is the list. The prettiest package and the most creatively crafted message will have no impact if it goes to the wrong audience. When feasible, organizations should segment targeted prospect pools into smaller groups in order to allow the tailoring of messages to each segment. For example, some planned giving messages may be appropriate for anyone over age 40 while messages about CGAs will be more appropriate for those over age 55.

Once the purpose of the mailing has been outlined and the prospect list has been assembled and segmented, it is time to design the package. One of the greatest challenges with direct mail is simply getting the intended reader to open the envelope. A brilliantly written message will never reach its target if the reader throws the piece in the trash without even opening it. Planned gifts are different than annual gifts. They are generally much larger gifts. Donors see these gifts as important. They take their time when considering them. The direct mail package should reflect this. The outer envelope and the letterhead used should, at a quick glance, alert the recipient that the mail piece is something special. Envelope size and stationery quality should also be considered. Instead of using a standard business-sized envelope, one should consider using a large envelope to mail a letter flat or a smaller, monarch-sized envelope that can convey a more personal sense. Using a higher quality paper will send the signal that this communication is special.

There are a number of effective ways to get an envelope opened. For mail that the recipient is expecting, perhaps in response to her request for information, many organizations include this simple statement on the front of the envelope: "Here is the information you requested." Recognizing that recipients will almost always first open mail that looks personal, many organizations give their direct mail pieces a personal look. One can hand address the envelope and use a live postage stamp instead of using metered postage. For larger mailings, there are electronic fonts that closely resemble actual handwriting. Some organizations have volunteers, with nice handwriting, address envelopes.

Handwritten notes are an effective way to capture someone's attention. In the electronic age, people are used to receiving countless e-mails and vast amounts of computer-generated letters. While a hand-addressed envelope will often get the envelope opened, a personal note inside will help ensure the message has impact. For example, if a newspaper publishes an article describing the safety of CGAs, one might want to send a copy of the article with a short, handwritten cover note. There are many potential applications for handwritten notes. For example, one can send a handwritten note to confirm an appointment, thank a prospect for a meeting, share a copy of the annual report, thank a prospect for his telephone inquiry, and so on. If one doubts the special impact that handwritten messages have, one can visit www.handwrittenletters.com, a web site devoted to this vanishing art form.

KEY CONCEPT

Christmas and Hanukkah cards are nice, but be sure to send the appropriate card. If you are unsure, send a generic Season's Greeting card. Also, consider sending cards at other holidays like Thanksgiving. For widows, send a Valentine's card; they will call you!

—Jim Brozo, Senior Gift Planning Advisor, Grossmont Hospital Foundation

When dealing with the obstacle that an envelope can create, some organizations have discovered that the best way to deal with it is to eliminate the envelope all together. Postcard mailings can deliver short messages very inexpensively. For example, the Philadelphia Museum of Art sent an oversized postcard to its members that featured an image of peaches from a painting by Pierre-Auguste Renior with the headline: "Enjoy the fruits of your giving!" The flipside of the postcard included the headline: "Establishing a Charitable Gift Annuity is like giving away the tree, but keeping the fruit." The card briefly described what a CGA is and provided some sample rates. Readers were invited to contact "Peggy Jackson, Director of Planned Giving" instead of being referred simply to the Office of Planned Giving. Providing specific contact information for an individual is one way to add a personal touch to a postcard. Jackson recognizes that good planned gift marketing involves much more than sending postcards. However, as one component of the overall marketing effort, postcard mailings are an inexpensive way to stay in front of prospective donors. While such mailings generate leads, they also create a great deal of awareness.

Whether using letters, handwritten notes, or postcards, it is important to remember that the target audience for planned giving messages is over the age of 40. Therefore, one should design such letters to be easily readable by eyes that are over the age of 40. For printed messages, this means using a font size that is large enough for most people to read without reading glasses. The font size should almost never be less than 12 point. Some believe that serif fonts (i.e., Times New Roman), though not as clean looking as sans-serif fonts (i.e., Arial), are actually more recognizable and,

KEY CONCEPT

Make sure that older eyes can read your messages. Use a large font size and maintain a high contrast between print and paper colors. Avoid reverse type because it is more difficult to read.

therefore, more readable. One should also use a high contrast between the written word and paper color. Using gray paper and black print will ensure that a letter is not read by many recipients.

If an organization is only going to send one planned giving direct mail message a year without any other marketing, it should probably not send it. Planned gift marketing requires a greater commitment on the part of the organization. Direct mail works best over time as one piece supports another and as the entire direct mail program supports other marketing activities. It is the cumulative effect of all marketing components that will yield strong results.

A marketing program that involves multiple direct mailings also provides an opportunity for testing. A postcard mailing might work well for one organization but not necessarily another. A postcard mailing with a tear-off response card might work better than one with only a call-in telephone number. To ensure that direct mail is working as productively as it can requires ongoing testing. Every mailing that is done should include some type

KEY CONCEPT

Send prospective bequest donors a letter with a postcard inside or simply substitute a different postcard for the one usually included in planned giving mailings. Instead of having the postcard come back to the organization, give the prospect a special postcard and suggest that it be sent to his attorney. On the address side of the postcard, it should have the appropriate number of address lines, with the top line ending in Esq. On the flipside, the postcard can say something like, "The next time I update my will, please remind me that I want to make a provision for XYZ Organization." Leave a line for a signature so the attorney will know who sent it. When the attorney receives the postcard, she will put it in the client file and remind the individual at the appropriate time. If the attorney is not busy, she might call the client and suggest that the will be changed right away.

—Donald W. Kramer, Of Counsel at Montgomery McCracken Walker and Rhoads and Editor of *Nonprofit Issues*®

of test element. For example, if doing a postcard mailing, one could divide the prospect pool in half and send one group a postcard that invites people to request more information online while the second group is sent a post-card with a tear-off response card to use when requesting more informa-tion; the difference in response mechanism would be the only variable. Then, the organization can evaluate the response rates to determine which style mailing generates the best result. The approach that works best would then be used exclusively in future mailings.

In addition to sending stand-alone letters or notes, direct mail can be used to provide an educational program. For example, an organization can invite people to enroll in an estate planning course. Those who enroll can receive periodic mailings with staged information. While the organization could send out a series of brochures about planned giving products (i.e., bequest brochure, CGA brochure, trust brochure, stock gift brochure), The Partnership for Philanthropic Planning of Greater Philadelphia's *Planned Giving Course*[sm] outlines eight donor-centered packages that are designed to help prospects meet their own personal planning objectives. Because they are donor-centered, prospects will be more likely to read the material. In addition, they will be more likely to appreciate the organization for sharing useful information that is not necessarily self-serving. The eight packages are: Crafting Your Legacy, Unlocking Value in Your Estate Assets, Using Your Real Estate Creatively, Increasing Your Retirement Income, Providing Income to Your Elderly Parents, Paying for College for Your Children or Grandchildren, Maximizing Your Children's or Grandchildren's Inheritance, Creating a Family Vision and Multi-Generational Plan.[13] Instead of sending prospects materials about planned giving products, donor-centered mailings help prospects deal with the real-life issues they must face.

Whenever writing letters, regardless of the core objective of the piece, development professionals should thank donors for their prior support and for caring. Regardless of how many people are going to receive the same letter, it should always be written as if written to one individual. The tone should be warm, personal, and conversational.

Almost every written communication should contain a call to action whether it is to visit the web site, respond to an invitation, request more information, or some other action. Organizations should make it easy for readers to respond. In addition to providing full contact information, a reply card and envelope can be included.

While direct mail can mean many things and have many applications, there are a number of important components to keep in mind regarding all mail:

- When preparing to mail, one should pay particular attention to the development of the mailing list.

- Ensure that the message is easily readable with older eyes.

- Make the package look and feel different and important compared to other mailings.

- Send handwritten notes to stand out and provide a personal touch.

- Use postcards as an inexpensive way to stay in front of prospects and donors.

- Employ donor-centered themes and messages.

Telephone

Every development professional has a telephone on her desk. It sits there for a reason, actually two reasons: (1) to receive calls, and (2) to make calls. These reasons might seem obvious, but a large number of organizations fail to use a donor-centered approach in conjunction with this old-school technology. The telephone is a very personal communication medium. People receive some of the best and some of the worst news of their lives via the telephone. Telephones are so important to people that most of us now carry one at all times. Yet, many development professionals treat the telephone as just another tool rather than the highly personal contact device it is.

Every organization should make it very easy for prospects and donors to call. This means including the development office or planned giving office telephone number on all marketing materials. It also means attaching a name to the telephone number. Prospects and donors would much rather call a person for information than some faceless, bureaucratic institution. And, they certainly do not want to hunt around to try to find the correct telephone number.

When a prospect or donor does call, she should be greeted by a live person. This will send the signal that the organization cares about and respects the caller. Organizations should not ask callers to navigate an impersonal, seldom well-designed, automated call director system. If the call is to one's direct line and goes directly to voicemail if not answered, one should give the caller the option of leaving a voicemail message or connecting to a live person. If an unanswered call goes to a live person, that individual should ask the caller if he can be of assistance or if the caller would prefer to go into voicemail. Where receiving calls is concerned, the objective of the organization should be to show people respect by making life as easy for them as possible.

When a telephone message is received, the development professional should return the call within 24 hours. When travel plans or other scheduling issues will make this impossible, callers should be alerted to this by the live assistant or by the recorded outgoing voicemail message. Alternatively, an assistant can call the individual back, apologize for the development professional's lack of availability, and determine if someone else can be of assistance or schedule a telephone appointment at a mutually convenient time.

If an organization plans a mailing or some other special planned giving promotion, it should anticipate an increase in the number of calls it will receive. The organization should prepare accordingly. For example, a development professional should not mail 10,000 CGA postcards the week before taking a two-week vacation. If one is going to drive people to the telephone, he should be there or nearby to handle the call when it comes in.

Good development people spend a significant amount of their time away from their desks doing productive things. This means that handling incoming telephone calls can be tricky. In addition to making sure that it is easy for a caller to leave a message or be directed to another person, organizations should make sure that other staff members can answer basic questions.

If you use the telephone wisely and offer prospects something of value with each contact, even simple information, they will look forward to your calls.

Every development professional should carefully train support staff so they will be prepared to answer very basic questions that the office typically receives. For example, if a woman calls in wanting to know what language she should use to include the organization in her will, an assistant should be able to provide that information or direct the caller to the information on the organization's web site.

When using the telephone to make calls, a priority should be to return calls promptly. In addition, the telephone can be used to set appointments for face-to-face visits and for general education and cultivation purposes including following up on information that was sent at the prospect's request. Regardless of the reason for the call, it is important to remember that the call is an intrusion. When making a call, the development professional should remember to identify herself and then ask permission to speak. If the prospect is unable to converse, an appointment can be set for a more convenient time. The prospect will be grateful for the development professional's flexibility and will be more receptive when called again.

Using a cell phone is fine unless one has a poor service or is in a poorly serviced area. If one is confident that the quality of both is good, then a call can be comfortably placed. However, if one is in a poorly serviced area or is unsure of the area, it is a good idea for one to alert the person on the other end that the call is being made from a mobile telephone in case the call is dropped. If one is using an unreliable service, one should change service providers, now.

Many development professionals put their mobile number on their business cards along with their office number. However, others do not include their cell number. When they present their card to a prospect or donor, these development professionals handwrite their cell number on the back of the card and present it with a statement like, "Here's my card. I've written my cell number on the back so you can feel free to reach me at any time." This underscores to the prospect or donor that he is special and important, someone worthy of receiving this privileged information.

Beyond the obvious uses of the telephone, some organizations are using the telephone to learn more about their prospects. As part of the prospect rating process, these organizations are calling prospects to survey them. They are finding out what interests prospects, what assets they have, whether they have a financial advisor, whether they have children, and other useful information. They are also confirming contact information and acquiring new details like e-mail address.

While the telephone is a powerful information-gathering tool, other nonprofit organizations are using the telephone to provide information to prospects. For example, one large, national charity called its planned giving prospects to ask them if they would like to receive monthly information about estate planning that could help them avoid taxes and better care for their loved ones. Prospects were first sent an opt-out letter that was followed by a telephone call describing the program and asking the prospect to enroll. Once enrolled, the communication switched to direct mail. The first "course" package included information about the importance of having a will and personal inventory. The second package provided helpful tips to prospects about how to select a financial advisor. Following that mailing, prospects received another call to see if they found the materials useful and if they had taken any estate planning steps. The third package included a third-party endorsement of estate planning, usually in the form of an article in an independent publication. The fourth and final cultivation package included a booklet outlining various charitable gift planning options. These cultivation calls and mailings set the stage for an ask, also by mail and telephone.

The telephone can also be used to ask for gifts and thank donors. These applications will be discussed later. When using the telephone to support the education and cultivation of prospects and donors, one should keep these key points in mind:

- The telephone is a highly personal medium and should be regarded as such in all cases.
- It should be easy for callers to reach a live person by telephone.
- Calls to prospects and donors should offer something of value.
- The telephone can be used to gather valuable information.
- The telephone can be used to engage and educate.

Newsletters

Newsletters are a practical way to communicate regularly with prospects and donors. An organization may have a general newsletter or magazine that can include planned giving content. In addition, when the budget permits, it is a good idea for organizations to also send a dedicated planned giving newsletter to prospects and donors. Such newsletters show prospects and donors that the organization cares about them, particularly if the content helps and benefits readers. It also helps to get prospective planned gift donors thinking about gift planning.

A dedicated planned giving newsletter can be produced quarterly, or even more often. It should be published no fewer than three times per year. The key is for the development professional to create a plan and then to stick to it. If people are accustomed to receiving an organization's newsletter on a quarterly basis and then, suddenly and without explanation, the newsletters stop coming for an extended period, people may, at best, begin to forget about the role planned giving plays for the organization or, at worst, may think something is wrong. People may even feel offended that they were dropped from the list, though they were not. Or, they may feel the organization did not send the newsletter because they can not afford to do so. Once a mailing schedule is started, it is difficult and awkward to alter it. Consistency is an essential component of using a newsletter for marketing.

Fifty percent of the marketing impact of a newsletter will depend on the list. Forty percent of the impact will be driven by content. Only 10 percent will be driven by design. Let these proportions guide where you put your effort.

—Viken Mikaelian, CEO and Founder, PlannedGiving.com

As with any marketing channel, it is important to identify the appropriate audience for the planned giving newsletter. Organizations should mail the newsletter to as many prospects and donors as possible given budgetary priorities. For organizations with limited budgets or other planned gift marketing priorities, newsletters should be sent to older donors as a priority group. Larry Stelter, President of The Stelter Company, suggests mailing, at a minimum, to annual donors age 55 and over who have given in three out of the last five years.[14] The mailing list should also include members of the organization's board, members of the organization's planned giving advisory council, staff, and volunteers. Budget permitting, the organization can mail to younger donors, those who have given less frequently, or even to those who have not given at all but have some type of relationship to the organization.

IN THE REAL WORLD

Less Can Yield More When You're Donor–Centered

A few years back, a colleague, Brian Sagrestano, killed most of a 40,000-piece quarterly newsletter mailing that his organization, University of Pennsylvania, was making. He pared his mailing list down to the 3,900 most loyal donors. Then, he developed a useful, fun-to-read newsletter.

The newsletter included columns such as what is necessary to prepare one's will, how to protect important documents while traveling, and other information anyone could appreciate and benefit from. Finally, he included focused, benefits-based planned giving articles such as "How to Establish an Endowed Scholarship with a Gift That Costs Nothing During Your Lifetime."

(continued)

> **IN THE REAL WORLD (CONTINUED)**
>
> The result? Even after eliminating more than 90 percent of his mailing list, the number of responses Sagrestano generated actually went up!
>
> "This was not a huge leap of faith for [Penn marketing guru] Colleen Elisii and me," Sagrestano explains. "The costs for the newsletter were exceptionally high and the yield was incredibly low. Changing the focus to a donor-centered approach inspired loyal donors to want to help. They were much more interested in what we were saying."
>
> —Viken Mikaelian, CEO and Founder, PlannedGiving.com

In contrast to the University of Pennsylvania, which significantly scaled back its newsletter mailing list to produce better results, Harvard University continues to send its planned giving newsletter to 54,000 people. However, Harvard does engage in periodic tests to determine ways to impact effectiveness or decrease cost. For example, Anne T. Melvin, Deputy Director of Planned Giving for the Faculty of Arts and Sciences at Harvard University, says that the university tested printing the newsletter in full color versus black-and-white. They found it made no difference in response rates. For other organizations, the outcome might have been different, which is why testing is so important.

The ideal newsletter will contain several short articles rather than just a few long pieces. People do not have time to wade through lengthy articles. People want to get useful information quickly and easily. Having several articles will also provide an opportunity to vary the subject matter, thereby enhancing the likelihood that the average reader will find something of interest. Content should be kept meaningful and useful to the reader. When sharing stories about donors, these stories should be real (and used with permission), rather than fictional or composite. Real stories convey greater emotion. Development professionals should be sure to highlight different types of donors so that prospects have a greater chance of eventually identifying with the donor and so that prospects also understand that gifts of all sizes are appreciated.

Extra! Extra! Read All About It!

The Stelter Company believes that organizations should carefully select content for planned giving newsletters in order to effectively educate and cultivate prospects and donors. Here is some of the content they recommend:

Reserve the front page for a donor testimonial story. Include a photo of the donor when possible. Place emphasis on why the gift was made as well as the benefits to the organization and the donor. Place less importance on the amount of the gift, the type of gift vehicle used, or the intricacies of how the vehicle works. Save such details for an inside article that outlines the gift in broad strokes.

Feature at least one article in each publication covering wills and bequests. People need to hear your message many times before it sinks in. Don't be afraid to consistently promote these basic components.

Include your organization's sample bequest language in each issue.

Provide clear instructions as to how your organization can assist donors. Give the name of a contact person and a toll-free telephone number.

At least once a year, include a list of the newest members of your legacy society.

Include a variety of topics in each newsletter—covered in three to five shorter articles, as opposed to one long piece on a single topic. The reasoning is that if a single topic you are sharing happens to bore your readers, they have several other articles to keep them interested.

If you don't want to put your readers to sleep, then limit what you say about life insurance. I can't think of any other topic in my experience that has pulled in a lower response rate. Let's face it. Talking about life insurance is dull.

Real estate can be another tricky subject. I've found that certain areas of the United States are more amenable to reading about gifts of real estate than others. If you live in an area where real estate values have catapulted, consider including the topic—but maybe on the back page.

Each newsletter should hit on the following four themes:

1. *A heartwarming story.* Include a testimonial from someone who has supported your organization with a planned gift or someone who has benefited from a donor's generosity.

(*continued*)

As with direct mail, newsletters should be printed with older eyes in mind.
High contrast will help ensure readability. Black print on white paper is easiest
to read. Avoid reverse type, white letters on a dark background, which is difficult to read, fax, or photocopy.

To enhance the look of newsletters and to make them more engaging, they
should contain photographs. However, avoid stock photographs that offer little
meaning. Readers would much rather see photographs of the actual people an

organization serves or buildings that are familiar and create nostalgia. While photographs of real, smiling donors are fine and a good donor recognition technique, readers prefer to see images showing how the organization fulfills its mission.

In this electronic age, many organizations have relied increasingly on Internet technology to communicate with people. While e-mail, web site, and social networking technologies can all be used effectively, good old-fashioned paper still has a place. While older people are increasingly using the Internet, their usage rates and comfort levels are still not as great as for younger people. Even when marketing to younger adults, paper newsletters allow organizations to capture an individual's attention in another way. Once again, it is all about multichannel marketing with one channel supporting another so that the organization can benefit from the cumulative effect of all efforts.

Readers should be encouraged to take some type of action. The newsletter should also provide readers with a number of easy ways to contact the organization, and encourage them to do so. The publication can suggest readers visit the organization's web site to read additional articles, use gift calculators, view photographs and videos. The newsletter can also include a clip-and-mail slip to request information, a pull-out reply postcard or, ideally, a response card and envelope to ensure personal information remains confidential. At a minimum, every newsletter should provide full contact information including name, title, address, telephone number, and e-mail address. The goal is not necessarily to

In the Real World

Executive Insight

Ironically, those who continue to use traditional communication channels as their primary communication with the conventional market for planned gifts may find great receptivity from older persons who begin receiving less mail as some organizations thin out the mail by opting to market planned gifts to a younger universe of donors through more active use of the web.[16]

—Robert F. Sharpe, Jr., President, The Sharpe Group

get the reader to make a gift. The goal is to engage the reader and to continue that engagement.

One northeastern university mails over 50,000 newsletters. From that, they might receive 30 requests for information that ultimately lead to four bequest expectancies. The primary purpose of a newsletter is to educate and cultivate. A high-volume response rate is not expected. However, four bequest commitments is certainly a strong return on investment despite the low, but reasonable, response rate.

While it is less expensive to mail a newsletter without an envelope, many organizations find that readership goes up when the newsletter is mailed flat, inside an envelope. When preparing planned giving newsletters, one should also keep the following points in mind:

- Plan to mail a newsletter at least three times per year.
- Once an organization starts sending newsletters, it should consistently maintain its production schedule.
- Mail to as many prospects and donors as the budget will permit with planned gift donors and older, frequent annual donors as the priority.
- Make sure the newsletter is designed for older eyes.
- Include several short articles on varied topics.
- Include photographs, particularly of those benefiting from services.
- At least once a year, recognize planned gift donors in the newsletter.
- Include full contact information in all newsletters.
- Call readers to action.

Web Site

Most nonprofit organizations have a web site. It is just common sense. The Internet is the clearinghouse for information that people need every day including researching stock performance, finding out the weather forecast, reading a film review, catching up on the news headlines, or getting driving directions.

People go online. Nonprofit organizations need to be represented on the Internet, and they are—some using the medium better than others.

While some nonprofit organizations new to gift planning do not have dedicated planned giving pages on their web site, they should nevertheless contain some vital planned giving information on existing pages. However, as the planned gift marketing effort grows, the organization will want to have a dedicated planned giving section on its web site.

Planned giving prospects of every type are online, even senior citizens. So, it is definitely time to meet them there with the highest-performance marketing tools one can muster, as well as an overall donor-centered strategy to make it all work.

It is important for every organization to know whether its web site is helping or hurting its marketing efforts. Not only are prospects online, but they are getting savvy about being online, so development professionals had better check exactly what it is web site visitors will encounter when they visit.

Viken Mikaelian, CEO and Founder of PlannedGiving.com and his team have helped nearly 500 nonprofit organizations launch web-based planned giving marketing programs.* In addition, the company conducts national surveys and publishes reports to assist fundraising and communications professionals. Mikaelian observes, "The phrase we use as shorthand for prospects' attitudes is 'Don't make me think.' Your web site should be reader-friendly and easy-to-comprehend on the first viewing. Otherwise, your prospects will click elsewhere, and fast. You don't want them to do that."

Development professionals should visit their web site and ask the following questions:

- Is the planned giving section easy to find?
- Is it reader-friendly and easy to navigate?
- Is text presented in easy-to-digest portions? Or, does unbroken text scroll, discouragingly, down and down the page?
- Is it visually appealing?

---

*Viken Mikaelian, CEO and Founder of Planned Giving.com, graciously contributed extensive material for the sections about Web, e-mail, and newsletters.

- Does it look as intended regardless of the Internet browser used and the type of monitor used?

- Are the gift descriptions clear, engaging and to the point?

- Is the focus on the benefits that a gift plan can provide the reader? Or, does it contain dry recitations of gift plan features, such as, "The second tier of income distributed to you by a charitable remainder trust will be treated as capital-gain income, to the extent that the trust has recognized capital gain within the relevant tax period."

Mikaelian recognizes that only 15 percent of people are "literal," while the remaining 85 percent are "visual." So, web site visitors should be visually engaged. Planned giving professionals should build illustrations into gift descriptions, incorporate graphically exciting callouts (blurbs pulled from the main text, set off in larger type or boxed for emphasis), and keep paragraphs short with plenty of breaks in between for easy reading.

Content should also take full advantage of technology. Simply converting a printed brochure into an electronic brochure is not enough. "Remember, there are exciting ways to convey information on a web page that never existed for the printed page," Mikaelian says. "For example, if you provide extensive gift descriptions, don't just dump them on the page. Feed the information to your readers via interactive 'Learn More' links. This kind of technique will make a web site 'sticky' by keeping prospects playing around on it. Meanwhile, you're building their interest in being a part of your program." Other ways to engage visitors are with videos and gift calculators.

Savvy corporate web sites offer surveys, online contests, and blogs as ways to engage visitors. In addition to gathering data, these tools keep customers from quickly leaving the web site. They help create a bond between the customer and the business product. Nonprofit organizations can achieve the same thing.

Most donors do not know what *planned giving* means. Most Americans do not really know what a *bequest* is. If they do, many think it is something only wealthy people or celebrities do. So, organizations should lose the technical jargon and focus on language that real people speak. Web sites should be more inviting with appropriate, useful messages along with exciting images including, when the budget permits, videos. One should not expect prospects to wade through masses of planned giving technical content. Instead, development professionals should consider this: Stories about people have human interest—they involve the reader in ways technical material never will. That is why one should highlight individual donors and "story-tell" the whys of their giving. The specifics about gift vehicles are not particularly relevant. Understanding what inspired the donor is more important. Donor stories can stimulate others to give and encourage second-time gifts as well. Creating an archive of donor stories is also a nice way to recognize donor support. When prospects identify with donors, they are more likely to follow in their footsteps. So, organizations should be sure to post stories about donors of every description who have given gifts of various sizes and types.

When building a planned giving section, some organizations use material supplied by vendors. Some have vendors supply stock material for the entire planned giving site. Some of these products are of reasonable quality.

 IN THE REAL WORLD

A Picture Is Worth 1,000 Words, and Some Chuckles

Donor stories not only help your prospects identify with people, they also give you the chance to be warm and fuzzy. A good example of this is a photo Oberlin College had online of three donors, two older women and a man, wearing their cheerleading outfits holding a football. When you clicked through, you saw the same three, wearing the same clothes but, in the photo from 1949, they were cheerleading at a football game when they were young. Oberlin used web technology to connect two pictures that tell an engaging, compelling donor story. It's web-centric, donor-centric, and creative!

—Viken Mikaelian, CEO and Founder, PlannedGiving.com

However, most will seem fairly dry and cookie-cutter unless the content is personalized to each individual organization. A truly powerful planned giving web site will be completely integrated with the organization's overall web site. A visitor should know that they have visited a particular web site by the character of the site and the content, not just the name at the top. Interchangeable web sites are not as compelling as customized web sites. However, for some organizations that have staff or budgetary constraints, standardized sites may be the best option.

If an organization uses stock content, there is one sin that should be avoided at all cost. Some well-intentioned vendors distribute composite "donor" stories. These are fictional stories based on typical donors. The accompanying photographs are of models not real donors. Unfortunately, some organizations try to pass these stories off as real rather than clearly labeling them as composite stories. Passing off a composite story as a real story is a lie and, therefore, unethical. If discovered, it will erode trust. Organizations should never lie to prospects and donors. While labeling a composite story as such solves the ethical problem, it also renders the story nearly useless, which may explain why some organizations skip the label. Identifying a story as a composite also makes the web site seem like a television commercial selling soap. By contrast, donor-centered planned gift marketing is not about trying to sell a product. It is about helping people realize their philanthropic aspirations in a meaningful way while protecting their loved ones. It is built on integrity. Real stories, used with the permission of donors, can be an emotional endorsement in a way that composite stories cannot. Real stories will show recognizable faces. Think of the Oberlin story in the previous "In the Real World." Virtually everyone from the Class of 1949 will remember at least one of the cheerleaders. As a result, their story will resonate and inspire. One will not have that advantage with a composite donor story. Furthermore, using real donor stories is a fantastic way to recognize donors. Not only do they get to leave a legacy through their gift, but they get to leave a lasting legacy by inspiring others with their story. Organizations should use real stories. If they truly cannot, composite stories should be clearly labeled as such.

Tell real stories about real donors to maximize emotional impact.

True communication involves a two-way flow of information. Once a visitor has viewed an organization's web site, it should be very easy for her to contact a planned giving officer. Visitors should never have to hunt for contact information. If they are forced to do so, they will not; they will simply visit another web site without bothering to contact the planned giving officer at all.

Contact information should be easy to find but it also should be done with a personal touch. Rather than providing a telephone number to the planned giving department, organizations should provide the names of planned giving staff, their numbers, and their e-mail addresses. Mikaelian also suggests, "Place your photo, and possibly your bio, online. Your prospects want to see who they will be talking to. If you are a one-person shop, get creative. If you're the only fundraiser at a veterinary hospital, say, include a photo of Tonka the black lab as your administrative assistant! And give Tonka a phone number and an e-mail address as well! Just be sure to answer when Tonka is out."

Planned giving does not have to be boring. As long as it is tasteful, a funny, corny web site will engage people and encourage them to call. However, even the most creative web site will be wasted if nobody knows it is there. Organizations must drive web site traffic. Unless prospects are prompted, they will only

Do not frustrate interested prospects who would gladly pick up the telephone and call you if they could simply find your name and number. Make contact names, numbers, and e-mail addresses easy to find.

find an organization's web site accidentally, or by their own hunting efforts. Donor-centered marketing does not place the burden on the prospect or donor.

Mikaelian advocates the following three-level approach to informing an organization's constituents that a web-based resource exists to help them plan their gifts.

Use external sources. It may be counterintuitive, but when a web site is ready, one should use traditional hardcopy, snail-mail materials to tell prospects and donors about it. This approach works because most Americans still prefer to receive their information via the U.S. Postal Service. One can also piggyback on the organization's other communications. Here are some ways to use traditional marketing to promote a web site:

- Send a special flashcard (i.e., "Want to learn more about the gifts that pay you back?").

- Highlight the web site in the fundraising newsletter or in the organization's general publication with an article.

- Print display ads in the organization's publications.

- Consider refrigerator magnets and coffee mugs bearing the URL.

- Add a line beneath the signature on every prospect communication that says, "Did you know that you can make a gift that costs you nothing during your lifetime?" Then, place a customized, easy-to-remember and easy-to-type referring-URL that takes them to the planned giving section of the organization's web site.

Use internal sources. Organizations already communicate with prospects and donors with an institutional web site. Promotion of the planned giving section of a web site can be piggybacked onto these other pages. Here are some options:

- Any place an organization's web site talks about new projects or opportunities, or about endowment, one can insert a link to the planned giving site. While a simple link is fine at a minimum, one should consider enhancing the transition with lines like: "You can support this research with a gift that costs nothing during your lifetime." "Many of our retired volunteers have established charitable gift annuities for the hospital." "You can place us in your will just like Mrs. Jones did. Click here to learn how."

- At the beginning of a web page describing research breakthroughs, one can simply mention: "Much of this research was funded through creative gifts made by . . . " with the words *creative gifts* hyperlinked to the planned giving pages.

- Below one's signature line, above the address, place a catchy phrase like "Make a Gift and Receive Income for Life" and hyperlink it to the corresponding page (in this example, the CGA page) on the planned giving web site.

Promote your web site personally. A no-cost, yet often overlooked way to promote a planned giving web site is for the planned giving officer to promote it personally. Here are some simple ways one can promote a web site:

- Add the URL to business cards.

- Show off the web site at a meeting of the planned giving advisory council during a regularly scheduled meeting.

- Mention the web site to prospects when visiting with them or, better yet, show them the web site on their computer or a laptop computer brought along for the purpose. Giving a little guided tour of the web site is the most powerful introduction to the web site a prospect can get.

- Mention the web site at events.

- E-mail the appropriate link to a prospect as part of the response to a request for more information.

A web site can be a useful tool for educating and cultivating prospects. Development professionals should keep the following in mind when including a planned giving web site in the marketing mix:

- Ensure that the planned giving section is easy to find.

- Create a planned giving section that is easy to use and easy to read.

- Provide information that is useful to site visitors.

- Think creatively when designing the web pages to make them engaging.

- Promote the planned giving section to drive traffic.

- Tell real donor stories to inspire others.

- Make full contact information obvious so prospects can effortlessly be in touch.

E-mail

E-mail represents a powerful and convenient communication tool. It can be used to send individual messages or for mass communication, particularly in the form of e-newsletters. Unfortunately, the enormous popularity of e-mail has actually become a problem. People are inundated with e-mails from friends, family, colleagues, vendors, retailers, and others. Some of these e-mails are wanted, some are not. For most people, the volume of e-mails they receive weekly is quite significant. This causes a condition known as "marketing over-load." People now receive so many e-mail messages that they scan them with one finger hovering over the Delete key, warns Mikaelian. Many e-mails do not even get opened. The last thing any development professional wants is a prospect or donor to actually press the Delete key when reviewing the subject line of her message, assuming it made it through the spam filter in the first place.

It is very easy for an organization's e-mail message to get lost in the crowd. And, if a nonprofit organization is guilty of adding to the clutter in someone's e-mail box, it can create resentment. Even many readers who have opted-in to an e-newsletter will grow tired or annoyed with it if it comes too frequently and if it fails to deliver relevant information of value to the recipient.

Part of the problem with e-newsletters is that they are often sent too frequently. For example, some vendors recommend sending e-newsletters on a weekly basis. Another problem is that they tend to be generic and dull. For example, many e-newsletters rely on boilerplate material rather than content tailored to the specific organization. While e-newsletters have admittedly gained popularity, they often are not utilized with a donor-centered orientation. Organizations tend to use e-newsletters because they are relatively inexpensive. If using a service, they are also simple to implement. While on the surface these may be two good organization-centric reasons for using e-newsletters, donors and prospects have largely been removed from the equation. Organizations often think that e-mailing is very inexpensive. However, these organizations usually fail to factor in the cost of nonresponse. Unfortunately, annoyed prospects are no longer prospects. That can be very expensive in a planned giving program. To understand this, one must keep in mind that prospects create value for an organization in two ways: (1) by contributing today, and (2) by increasing their intent to contribute in the future.

If an organization sends out 10,000 e-newsletters and gets a 0.05 percent response rate—five responses (i.e., inquiries)—the organization has done pretty well. However, one needs to look at the flipside. In this scenario, 9,995 people did not respond. While some may nevertheless still have been interested in the e-newsletter content, the fact remains that thousands were, at best, indifferent to it or, at worse, were annoyed by it on some level. These recipients may be high-value and high-potential prospects, and if they perceive the e-newsletter as annoying spam and an unwelcome intrusion in their inbox, the sender has just shot herself in the foot. When one factors in the cost of potentially alienating thousands of prospects, it turns out that e-newsletters can actually be quite expensive.

IN THE REAL WORLD

Executive Insight

Spam by any other name is still spam. Promotional material automatically mass mailed to a list of e-mail addresses will quickly tire prospects, even if they have given the organization permission (opted-in) to send them e-mail blasts. Soon, they'll be punching the delete key. Dressing pseudo-spam up and calling it a newsletter is a technique that doesn't fool anyone on the receiving end. In the technical world, opted-in spam is called bacon. Just remember, it's still junk food.

—Viken Mikaelian, CEO and Founder, PlannedGiving.com

E-mail messages are immediate, intimate, and timely. They are quick blasts from a friend or coworker that share something that is happening now that one should not miss. People open e-mails, read them, and act on them. If one wants his e-mails to planned giving prospects to be read, he must write the content with those specific traits in mind, advises Mikaelian.

"Even more than with print materials, e-mails are subject to a quick thumbs-up/thumbs-down verdict by their recipients, based on their relevance and impact. In other words, they're a great medium to announce, 'Gift annuity rates are now three times the average yield on a share of common stock!' But on the other hand they're a very poor way to inquire, 'Do you know what a gift annuity is?' Your e-mail messaging should work with this, not against it," according to Mikaelian.

One should use e-mails to share news—even if the topic is not news to the sender. What matters is how the recipient views it. Some headlines might include:

- "Our Campaign is halfway toward its goal!"
- "Here's how Dr. and Mrs. Smith used a gift of life insurance and a 1955 Corvette to create their research fellowship."
- "Alumni will honor Coach Blitz with an endowment for the team in his name."
- "Leaving your IRA to your kids? Most of it will go to Uncle Sam."

Development professionals should tell e-mail recipients what exciting things are happening and how they can be a part of them. Mikaelian recommends e-mailing when there is an important reason to do so, perhaps four to six times a year at most. Message copy should be kept to under 10 lines. This is where one really gets traction with a less-is-more approach. Think new, exciting, concise, easy, and fast while keeping the topics grounded in the mission and needs of the specific organization.

The other application for e-mail messaging is one-on-one communication. E-mail can be a great way to stay in touch with a donor, confirm a meeting,

KEY CONCEPT

Consider timing an e-mail message to echo a direct mail message about a week or two after the mail is sent. One message will reinforce the other.

—Anne T. Melvin, Deputy Director of Planned Giving, Faculty of Arts and Sciences at Harvard University

quickly exchange simple information, and so on. When using e-mail for one-on-one communication, one must find out the recipient's preferred e-mail address and should make the e-mail as personalized as possible so that it does not resemble an e-blast. The subject line should also be carefully written to create a unique identity for the e-mail. Development professionals should still be careful not to inundate recipients with even personal e-mails.

When sending any type of e-mail, it is important to do so at a time when recipients will be most receptive. The prevailing wisdom is that e-mail messages should be sent on Tuesdays, Wednesdays, or Thursdays when recipients are less likely to be distracted. Since many e-mail users quickly delete "junk" from their overstuffed inboxes at the beginning of each day, it is better to send e-mail messages from mid-morning through mid-afternoon. However, testing is warranted since readership rates and readers' habits may vary from organization to organization and constituency to constituency.

While services exist that can append e-mail addresses to one's prospect or donor file, there are a number of problems with such efforts. First, the match rates are usually very low. Second, even if there is a record match, the accuracy rate for the e-mail addresses provided are also low. Third, before one can begin using the addresses, recipients should be given an opportunity to opt-out of receiving e-mail messages; obtaining the recipients, permission is extremely important in donor-centered marketing. Therefore, the best way to obtain e-mail addresses is from prospects and donors themselves.

When creating any type of e-mail message, one should keep the following in mind:

- Collect e-mail addresses on an ongoing basis.

- Get permission to send e-newsletters.

- Make it easy for people to opt-out whenever they might choose to do so.

- Remember that less is more. When designing an e-mail, keep it simple. Many people read e-mails on their phones. The overuse of graphics can render the message unreadable in that format. Even on a desktop computer, some browsers and e-mail software will fail to display fancy messages as intended.

- Mail-merge messages to allow a personal salutation to be included in each one, just like a letter.

- Minimize the chances of your e-mail messages being tagged automatically as spam by staying away from e-mailing through bulk senders. This means, if one has 1,000 prospects on a list, one sends 1,000 individual e-mails, and not a copy of one e-mail to all 1,000.

- Use a familiar sender, and do not change senders.

- Write an intriguing subject line.

- Combine a planned giving message with someone else's e-mail in the organization. For example, an organization might be preparing to send an article about a project it is working on. At the end of the article, the planned giving officer could mention how a gift through a donor's will could endow it.

- Do not overwhelm donors or prospects with e-mails.

- Use e-mail to remind people what the organization does. Send information about how the organization is making a difference. Do not just use e-mail to promote giving directly.

- When writing an e-mail message, remember to make it sound like it is being sent to just one person no matter how many will receive the same message.

- Development professionals should be prepared to follow up on e-mail responses immediately. E-mail is an immediate form of communication that requires immediate response.

Social Networking Technology

Social networking refers to a variety of technologies and services that allow individuals and organizations to interact via the Internet. Popular social networking services include Facebook, Twitter, MySpace, and LinkedIn. Whether or not a nonprofit organization chooses to actively participate on these social networking sites, they are impacted by them for one reason: Many people are using these sites and some are talking about the organizations they like and the ones they do not.

Social networking sites are attracting millions of participants. Facebook, just one site alone, boasts the following numbers:[17]

- More than 400 million active users.

- Fifty percent of active users log on to Facebook in any given day.

- More than 3 billion photographs are uploaded to the site each month.

- More than 3.5 million events are created each month.

- More than 1.5 million local businesses have active pages on Facebook.

- More than 20 million people become fans of pages each day.

In February 2010, Twitter achieved a new milestone by processing more than 50 million Tweets, messages of a maximum of 140 characters, in one day.[18] Social networking is not just for the young. For example, one of the fastest growing segments of the population on Facebook are women from age 55 to 65.

While electronic social networking should not and cannot take the place of more personal human interaction, the technology can be used to build trust by educating and cultivating prospects and donors. This is particularly true in cases where geography might make it difficult to do this any other way. Development professionals can use social networking sites to remind the public how the organization is making a difference. For example, a disaster relief agency might post pictures and videos of its staff helping to provide relief to flood victims. If an organization is going to be featured on the local news, sending a Twitter message can encourage more people to tune in.

Social networking technologies are an informal way for organizations to stay in front of prospects and donors, provide useful and immediate information, and show people how the organization is making a difference. It is also a good way to encourage positive word-of-mouth. For example, an organization might post photographs from a recent fundraising event. Some of those who attended the event might then in turn share the pictures with their friends thereby exposing more people to the organization and reinforcing the positive experience for the attendee.

Even if an organization does not actively participate in social networking sites, it is important for these sites to be monitored. The average Facebook user has 130 "friends" on the site with some users having thousands. Some Twitter users have thousands of followers. If one of these people has a bad experience with an organization and broadcasts that fact, it could create a public relations nightmare for the organization. Organizations should have a plan in place for dealing with such challenges, though sometimes the best strategy will be to ignore it. For example, unfounded rants may be best ignored, but organizations should consider correcting factual errors. Conversely, someone might surprise an organization with unexpected, gushing praise. That would be a prospect worth contacting and thanking. At an absolute minimum, organizations should be aware of what the public is saying about them and, therefore, should monitor the popular social networking sites.

IN THE REAL WORLD

Social Networking Meets Prospects Where They Are

At Chapman University, I created a Facebook page. After six weeks, the Charles C. Chapman Heritage Society fan page had nearly 100 fans. This number is expected to grow significantly over time given that other official Chapman Facebook pages reach thousands of people.

I initially promoted the page by suggesting to my own Facebook friends associated with Chapman University (via the site) that they should become fans of the page. Within a few hours, I started seeing unfamiliar names also becoming fans. It had gone viral that quickly!

The Charles C. Chapman Heritage Society fan page provides estate planning information for people of all ages, but I made a special effort to keep most of it targeted at the under 40 demographic, planting the seed; however, the page has attracted a number of people from as far back as classes from the 1950s. Periodically throughout the week (at different times of the day), I post a teaser and then link it to the related page on our web site: www .chapman.edu/plannedgiving. I try to make sure I keep the page visually interesting by making sure to periodically include articles with graphics.

I also have a few more ways that I'm currently promoting the Facebook page (and thus planned giving):

1. Our monthly planned giving e-newsletter includes a "Become a Facebook Fan" link.

2. When I post a spotlight on the Facebook page, I tag the Facebook profiles of the individuals for whom I am connected. As their friends spot the tag, they may also want to become fans.

3. The current signature file on my e-mail now promotes the Facebook page.

4. I post the teasers on the official Facebook fan pages of various audiences around campus: Chapman Alumni Association, Church Relations, Athletics, Chapman University.

5. I plan to include a post as part of the faculty/staff online newsletter/blog at www.chapman.edu/happenings.

6. The planned giving web site includes a "Become a fan on Facebook" promo on the left sidebar.

I don't include anything about the Facebook page in print publications because I don't think it would elicit a response—to be effective, the promotion has to involve a simple click of a hyperlink.

The thing I like most about the Facebook page is that it allows me to get information out to our page fans rather than relying on them to discover the planned giving web site on their own. Someone has to be pretty mature in their legacy thought process to find the planned giving web site but, via Facebook, I can plant seeds and generate nontraditional traffic to our web site. Of course most people don't follow the link or perhaps even see the post in the first place, but this is a long-term strategy of engagement.

(continued)

> **IN THE REAL WORLD (CONTINUED)**
>
> Similar to Facebook, I have also started posting information to my status on my LinkedIn profile. I don't do this on my personal Facebook page, but the professional focus of LinkedIn makes these "status posts" feel appropriate.
>
> I also like that the Facebook "insight" feature of my fan page breaks down the demographics and related page activity of the fan membership. This is a very useful marketing feature.
>
> —David B. Moore, Director of Planned Giving, Chapman University

When thinking about social networking technology, one should remember:

- Whether or not an organization chooses to use social networking technology, millions of charity supporters already are.

- It is important for organizations to know what is being said about them.

- Organizations should consider sharing timely information that reinforces the message about how the organization is making a difference.

- Social networking sites can provide an informal venue to help prospects and donors better get to know the development staff.

- Electronic social networking is not a substitute for real human contact.

Events

Events can be a great way for organizations to educate and cultivate prospects. Planned gift marketing can piggyback on existing events. Such events can include recognition of planned gift donors, brief information about gift planning, or the dissemination of printed material about gift planning.

Events specifically focused on gift planning should be centered on the needs and interests of donors. For example, donor-centered seminar topics can be in alignment with the fundamental information disseminated through direct mail, as mentioned previously in *Planned Giving Course*: "Crafting Your Legacy," "Unlocking Value in Your Estate Assets," "Using Your Real Estate Creatively," "Increasing Your Retirement Income," "Providing Income to

Your Elderly Parents," "Paying for College for Your Children or Grandchildren," "Maximizing Your Children's or Grandchildren's Inheritance," "Creating a Family Vision and Multigenerational Plan." One should also remember that it is never too early to begin educating and cultivating prospective planned gift donors of any age.

Other types of events can tie into organizational mission. Prospects and donors can be invited to special research briefings, meet and greets, and behind-the-scenes tours designed to demonstrate mission fulfillment made possible through donor support. For example, the Foundation Fighting Blindness hosts periodic lectures about the latest scientific research involving vision. While not specifically a planned giving cultivation event, such programs cultivate support of every type in two important ways. First, prospects and donors can hear directly from scientists and learn how contributions have funded vital research. Second, attendees, many of whom either suffer from an eye disease or have a loved one who does, can learn the latest information that could impact their condition. By giving prospects and donors this "insider" status, the Foundation is educating and cultivating.

When hosting education and cultivation events, there are a number of things to keep in mind. When attempting to attract a more senior audience, one should remember that many older adults do not like to drive after sunset. Therefore, events targeting senior citizens should be held earlier in the day or in the spring and summer when the sun sets later. Other seniors no longer drive at all. If one knows who these individuals are, arrange transportation for

KEY CONCEPT

When hosting senior citizens at an event involving a meal, never serve spinach or grapefruit as a couple of common senior medications prohibit these foods.

—Ann Barden, Gift Planning Director, Oregon Health & Science University Foundation, Doernbecher Children's Hospital Foundation

KEY CONCEPT

Always provide plastic storage bags or other packaging at events for people to pack with treats for later. Many people live in facilities that do not have lemon bars or brownies, and these little treats are most appreciated—and often shared with a story. Even if someone does not live in such a facility, having the opportunity to take home a few treats will be appreciated.

—Ann Barden, Gift Planning Director, Oregon Health & Science University Foundation, Doernbecher Children's Hospital Foundation

them to the event. However, since it is unlikely that one will know all of the nondrivers, it is helpful to include a line in the event invitation that encourages individuals to contact the organization for assistance in arranging transportation if necessary.

When doing event planning, one should consider ways to be of service to attendees. For example, the venue should be not just handicap accessible but truly easily accessible. Lighting should be appropriate for the audience. If a program book is distributed at the event, the print should be large enough to be easily read by all in attendance. "Runners" should be available to assist attendees who are not completely ambulatory. Every event is an opportunity to share useful information with prospects and donors, show them the respect they deserve, educate them, and cultivate their support.

Event planning can be tricky. Here are some basic tips:

- Send an upcoming events listing as an e-mail, e-newsletter, print newsletter, postcard, or insert into another mailing at least four to six weeks in advance.

- Send the event invitation three weeks prior to the event.

- Ask people to respond up to one week prior to the event. However, always be prepared to make exceptions since the objective is to get people to the event.

- For free events, anticipate that only half of the respondents will actually attend with an additional 5 percent showing up who never responded.

- To maximize attendance, have a friend or colleague invite friends and colleagues. Someone is more likely to accept an invitation from a friend or colleague and then is more likely to actually show up than if they were simply invited by the organization.

- It is critical that the development professional recognizes that he is the host of the event. That means he must make sure that the needs of attendees are met, that attendees are greeted by staff or volunteers, and that attendees are engaged and introduced to one another.

- Follow up invitations with a friendly telephone call. The idea is to keep it casual, make sure the individual received the invitation, and see if she needs assistance getting to the event.

- After the event, send a letter or note to attendees to thank them for attending, to invite their feedback about the event, and to request their recommendations for future events. Follow-up telephone calls can also be made for the same purposes.

Face-to-Face Visits

If a nonprofit organization had unlimited resources, every prospect would receive a personal visit on a regular basis. Unfortunately, no nonprofit organization has such resources, so development professionals must prioritize and use other communications tools to fill the void. Nevertheless, the number one most effective method of communication in the development effort has been, is, and will always be face-to-face visits. This is true with development in general, and is particularly true with gift planning.

Visits with prospects and donors are important because it helps build trust. The more confidence a prospect has in the development professional and in the organization, the more likely she is to support the organization and the more likely that support is to be substantive. From the organization's

Visit with Prospects to Build Trust

When making an introductory visit, I try to make it clear (using whatever language comes to mind at the moment and jibes with the flow of the conversation) that:

1 My job is helping people build their charitable legacy.

2 The timing of a legacy gift has everything to do with the donor's circumstances and almost nothing to do with the charity's.

3 The sole purpose of my visit is so when the time comes for them to consider their legacy gift, they will have a face to go with the voice on the other end of the line.

My experience using this approach has, I think, been pretty good. It often leads to an open discussion in which the prospective donor tells me pretty much what he's thinking and gives me a chance to respond. My goal is to leave the first meeting not with a gift commitment, but with the donor's trust.

—John Gillon, Senior Director of Gift Planning, Wake Forest University Baptist Medical Center

perspective, face time with a prospect allows the development professional to gain a better understanding of the prospect's interests, concerns, and ability to make a planned gift.

There are a number of different types of face-to-face visits. The obvious type is the visit with a prospect that may or may not include the spouse and other family members. Such meetings will ideally take place in the prospect's home where they will likely feel most comfortable and the development professional is likely to uncover more clues to better understand the prospect. However, such visits can take place anywhere the prospect feels comfortable. For example, some will prefer to meet in their office. In that case, some clues will still be available, but interruptions are probably likely. Some prospects will prefer to meet in a restaurant. While breaking bread with someone is a good way to build rapport, the neutral setting will not provide many insights about the prospect and the noise level may make a meaningful conversation difficult. If the prospect prefers to meet at the organization's office, it provides an opportunity to offer her a behind-the-scenes tour so she can see the organization in action.

During individual visits, the development professional can learn more about the prospect or donor and can provide the individual with the information they seek. For example, an article in a newsletter may touch on the benefits of a charitable remainder uni-trust, but certainly will not be able to go into any detail about how that mechanism works given the space constraints. On the other hand, if a prospect expresses an interest in trusts during a visit, the development officer can provide as much detail as the prospect wants. The prospect's financial advisors can even be encouraged to attend. Visits are an effective way of identifying what information a prospect needs to aid his philanthropic planning and then providing that information then or at a follow-up meeting.

Guy Kawasaki, in his book *Rules for Revolutionaries*, identified five barriers to action:

- Ignorance.
- Inertia.
- Complexity.
- Cost.
- Response Channel.[19]

Personal visits can provide the education and cultivation necessary to overcome each of these obstacles to the gift. During a visit, the development professional can overcome ignorance by introducing gift planning concepts to prospects that they might not be aware of. A person cannot make a planned gift if he does not know what the options are. One must remember that a majority of people do not even know what the term *planned giving* means.

Inertia is a real challenge. People have existed perfectly well before the development professional came knocking. To deal with inertia, the development professional will need to identify the prospect's needs and objectives, and show her how those needs or objectives can be met with a planned gift. A visit is a good setting for this. If there is some sense of urgency the organization can create (i.e., a limited time challenge grant that will match planned gift commitments such as the one used by the Natural Resources Defense Council), a visit is a very good forum for explaining that immediate need.

Even relatively simple planned giving methods can appear complex to those who are unfamiliar with them. With other forms of communication, it can be cumbersome to go into sufficient detail and, no matter the volume of detail, it is often difficult to determine if the recipient of the information truly understands it. With a visit, the development professional can be sure to provide the information that is most relevant to the individual prospect and learn, through immediate feedback, whether the prospect is understanding the information. Even the most complex issues will be more easily demystified during a face-to-face conversation.

One particular area of confusion for many prospects is the cost of making a gift. A donor's number one priority will almost always be taking care of loved ones. Therefore, it is important to show prospects how gift planning can achieve their philanthropic desires while protecting loved ones. During the visit, development professionals can show prospects a variety of ways various gifts can save taxes and preserve wealth. By demonstrating for donors how they can effectively become a major donor today with little or no sacrifice today, development professionals will remove a major barrier to giving.

If a prospect is not sure how to respond, how to make the gift, they will likely not do so. Prospects should be given many avenues for giving. The visit is just one potential avenue. During the visit with a prospect, the development professional can ask for the gift when appropriate, seldom on the first visit. However, a formal ask is often not necessary once the other barriers are removed. The gift will often evolve organically from the ongoing conversations.

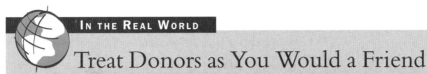

IN THE REAL WORLD

Treat Donors as You Would a Friend

I consider donors as our friends. I believe the best way to thank a friend for their generosity is to do so personally, face-to-face. When marketing responses are insufficient to create introductions, I simply "drop-by" to visit with our friends. The pattern of those drop-bys is rather simple:

1. Introduce myself.
2. Offer appreciation on behalf of the President.
3. Describe what I do.
4. Do a lot of listening and a little bit of talking.
5. Repeat the appreciation as I depart.

To successfully do this, you have to do some careful thinking, as well as some research, about your charity, its friends, and yourself. You have to clear your head of a lot of flotsam, do some real introspection, and practice your craft diligently. Your commitment to the best interests of your friends and absolute integrity are paramount.

I've been doing this for going on 17 years now, and I've found great success. Oh, I've stubbed my toes a few times. Typically, however, I can walk away from that visit with a relationship begun and a pretty good idea as to whether I should invest the time and energy to pursue a planned gift.

Somewhere in my initial contact—typically at the end—I might say, as I hand them my card:

"If anything we have discussed today might be interesting to you, I'd love to be of assistance."

"I don't know if you have ever considered including the Rehab in your plans, but if that might be a possibility, I'd love to be helpful."

"Here is my card. You know what I do. When the time is right, let me be helpful."

"You seem to have an interest in (life income, including us in your plans, etc.). Perhaps we can discuss that next time we visit. Shall I call in advance?"

"How can I be helpful to you?"

(continued)

Another type of face-to-face contact happens at events. Whether an organization's event is planned-giving focused, the planned giving officer should know which gift planning prospects will be in attendance and should make a point of greeting them and hosting them. This is a great way to make prospects and donors feel appreciated and important. For example, the executive director of a theater company makes a point at almost every performance of "running into" prospects in the lobby or even visiting subscribers at their seats before the curtain goes up. Some of her visits are random, but others are carefully planned. She knows which subscribers are coming, which performance they are attending, and she knows exactly where they are seated.

Organizations can also host informal focus groups designed to generate feedback from a target audience. People like being asked to provide advice. It makes them feel important and creates a sense of ownership. Such events are also a great opportunity to learn how the target audience perceives the organization and its planned giving program. If one invites 100 people to attend a discussion group, five to 10 may come. This is a great educational and promotional opportunity for those who attend. However, even those who do not attend will have received some basic contact about planned giving and will appreciate the invitation even if they do not take advantage of it.

For some organizations, geographic obstacles and tight budgets limit the number of visits. To deal with these challenges, these organizations have adopted the concept of the extended telephone visit. While not a true replacement for a face-to-face visit, such contacts are more than a quick telephone chat. With video telephony and Internet conferencing, these extended telephone conversations can be made a bit more personal and dynamic.

Face-to-face contacts will help development professionals earn the trust of prospects and donors. The two-way communication that takes place during visits is the best way to ensure that people are receiving the education they need and the cultivation they deserve. Visits also ensure that the development professionals gain greater insights about prospects, their interests, desires, and needs.

In development offices where the planned giving officer wears many hats or where many other development officers or major gift officers have contact with donors and prospects, it is important to try to have philanthropic planning be part of the conversation. The people responsible for planned giving need to educate colleagues about planned giving so these individuals can have a holistic conversation with prospects and donors. In addition, the planned giving professional needs to get the buy-in from colleagues to ensure that relevant information is shared.

When thinking about face-to-face visits, there are many things to keep in mind. But, the most critical point, the one never to lose sight of, is:

- Development professionals should get out from behind their desks to see as many people as humanly possible.

Advertising

While newspaper, magazine, radio, and television advertising can be done, such promotion is expensive if done properly. An isolated advertisement will not produce much response. Advertising must be sustained in order to be truly effective. Precious budget dollars will almost always yield greater results when invested in other marketing channels.

If advertising in external media, consider smaller advertisements or shorter commercials. Consider advertising in the regional edition of a national magazine. Consider advertising on cable instead of network television.

One way to advertise cost-effectively is for one to do so using the organization's existing media. For example, gift planning can be advertised in a general organization newsletter, an alumni magazine, a campus radio station, or other media.

When writing headlines for display advertisements, consider these tips:[20]

- Realize that your headline must either convey an idea or intrigue the reader into wanting to read more of your writing.

- Speak directly to the reader, one reader at a time, even if 20 million people will read your headline.

- Use words that have an announcement quality.

- Offer information of value.

- Start to tell a story.

- Begin your headline with *How to*.

- Begin your headline with *How, Why, Which, You,* or *This*.

- Begin your headline with advice.

- Use a testimonial-style headline.

- Offer the reader a test.

- Use a one-word headline.

When designing a print advertisement, one should keep the following items in mind:

- Use plenty of white space and avoid clutter. Less is definitely more.

- Make sure that one thing dominates the advertisement. It could be a picture or headline, but not both. You want to catch the reader's eye, not confuse him.

- Limit the use of fonts to avoid distracting readers. Use one or two at the most.

- Remember to use easy-to-read text. That means a large font size. It also means short sentences and short paragraphs.

- Use an appropriate image, either a photograph or graphic to engage the reader.

- Be specific rather than general or vague.

- Make sure the advertisement contains a call to action.

- Include a clearly visible logo.

- Include complete contact information.

Summary

To maximize planned giving results, nonprofit organizations must effectively educate and cultivate potential supporters. Even among donors to nonprofit causes, the vast majority do not understand the term *planned giving* and have never been approached to make a planned gift. The nonprofit sector cannot expect people to make planned gifts when they have little understanding of what they are and are more often than not never asked. The sector must more effectively reach out to potential planned gift supporters.

Once an education or cultivation objective is defined, the development professional can identify the most appropriate audiences. In some cases, the audience may be almost universal while in other cases the target group will be fairly small. Next, the development professional needs to think not only of the organization's objective but also what value she can bring to the prospective donor. Once these steps have been taken, the planned giving professional is ready to select the appropriate media for delivery of the marketing message. The next step involves developing an effective message that is meaningful and memorable. Once the appropriate timing is identified, the message can be disseminated. Usually, the best time to disseminate a planned giving message will be as soon as the organization is ready to do so, provided it will not compete with the organization's other marketing and fundraising efforts. To ensure that communication is ongoing, the development professional should also put in place an appropriate follow-up plan.

As Frank Luntz suggests, there are a number of communication elements of particular importance to good marketing. The development professional must remember to remain focused on what interests her prospects and donors rather than on what interests her. The process is about matching the interests of the donor with the needs of the organization. In a general sense, donors want value; expressed another way, they want to have a positive impact while protecting their loved ones. One should use language that prospects and donors will understand and that will resonate with them. Development professionals should speak from the heart and seek to make emotional connections with prospects and donors. Communications need to be individualized, personalized, and humanized. Prospects and donors are living full, generally fast-paced lives. They expect everyone else to do the same. That means messages must be ubiquitous, planned giving officers need to be accessible, and information must be easy to access and understandable. Good marketing involves appealing to the head and the heart; it also involves thinking creatively to appeal to all five senses.

Educating and cultivating prospects and donors will be most successful if multichannel marketing is used. While limited budget resources may limit the number of channels used and the frequency with which they are used, organizations must make a commitment to communicate regularly if they want a productive marketing effort. By piggybacking the planned giving message onto existing communication channels, organizations can get planned giving messages out in a cost-effective manner. Additionally, development professionals can use direct mail, telephone, newsletters, web site, e-mail, social networking sites, and events as communication channels. However, the single best way to educate and cultivate prospects and donors is to visit with them face-to-face. Personal visits will help earn the trust of prospects and donors while giving the development professional the opportunity to learn more about the individual and how they can best be helped.

Planned giving takes patience. Sometimes, gifts can be secured quickly. However, more commonly, gifts of substance will take some time to develop, sometimes years. While organizations will want to make their planned giving messages ubiquitous in the most cost-responsible ways possible, visits with a refined group of prospects will yield strong outcomes over time for both the donor and the organization.

Exercises

- Using powerful language that resonates with prospects is important. To practice using language that resonates, pull out an old marketing letter or newsletter article and rewrite it using Luntz's power words without making many other changes.

- Conveying passion is not easy. We may know what we intend to say, but we might miss the mark. Before sending a letter or printing an article, run it by your parents or your in-laws to get their reaction. Do they understand it? Did they find it emotionally stirring? Were they bored senseless?

- Communication, by definition, is a two-way street. Organizations should make every contact easy and warm. To discover what kind of experience people are having when they try to call you, try calling yourself through the organization's main number. Is it a pleasant or tedious experience?

- A web site is a cost-effective communications tool particularly if you use other media to drive traffic to the web site. Take a moment to visit your organization's web site from its home page. If you have a planned giving page, how many clicks does it take to get there? Better yet, ask a parent or in-law to find your organization's planned giving page and time how long it takes. If it cannot easily and quickly be found, it is simply worthless.

- Planned giving messages can be easily piggybacked onto other communications. Review your organization's last general newsletter or magazine. Is there an article that could have been appropriately tagged with a planned giving message? Is there some other way a planned giving message could have been inserted somewhere?

- Face-to-face visits are the most effective way to educate and cultivate people while giving the development professional the opportunity to gain insight. Think back to your last visit with a prospect, hopefully not that long ago. What were the most important things you learned that you did not know before the visit? Now, multiply that by your prospect and donor universe, and you will begin to better understand the potential power of visits.

- It is important to know what is being said about your organization. There are many ways to research how your organization is perceived, from focus group studies, to surveys, to feasibility studies. But, an inexpensive and simple way to start is to check several online sites starting, perhaps, with Twitter.com and do a search for your organization. You may be surprised with what you find, or do not find, being said about your organization.

CHAPTER 5

Educate and Cultivate Professional Advisors

Many hands make light work.

—John Heywood

After reading this chapter, you will be able to:

- Understand the need for educating and cultivating professional advisors.
- Identify key points to consider when creating a Planned Giving Advisory Council.
- Understand the responsibilities of a Planned Giving Advisory Council.
- Utilize various methods for engaging professional advisors.

One of the most effective ways to secure planned gifts is to work effectively with donors' professional advisors. The philanthropic planning process will often involve a donor's lawyer, accountant, stockbroker, financial planner or other advisor. At a minimum, learning how to work effectively with these individuals is important to meeting the needs of the organization's donor and the advisor's client on a transactional basis. However, developing relationships with the advisor community in advance of an individual donor conversation can yield dramatic, broader long-term results for an organization.

Build Win-Win Relationships with Donor Advisors

Professional advisors are already talking with their clients about philanthropy. A 2008 survey of professional advisors from seven leading financial institutions revealed that "90 percent of wealth advisors ask clients about their interest in philanthropic planning or charitable giving," while 53 percent report "always" raising the issue with clients and 41 percent report that they only feel comfortable bringing up the subject with certain clients.[1] The nonprofit sector should help the advisor community to: (1) have the most meaningful conversations about philanthropy that are possible with their clients, and (2) help advisors feel more comfortable talking about philanthropy more often with their clients.

Just as nonprofit organizations must educate and cultivate the support of prospects and donors, they should also educate and cultivate the advisor community. Doing so will benefit the planned giving program in a number of ways:

- Advisors who are better educated about planned giving can better assist their clients when it comes to philanthropic planning.
- Advisors can generate new prospects and new gifts for organizations.
- Advisors can assist development professionals with complex gift arrangements.
- Advisors can provide educational programs for prospective donors.

IN THE REAL WORLD

Cultivating Donor Advisors Helps Everyone

I have come to see that nonprofit and for-profit organizations can work perfectly together. Over a seven-year period, I met with 682 professional advisors in New Jersey as a planned giving officer with the American Cancer Society. As a result, I had the good fortune to close several gifts due to these relationships.

As charitable gift planners, we can be a tremendous resource to those allied professionals such as estate planning attorneys, accountants, financial planners, and insurance specialists, to name a few. If we can become a valued asset for them in their practice, then they will seek out our counsel when their clients come to them with questions about philanthropy. In turn, they offer a wealth of knowledge in the areas of their specialty and can also be great partners when we can consider joint marketing to our donor prospects and their client prospects. When we realize that networking with those who are having discussions about the management of wealth and those who are affecting the decisions of the same individuals that we call upon, then we can achieve greater success.

When advisors and development professionals come together, each can benefit. More important, the client/donor will benefit. Ultimately, this will mean a greater flow of philanthropy.

Some of the tools I have used to cultivate advisors have been newsletters, legal updates, a federal tax pocket guide, and a mercifully simple guide to gift planning options. When I worked at American Cancer, we had a healthy eating cookbook. I would provide advisors with extra copies that they could give to their clients who had done a gift with American Cancer. I have also organized golf outings where the advisor brought along a client, and I brought along a donor; it was a great way for everyone to get to know one another.

I'm reminded of a quote by Dale Carnegie that has guided me as I work with advisors: "The rare individual who unselfishly tries to serve others has an enormous advantage. He has little competition."

—Robert E. Wahlers, Senior Director of Development and Gift Planning, Meridian Health Affiliated Foundations

Donor advisors can help nonprofit organizations reach their fundraising goals. Scott R.P. Janney, President of PlannedGiving.com and Director of Planned Giving at Main Line Health, has found that throughout his career, he has known bankers who have been instrumental in sending gifts to the charities where he worked.[2] This is especially true of trust officers who administer gifts made through estates. When most organizations receive notice of a bequest or the actual check from a trust officer, they reply with only the standard form letter. The reasoning behind this impersonal response is that some other person made the gift, and the banker is only doing her job. Many development professionals fail to think through the transaction. When one is contacted by a person who gives away money for a living, one should be asking, "What other charitable gifts might they control?" These professionals may have certain discretionary powers to direct donations to certain specific charities or causes. Since one's organization has obviously fit the requirements for at least one gift, it only seems logical that one would want to know if there are other gifts that might be directed toward the organization's mission.*

Janney has also presented certain specific gift options to potential donors that were met with the reply, "My accountant/broker/attorney says I shouldn't do it." Sometimes the prospect's professional advisors will advance the development professional's efforts, and sometimes they will thwart them. Organizations typically look only at what these advisors can do for the charity, or what they can do to frustrate the best gift proposals. However, nonprofit organizations would benefit from looking at the relationship from the advisor's perspective by asking, "What can development professionals do for advisors?"

Janney has developed a well-thought-out plan for enhancing relationships with the advisor community that includes the creation of a Planned Giving Advisory Council. His work and proven methods inform much of this entire chapter.

KEY CONCEPT

Do not ask what a professional advisor can do for the organization. Instead, development professionals should ask what they can do for professional advisors. That is what builds relationships.

—Robert E. Wahlers, Senior Director of Development and Gift Planning, Meridian Health Affiliated Foundations

---

*Scott R.P. Janney, EdD, CFRE, RFC, President of PlannedGiving.com and Director of Planned Giving at Main Line Health, graciously contributed extensive material throughout this entire chapter.

Six Exchanges of Value

The relationships development professionals have with accountants, attorneys, bankers, estate planners, financial planners, real estate agents, stockbrokers, and other advisors can be marked by exchanges of value where the professionals on both sides of the table benefit. Development professionals can help donor advisors improve their skills, reputations, and bottom lines while helping them provide better service to their clients. At the same time, development professionals can serve the charities they represent more effectively.

IN THE REAL WORLD

Offering Value to Advisors Can Yield Dramatic Results

The Philadelphia Foundation, a community foundation that manages more than 775 charitable funds, has been serving communities in southeastern Pennsylvania for more than 90 years. Not long ago, the Foundation made its number one priority the education and cultivation of professional advisors.

The first step was to create a database of advisors interested in philanthropy. By early 2010, the database included over 3,500 advisors throughout the region. As advisors were identified, the Foundation introduced itself and began the process of trying to get to know them. The Foundation's e-newsletter delivers information of value to advisors and reminds them that the Foundation is a resource for them. One way the Foundation serves as a resource is by offering regular education programs that provide advisors with meaningful information that can help them help their clients while giving the advisors the opportunity to earn needed continuing education credits. During the educational programs, the Foundation takes a few moments to describe what the Foundation does and how it can serve the philanthropic needs of donors/clients.

In 2009, half of all new gifts that came into the Foundation came in from advisor referrals.

—Heather Gee, Vice President for Development Services, The Philadelphia Foundation

There are at least six areas where development professionals could use help from donor advisors. A successful charity will recognize that these professionals can also benefit from the organization's help in the same areas. Each of these areas is full of opportunities for exchanges of value that are beneficial to the charity, the donor advisor and, ultimately, the donor.

Access. Some organizations have been approached, from time to time, by financial planners who wanted to "give free seminars" to the organization's donors. All that was required was that the planner be provided with the organization's mailing list. Smart development professionals, however, recognize that this exchange would violate the trust of donors. Nevertheless, donor advisors can achieve very practical and profitable access to many of an organization's donors, but in ways that will benefit the charity, the advisor, and the donors without crossing any ethical boundaries.

Any time advisors' names are associated with an organization, people who believe in the cause take a closer look at them. When they sit on a board or attend a function that the charity hosts, they associate with people whom they may be able to help make a gift to the organization while increasing their own business opportunities. When a nonprofit organization has a list of prominent professionals on its board or planned giving council, other donor advisors may wish to spend time helping the organization and associating with those same professionals.

For its part, the nonprofit organization also wants access to the advisor's clients. One does not need to ask for direct access to their clients. However, any time the advisor's name is associated with the charity, people who know him may take a closer look at the organization. This refers not only to the advisor's clients, but to other professionals with whom the advisor associates. If one creates the impression of being a well-run charity that makes donors feel good about their gifts, is easy to work with, and recognizes donors and their advisors in sensitive and appropriate ways, more advisors and donors will give the charity serious consideration.

Publicity. Publicity is an important motivator for advisors and a strong benefit for nonprofit organizations. Partners and employees of large advisor businesses see the world through different lenses than small business owners or independent agents. People who work for a large corporation often need to demonstrate community service to move up in their organization. The corporation is interested in promoting its reputation and may include measurements of corporate citizenship in job reviews. Larger firms may also have policies that encourage their professionals to help nonprofit organizations, and the firm may make corporate donations based on this participation. Perhaps even more compellingly, more independent or entrepreneurial advisors need to be involved in the community to build their credibility and bottom line. It is important for development officers to be aware of the motivations of different professionals.

When an organization publicizes a large estate gift, it should consider ways to mention the name of the donor advisor(s) who helped facilitate it. This would send the message that these professionals are good members of the community and it helps other people who may be interested in donating to the charity find the professional advisors who have a particular affinity for philanthropic planning.

Organizations can also recognize donor advisors through the publicity given to the group's planned giving advisory council and board in newsletters and on the web site. Web access traffic reports often show that the names of donor advisors associated with charities are common search strings people use both to find charitable organizations and discover information about advisors. An advisor's associations with charities builds her reputation and provides important exposure to communities where she works and hopes to gain attention.

Donor advisors can also help build a nonprofit organization's reputation and provide important exposure in the communities where it is interested in building relationships, particularly with the highest net worth donors. Not all wealthy individuals rely on professional advisors, but this practice becomes more common as wealth increases. The Philanthropy Roundtable (Boston College Social Welfare Research Institute and Bankers Trust) found that 93 percent of the affluent would increase giving if they found additional causes they felt passionately for; 66 percent would give more if they were better informed about giving options and the effectiveness of their contributions; and 85 percent would be anxious to receive guidance on philanthropy from their advisor.[3] The publicity donor advisors give an organization may not turn a great number of heads. However, since a great deal of wealth is concentrated in the hands of people who use advisors and make disproportionately large charitable gifts, the right word from an advisor is exactly the kind of publicity most charities need. The number of contacts might be modest, but the size of resulting gifts could be quite substantial.

Credibility. Many donor advisors see themselves as "pillars of the community." Joining a board or planned giving advisory council of a respected nonprofit organization or helping out an important charitable cause adds to this public image while validating one's sense of self.

The issue of credibility is a two-way street. A nonprofit organization also can gain or lose credibility through its associations with donor advisors. In the same way that good donor advisors will want to associate only with respected charities, development professionals must protect their organizations from close associations with people of questionable reputation.

Credibility is in the eyes of the beholder. In the philanthropic process, that means the donor's eyes. To be perceived as credible involves, in large part, fulfilling the donor's expectations. Therefore, it is important for professionals, both advisors and development officers, to understand how donors perceive the role of each and then to make sure to live up to those expectations. For planned giving professionals, it is important not to try to stand in the place of the allied professionals who serve the organization's donors, their clients. It is clear from the results of a survey, involving 603 donors who had made planned gifts worth at least $75,000 and had a net worth of $5 million or more, that donors expect different services and a different set of skills from the planned giving officers they work with than from their professional advisors (see Table 5.1). It is important for people who raise money for charities to recognize the lines that are defined by the differing areas of expertise and roles in order to maintain credibility and achieve effective comfort levels with prospects and donors.

TABLE 5.1		
What Donors Want in Their Charitable Advisor		
	Planned Giving Officers	**Professional Advisors**
Expertise in the technical details of executing the planned gift	16.0%	97.9%
Skill and efficiency in working with the donor's professional advisors or with the charity	60.3%	75.2%
Willingness to let the donor set the pace in the planned giving process	67.2%	86.0%
Help in deciding what type of planned gift to make	85.5%	96.8%
Knowledge about the advantages and disadvantages of each type of planned gift	94.7%	99.4%
Sophisticated understanding of the donor's personal motivations to give	99.2%	82.2%
Effectiveness in getting the charity to treat the donor as he wants to be treated	69.5%	11.2%
Source: Prince & Associates and Private Wealth Consultants, 1997		

Free Advice. Development professionals do not need to be experts in every facet of philanthropic planning. Creating a planned giving advisory council provides an organization with a group of in-house experts prepared and on-call to offer advice when needed. Whether dealing with closely held businesses, mortgaged real estate, or hedge funds, there are professionals who specialize in each area. In order to give potential donors the best service possible, the development professional needs to know his knowledge limitations and when to seek guidance.

When starting a discussion about a complicated gift, development professionals can ask a number of advisors for their input via e-mail. In addition to getting sound advice, this will put ideas into the heads of some advisors who have not thought about a certain type of gift before and bring them up to speed about the charitable giving methods that may be useful to their clients.

Janney has also found that advisors need the types of information planned giving professionals can provide to help them and their clients make the best decisions. Many donor advisors want information about planned giving vehicles. Those who feel confident about the vehicles need to understand the missions of local and national charities so they can help their clients make the connections that result in charitable gifts.

Many planned giving professionals have found receptive audiences among professional advisors when they offer to make anonymous gift illustrations and provide information about their charities. For example, planned giving professionals can review trust documents for advisors looking for ways they can be better drawn to provide more benefits to the donors. This is insight the gift planning professional can provide since she has access to and familiarity with the types of software that advisors do not usually have.

Advice goes both ways, but always with an eye to better serving the client/donor.

Increasing the Bottom Line. The wealthiest individuals are interested in their charitable giving. Generally, among the wealthy, the greater someone's wealth, the greater the percentage of income and assets they will donate through a planned gift. Donor advisors are getting the message that the professionals who offer the best advice in the area of philanthropic planning are experiencing an increase in business from the highest net worth clients. The simple dichotomy between money in the account versus money given to charity fails to explain many of the dynamics that lead wealthy individuals to choose their advisors. Those advisors who are able to best meet the needs of their philanthropically inclined clients often see their assets under management increase dramatically, a dynamic expected to increase as we progress through the $41 trillion intergenerational wealth transfer. The success of the Fidelity Charitable Gift Fund and its many competitors show that brokerages and brokers are learning how to do well by doing good. Of the professional advisors surveyed, 42 percent indicated that a philanthropic services offering "significantly helps generate revenues." Ninety-one percent of the advisors indicated that "being able to address philanthropic needs would help differentiate themselves in the eyes of existing and would-be clients."[4] When development professionals help advisors understand gift planning and are seen as knowledgeable about charitable giving, they help them reach an important constituency that can drive their success.

Building more points of contact between potential donors and nonprofit organizations will create more opportunities for larger gifts. If the planned giving professional desires to build a team to solicit planned gifts in addition to having an advisory council, he should be sure to invite appropriate members of the council onto that team. Even if they are two distinct groups, make sure that they have open lines of communication, since *team* members may not possess the expertise of *council* members. Development professionals also need to remember that people who decide to make a planned giving commitment to an organization will need to seek professional advice. One should always encourage current and prospective major donors to seek professional advice. One should urge them to discuss planned gifts with their current advisors and, if they have no professional advisors, the development professional should provide them with a list of appropriate professionals. Development professionals should always supply donors and prospects with more than one advisor's name. It is preferable to provide three or more referrals.

As a development professional is building a circle of helpful and influential donor advisors, she should be aware that each professional has potential business and consulting relationships that also may support the charity. Bankers need to have positive relationships with attorneys, and financial planners just like development professionals need those relationships.

Philanthropy. Donors are often motivated by a mix of motives that can include tax consequences, family considerations, and recognition. The same complicated mix of motives is present in donor advisors. In fact, many professionals derive the same satisfaction facilitating gifts that their clients receive from making the gifts. Most advisors would like to be respected by the community and their peers, and they naturally want to increase their business, but the people from all walks of life who do the most good for their communities share a strong motivation to help their fellow human beings and improve their communities. As an advocate for a nonprofit organization, the development professional has a special role in helping donor advisors achieve their own philanthropic dreams along with the dreams of their clients.

Those who lead charities need to remember that unless there is a philanthropic interest on the advisor's part, the organization may not benefit from the

Relationships Build the Bottom Line for All

Not only is it important to look at ways to build relationships between the advisor community and the organization, it is important for the development professional to look for ways to help advisors build relationships with one another. This will enhance the value of the relationship for them and encourage even greater levels of involvement with the organization. This idea was impressed on me when I had lunch with a banker and an attorney who were both advisory council members for my organization. The purpose of the lunch was to review items we had discussed at our most recent council meeting, which they had both missed. Although this topic drove much of the agenda, one important part of the conversation revolved around an aspect of hedge fund management that had nothing to do with my charity. These two prominent professionals had potential business opportunities in common, along with a dedication to the advancement of the charity. After lunch, one of them said that if I could set up meetings of related professionals like that on a regular basis, I would have professionals "knocking down your doors" to associate with my charity.

—Scott R.P. Janney, President of PlannedGiving.com and Director of Planned Giving at Main Line Health

relationship. Without a strong philanthropic intent, the gift may not materialize or the benefits to the organization will be greatly minimized.

It also is important to work with the right advisors. One should look for professionals who are part of the organization's existing network. Look at which attorneys have written wills for clients who have named the organization as a charitable beneficiary. Look at which brokers donors used when they transferred stocks to fund CGAs or trusts. Look at which financial advisors board members turn to for advice, and which advisors are in their circle of friends. One should be sure to ask members of the board development committee, and particularly the committee's chair, to identify the most important players in the community, and identify relationships these professionals have with existing board members and significant donors.

The Planned Giving Advisory Council

While informal relationships can be developed with advisors, creating a Planned Giving Advisory Council can help form the foundation for a successful planned giving program. It can be a source of valuable advice and credibility for the gift planning program, and it can help market and close planned gifts. However, to be beneficial to the organization, it must be carefully developed and managed.

It is important to consider the stage of development of the planned giving program when looking to start, or reinvent a *council*. One must also consider the strengths and goals of the organization, as well as one's own personal strengths and desires as a development or planned giving officer. One can start by taking a careful look at the level of experience and maturity of the program and staff.

One way to plan the development of the council is to start out small and intimate, then add to the number as the planned giving program matures. Table 5.2 provides an illustration of this progression.

When reviewing Table 5.2, one should consider personal experience level as well as the planned giving program's maturity when identifying the current stage along the continuum and whether the current council, or the one being started, fits the current stage. One may be working with a council that fit five

IN THE REAL WORLD

Executive Insight

I advise people who are new to the field and in newer programs to gather an intimate group of advisors to augment their limited experience and use them as a resource and sounding board. For those with more experience or who work in an established program, it may be better to have a larger advisory council that often is more visible, that publishes articles and offers seminars and free consultations to prospective donors. The most seasoned planned giving officers often nurture a broad network of experts for referrals (both directions), credible advocacy among board and senior management, and current information about planning, law and finance.

—Tom Cullinan, President, Schola Donum Inc.

TABLE 5.2		
Program Status Relative to Advisor Group Size		
Stage 1	Stage 2	Stage 3
New planned giving officer and planned giving program	Some planned giving experience and an established program	Mature planned giving officer and planned giving program
Small number of intimate professionals for advice and direction	Eighteen to 24 members and two to three meetings per year	Large professional network for referrals, advocacy, and information

Source: Scott R.P. Janney, "Get Donor Advisors onto Your Team: The Planned Giving Advisory Council and Other Strategies." Univest Foundation Planned Giving and Development Spring Seminar, May 9, 2007.

years ago, but not today. Or, one may have inherited a council that is not the right size or structure. Two examples of mature councils are those at the Morton Plant Mease Foundation and the Philadelphia Orchestra.

The Morton Plant Mease Foundation grew its planned giving advisory group from a 12-member council in 1979 to a Stage 3 organization with a formal structure that facilitates its 170-member Financial Counseling Services (FCS). This professional network is supervised by a 13-member executive committee that meets four times per year, with each member of the executive committee acting as a team captain for a group within the FCS. The Foundation has allocated significant resources in support of this council, including a full-time director of FCS. It publishes and distributes an annual membership directory, and sponsors various receptions, networking opportunities and social events throughout the year. Members receive a monthly newsletter and a weekly e-newsletter. Although this is a significant investment of time and resources, it has shown significant results. Since tracking of their participation was started in 1996, this group has raised over $75 million in revocable and irrevocable gifts, including the Foundation's largest gift of $5 million received to fund its new Heart Hospital.

The Philadelphia Orchestra's 70-member council attracts attendance of about 40 professionals to its 8:00 a.m. biannual meetings. The Director of Planned Giving gives members specific information about the concert schedule and encourages them to use Orchestra performances as cultivation events.

Building Robust Councils Leads to Success

During the early part of my tenure as President of Arkansas Children's Hospital Foundation (1980–1997), I hired the hospital's CFO, Steve Reed, to become Vice President of Planned Giving. We wanted to create a robust planned giving program. To help accomplish this, we wanted to involve a large number of allied professionals. We started five councils throughout Arkansas ranging from 35 members in the smallest community to 125 in Little Rock. The Little Rock Chair was a long-time hospital board member who headed one of the South's largest law firms. Initially, 100 were invited to join the Little Rock Council and 95 accepted.

We sought attorneys, trust officers, financial planners, stock brokers, and life insurance agents, and more than one person from a firm could join. The Councils met three to four times a year. The Little Rock Council heard brief talks by our hospital CEO and a physician, and then Steve or a Council member discussed an unusual planned giving situation. When members joined, they were given a large, childlike certificate, matted and framed, and every person hung it in his or her office.

The out-state councils followed the same schedule, but I carried the CEO's role. We had a physician speak at one of the meetings. Once a year, we would bring in a national planned giving expert to talk to all five councils. Nonmembers could join the councils simply by asking.

Steve and one or two members of the Little Rock Council presented two different estate planning seminars annually for noncouncil professionals, and continuing education credits were provided. The CEO or I would welcome the group and talk briefly about the hospital. On occasion, a patient family would speak.

Seminars for donors and the general public were conducted by Steve and Little Rock Council members and consisted of estate planning information and planned giving opportunities. Professional and general public seminars were held at the hospital, and tours were offered each time.

Our goals were to: (1) win over council members as ambassadors for the hospital, and (2) have them recommend us to their clients. On many occasions, Steve was asked to join a council member and his or her client to discuss planned giving opportunities.

(continued)

> **IN THE REAL WORLD (CONTINUED)**
>
> Our approach worked well for us. We significantly increased our number of estate donors and the amount of planned giving revenue. When the five councils were fully developed, almost 60 percent of our average of 45 annual planned gifts were either referrals from or cooperative efforts with council members.
>
> —Larry C. Woodard, a senior fundraising executive is former President of the Arkansas Children's Hospital Foundation

Another way to envision an advisory group is to look at the goals for the planned giving program, the areas where help is needed, and the overall functional model that should be adopted. Table 5.3 gives a functional description of various useful work groups for planned gifts. They are arranged along a continuum from a planned giving committee of the board, through a professional advisory council, to a fundraising team that asks for life-income gifts and bequest designations. These groups have different responsibilities that can be broadly defined as governance, advice, and solicitations. The need for each type of volunteer committee changes as the development professional and the program grow.

TABLE 5.3

Functions of a Committee versus Council versus Team		
Planned Giving Committee of the Board or "Committee"	**Professional Advisory Council or "Council"**	**Team to Solicit Planned Gifts or "Team"**
Main Functions: Governance and internal advocacy	**Main Functions:** Advice, publicity and referrals	**Main Functions:** Direct solicitation of planned gifts
Most Pressing Needs: Policies and standards Accountability	**Main Functions:** Advice, publicity and referrals	**Main Functions:** Direct solicitation of planned gifts
Membership: Mostly board members	**Membership:** Financial professionals from the community	**Membership:** People who ask for planned gifts

Source: Scott R.P. Janney, "Get Donor Advisors onto Your Team: The Planned Giving Advisory Council and Other Strategies." Univest Foundation Planned Giving and Development Spring Seminar, May 9, 2007.

The terms *committee, council,* and *team* describe the three basic types of volunteer groups. The committee is typically a planned giving committee of the board or some type of committee with governance responsibilities. The council is a group of professionals who can give expert advice in estate and financial planning. The team is a group of volunteers who make planned giving solicitations, but who are not necessarily experts in planned giving or a related field. These terms will vary from organization to organization, but will provide useful shorthand as one explores the functional differences which are outlined in Table 5.3.

Committee. In organizations where fundraising is the main mission of the board of trustees, such as hospital foundations and social service organizations, the board of trustees should have a planned giving committee. However, not all boards will have a planned giving committee, especially organizations that do not see fundraising as a primary board function and larger, more complex organizations. In some organizations, supervision and governance are the responsibility of a group of senior staff members or a gift acceptance committee. In this case, policy decisions are brought to the board by the vice president through the development committee.

Council. The council is usually made up of a variety of professionals from a number of donor advising capacities, including wealth managers, financial planners, attorneys, bankers, real estate agents, and insurance professionals. One may also wish to include a staff member with program responsibilities within the organization and a planned giving donor who is not a planning professional on the council. The development officer and charity set up the council for advice, but there are numerous other benefits. These benefits include the credibility the organization gains when community members see respected professionals working with its planned giving program, the direct or indirect access one gains to advisor clients, and the publicity generated through advisor involvement. The council of allied professionals opens doors to wealthy donors that ultimately lead to more planned gifts.

All members of the planned giving council should have the best interest of the organization at heart and look for opportunities to make referrals and help their clients make charitable commitments to the organization. However, on each council, there will be just a select group of members who are fully engaged. With proper cultivation, many professionals will grow in their commitment to and effectiveness for an organization over time as a result of serving on a council. Therefore, it is not a good idea to impose performance expectations. For example, if one institutes an expectation that all candidates for the council actively solicit gifts for the organization, one could easily drive many highly qualified and valuable professionals away. The council itself is a cultivation tool.

Team. The leaders of some charities dream of a council made up of highly respected and successful financial professionals who continually provide leads and solicit their wealthiest clients on the organization's behalf. Unfortunately, it does not work that way. Nevertheless, there will be times when the planned gift program can benefit from a group of volunteer solicitors who work like capital campaign volunteers. While the members of this type of team do not need to be financial or planning professionals, a number of council members may be exceptional candidates for the team. The team to solicit planned gifts does not need to be limited to a special project. It can also be organized to operate on an ongoing basis.

IN THE REAL WORLD

United Way Endowed and Planned Gifts Committee, Volunteer Job Description

CHARGE:

To ensure sufficient community support in future generations, grow United Way's endowment fund by developing, implementing, and evaluating planned giving efforts.

RESPONSIBILITIES:

1. Make a personal planned giving commitment to United Way to demonstrate your commitment to the program.
2. Attend regular planned giving committee meetings.

❸ Develop and comply with gift acceptance and planned giving policies.

❹ Participate in programs to educate and cultivate relationships with financial and estate planning professionals.

❺ Leverage professional and personal networks to identify and cultivate planned giving prospects.

❻ After receiving appropriate United Way training, solicit five planned giving prospects per year.

❼ Champion planned giving efforts within United Way and throughout the community.

❽ Develop and execute annual recognition and marketing programs.

❾ Evaluate the outcomes of the planned giving program and make recommendations to strengthen it.

TIME COMMITMENT:

Each committee member serves a two-year term. Four committee meetings are held per year. Additional time is required to conduct at least five individual cultivation calls per year.

—United Way Worldwide, "Of Legacy Builders and Planned Givers: United Way's Toolkit to Increase Endowed and Planned Gifts," p. 30, www.brattleboromuseum. org/pdfs/epg_toolkit.pdf

There is no solid "wall of separation" between the various groups. Certain important activities can fit into more than one group, but it makes the job easier when the roles of the committee, council, and team are clearly defined and communicated to all participants. For instance, there is an important distinction between advice and approval. Does the development professional really want a frank discussion about a new marketing plan at the council meeting? Does the planned giving professional want the members to feel free to speak their minds and offer creative ideas? Their creativity will be stifled if one asks them to approve the final product, expect their peers to vote on their ideas, and ask them to bear responsibility for the final product. This is one good reason to get ideas and advice from a council of professionals who do not carry the same responsibility as the planned giving committee.

IN THE REAL WORLD

Use a Volunteer Team to Secure Planned Gifts

One of my first projects when I started as the director of planned giving at St. Mary Medical Center was to form a legacy society. The Foundation had a large annual fund program but had only received 17 legacy gifts in its history. It was also gearing up for a capital campaign, and I realized that we had a small window of opportunity to focus board attention on the legacy society before the capital campaign began. I formed a small group of trustees who solicited their peers to become charter members of the St. Mary Legacy Society. This team was made up of the chair of the board, chair of the planned giving committee, vice president for medical affairs, and me. Each of us made a personal bequest commitment. Then we divided the list of board members among us and called, wrote, and visited all board members. I set a goal of 50 percent immediate participation, and this effort resulted in 11 out of the 21 board members signing up as charter members by the date of the vote to establish the St. Mary Legacy Society. By the end of the nine-month charter membership period, we had 33 legacy commitments!

—Scott R.P. Janney, President of PlannedGiving.com and Director of Planned Giving at Main Line Health

Defining and Evolving Roles

The previous section showed the distinctions between a committee, council, and team. These distinctions can be a helpful window for looking at the type(s) of group(s) that will offer the most help. A planned giving committee of the board is interested in the growth of the planned giving program and is responsible for monitoring financial success or failure. However, this committee may have a limited involvement in actually growing the number of participants in the program or directly raising planned gifts.

A team may be employed to solicit planned gifts, but it may not be qualified to offer professional advice or supervision. As the development professional matures and develops more expertise, and as the planned giving program matures, one's areas of most pressing need will evolve. The development professional will never be at a point in her career where policies and procedures are no longer important. As she explores more gifts, and more complicated gifts, with donors, she will face a continual need to revisit policy issues. However, as the need for many types of advice will diminish, other things that are offered by a council of professionals cannot be replaced. It is shortsighted to focus exclusively on internal issues at any time in one's career, especially when launching a new planned giving program. The development professional needs to be cognizant of moving through the middle column in Table 5.3 and begin soliciting and closing gifts.

The group structure should be related to the most pressing needs of the planned giving program. The planned giving professional should ask, "Which type of volunteer group does my program need now?" This question should be revisited periodically. One may not be anxious to form an additional volunteer group and, therefore, may decide to disband one type of group or change the way the group functions. However, if one decides to steer the activities of the current council toward those of a team, or divide the committee into different groups for governance and advice, one should be sure to respect the commitments that current members have made. If one is missing any of these three volunteer groups, one may want to form a working group of members with specific abilities, connections, and interests to serve in the areas of greatest current needs.

The Planned Gift Advisory Council and Its Members

The following questions should be clearly addressed by the nonprofit organization's job description for Planned Gift Advisory Council members:

- What does the council do?
- What benefits does the council bring to the organization?
- What can the organization expect from council members?

Two items that should be included on the list of expectations are: (1) all council members should be donors, and (2) within the bounds of the ethical guidelines of each advising profession, there are plenty of ways these advisors can promote the cause and, therefore, they should do so.

IN THE REAL WORLD

United Way Professional Advisory Committee, Volunteer Job Description

CHARGE:

To cultivate and educate planned giving prospects and the financial and estate planning community. Also, to develop and update United Way's planned giving policies.

RESPONSIBILITIES:

1. Make a personal planned giving commitment to United Way.
2. Advocate for United Way's planned giving program in the community and within United Way.
3. Develop and annually review planned giving policies.
4. Educate and cultivate other financial and estate planning professionals by hosting at least five one-to-one breakfast or lunch meetings.
5. Participate in United Way activities, including seminars, presentations, writing articles, or reviewing proposals.

TIME COMMITMENT:

Two-year term. The Professional Advisory Committee meets twice per year. Other time commitments include participation in seminars and other prospect cultivation activities.

QUALIFICATIONS:

Volunteers should be highly respected in their fields and possess the highest ethical standards. Knowledge and personal support of United Way, including volunteer and/or financial contributions, is highly desired.

—United Way Worldwide, "Of Legacy Builders and Planned Givers: United Way's Toolkit to Increase Endowed and Planned Gifts," p. 31, www.brattleboromuseum.org/pdfs/epg_toolkit.pdf

The council exists to involve members of a very important constituency. It is more than just another meeting to be planned. One should offer opportunities for advisors to share their own stories. They bring more credibility and a higher interest level from their peers than development professionals are able to produce without their assistance and leadership.

When recruiting council members, one should keep diversity, in the broadest sense of the word, in mind including seeking advisors from varied professions and from across geographic areas as appropriate for the organization.

When looking to work with councils, one should keep the following elements in mind:

- If one has regular meetings, keep in mind the donor advisors' question, "What's in it for me?" as the agenda is set. Make sure that meetings are helpful to the professionals and respectful of their time commitments. Make sure to clearly communicate the "take-away value" of the meetings.

- Refreshments are an important part of the meeting; plan to have much more than just enough. Do not settle for the usual fare. Make it inviting, special, pleasurable, and memorable.

- Make the meetings interesting. Do not bore the council with reports that they do not need to hear. Mix in humor; include visual reinforcement such as PowerPoint presentations, bulletin boards, and short video clips.

- Keep the meetings to one hour.

- Offer tours of the facility and presentations by important leaders.

- Give members a binder and provide copies of additional materials to use or give to interested clients.

- Every time one sends out a planned giving publication, send members additional copies with a personal note.

- Meet with members personally, on a regular basis.

- Be prepared to suggest the best members to serve in governing capacities at the organization.

Five Practices for Working with Donor Advisors

A helpful set of practices that are particularly important in working with donor advisors are the Five Practices of Exemplary Planned Giving Officers, adapted by Janney from *The Leadership Challenge* by James M. Kouzes and Barry Z. Posner.[5] Finding ways to exercise these Five Practices will help make the council experience more beneficial for donor advisors and more beneficial for the organization.

1. *Model the Way.* Since the development professional will be asking advisors to help the organization by donating their expertise, he needs to model a self-giving posture as he helps them make philanthropy fit into their professional services. One should lead by one's actions. Development professionals should make educational presentations relevant to the advisors, and help them answer the question, "How can I use this to help my clients and my business?" One also needs to "walk the walk" as a professional who exhibits clear standards of professionalism and ethical best practice. One should be the first to offer a helping hand, and never ask others to do things that she is not willing to do herself.

2. *Inspire a Shared Vision.* A vision is more than a financial goal. The charity is an important resource in the community and, perhaps, the nation or world. Many area professionals want to see it maintained and strengthened. In order to inspire a shared vision among donor advisors, one must listen to volunteer leaders to find the points where their vision and the organization's intersect just as one would do with donor prospects. For example, when Janney was at St. Mary, the senior partner of a physician group told him that a member of the council was the practice's attorney and had spoken with him about the importance of estate and charitable planning. When Janney made a presentation to the 25 partners of that group, he asked that attorney to review the presentation, and then expressed his appreciation for the attorney's help in front of the partners. Proper planning, with a charitable element included, is in the best interest of the organization, the donor/client, and the advisor.

3. *Challenge the Process.* If one is working with a committee when her professional and organizational needs call for a team, something is going to need to change. Challenging the process does not consist of change for its own sake, but of making the process work to serve the organization's purposes. One does not need to move to the perfect organizational structure in one quick step. Change is often accomplished with incremental steps and small victories. One should carefully choose which changes to make first, and build on a record of successful transitions before challenging the major structures or becoming embroiled in turf wars.

4. *Enable Others to Act.* The development professional should ask himself what he can do to make it easier for the professional advisors in the community to facilitate planned gifts to his organization and which barriers he can minimize or remove. Also, he should find appropriate ways for the organization's donors to learn about the expertise and services of the council members and other qualified professional advisors. One can create a climate of trust in order to help donor advisors work better through interdependence.

5. *Encourage the Heart.* Recognition is a very important part of building coalitions with the donor advisors in the community. One can start by listing the names and professional affiliations of council members in the organization's newsletter and web site. A word of encouragement and appreciation at meetings is also important. The planned giving professional should publicly thank specific members for their advice about particular questions and for their service on specific projects. This not only makes the members feel appreciated, it also gives their colleagues on the council ideas for how they can help the cause. One should also be sure to include council members in other donor events, especially if these events involve members of your board or legacy society. These two groups are especially important to council members, and it is also important to impress the board and legacy society members with the caliber of the council members. Development professionals should look for imaginative and authentic ways to say "thank you,"

both publicly and privately. Focusing on success stories at a meeting of the council could lead other professionals to follow the example.

IN THE REAL WORLD

Advisors Really Can Facilitate Philanthropy

Oseola McCarty was a quiet, 87-year-old African American woman living in Haittesburg, Mississippi. Even as a young child, she worked and she saved. "I would go to school and come home and iron. I'd put money away and save it. When I got enough, I went to First Mississippi National Bank and put it in. The teller told me it would be best to put it in a savings account. I didn't know. I just kept on saving," McCarty said.

Unfortunately, when McCarty was in the sixth grade, her childless aunt became ill. McCarty left school to care for her and never returned to school. Instead, she spent a lifetime earning a living by washing and ironing other people's clothes. And, she continued to save what she could by putting money into several local banks. She worked hard, lived frugally, and saved.

Nancy Odom and Ellen Vinzant of Trustmark Bank worked with McCarty for several years, not only helping her manage her money but helping look after her personally. They eventually referred her to Paul Laughlin, Trustmark's assistant vice president and trust officer. "In one of our earliest meetings, I talked about what we could do for her," Laughlin said. "We talked about providing for her if she's not able. Then, we turned naturally to what happens to her estate after she dies."

Laughlin continued, "She said she wanted to leave the bulk of her money to Southern Miss, and she didn't want (anybody) to come in and change her mind. I called Jimmy Frank McKenzie, her attorney—she'd done laundry for him for years—and he talked to her. He made sure it was her idea. Then, I met with her to let her decide how to divide her money up."

McCarty said, "Mr. Paul laid out dimes on the table to explain how to divide it up."

Laughlin explained, "I got 10 dimes (to represent percentages). I wrote on pieces of paper the parties she wanted to leave her money to and put them on the table. Then, I asked how she wanted her money to be split up. She put one dime on her church and one each for several relatives. Then, she said she wanted the rest—six dimes—to go to the college. She was quite definite about wanting to give 60 percent to Southern Miss. To my knowledge, she had never been out there, but she seems to have the best of the students in mind. The decision was entirely hers.''

McCarty said, ''I just want the scholarship to go to some child who needs it, to whoever is not able to help their children. I'm too old to get an education, but they can.''

McCarty signed an irrevocable trust agreement stating her wishes for her estate and giving the bank the responsibility for managing her funds. ''Mr. Paul gives me a check, and I can go get money anytime I need it. My lawyer gave them permission to take care of me if something happens to me,'' McCarty said.

Laughlin said the bank normally keeps such transactions in strictest confidence, but because of the uniqueness of McCarty's story, he asked for her permission to make it public. ''Well, I guess that would be all right,'' she said with her typical calm acceptance.

Laughlin notified The University of Southern Mississippi in 1995. McCarty, a washerwoman for over 75 years, donated $150,000 to Southern Miss to establish the endowed Oseola McCarty Scholarship.

Southern Miss recognized McCarty's generosity, and she finally got to see the university. She also got to meet some scholarship recipients before her death in 1999. As a result of the publicity about her extraordinary gift, Southern Miss raised over $200,000 in current gifts for the Oseola McCarty Scholarship Fund, which allowed for the immediate awarding of scholarships.

By working together, McCarty's advisors—her bankers and her lawyer— were able to protect her interests and assist her in realizing her philanthropic aspirations. Without the wisdom of the advisors, the gift to Southern Miss might never have been. Or, if it had been made, might not have been done in a way that would give the donor so much joy and the university the opportunity to leverage the story. By working together, advisors and non-profit officials were able to ensure that McCarty's wishes were honored, and that she was appropriately recognized while still alive, bringing her much deserved joy. With McCarty's story, Southern Miss was also able to inspire others to be philanthropic. Students benefited sooner, and more students have benefited than otherwise may have been case.

—This story was compiled with material from the Oseola McCarty memorial page at The University of Southern Mississippi web site (www.usm.edu/pr/oolamain.htm).

Summary

Development professionals and the organizations they represent should be mindful of the position occupied by legal and financial professionals. They are often the gatekeepers into the wealth of a community; they often possess considerable personal wealth, and they may be excellent candidates for making planned gifts with their own private assets.

By engaging them in ways that respect their expertise, time, and client relationships, development professionals can build relationships that benefit the nonprofit organizations they serve, the organization's donors/advisors' clients, and the professional advisors.

Just as organizations must educate and cultivate the support of donors, professional advisors must be educated and cultivated. When doing so, it is essential to adopt an advisor-centered posture and look at what value the organization can bring to the relationship that will ultimately best serve donors/clients. As trust and value blossoms, so will philanthropy.

Exercises

- Professional advisors can provide a number of benefits to nonprofit organizations. However, before approaching advisors to cultivate a relationship, you need to know what your objectives are. Review Tables 5.2 and 5.3 and determine where your organization currently falls and where it aspires to be.

- Most nonprofit organizations already have relationships with some professional advisors. Look at your organization's board list and identify the advisors that are serving. These individuals can be engaged to assist with advisor outreach.

- Other advisor relationships already exist. Develop a list of lawyers and accountants who have already facilitated gifts to the organization. This is a good group to cultivate.

- Offering professional advisors a relationship based on a fair exchange of value is important to building a successful partnership. List 10 ways your organization can provide value to professional advisors.

CHAPTER 6

The Ask

You may be disappointed if you fail, but you are doomed if you don't try.

—Beverly Sills

After reading this chapter, you will be able to:

- Recognize three different approach methods to solicit planned gifts.
- Identify key features of each approach method.
- Understand when to use each approach method.
- Appreciate how a prospect approaches the ask conversation.
- Ask for gifts with confidence.

Planned gifts allow donors to leave a lasting legacy. While such significant gifts are valuable to the nonprofit organization, they are also extremely valuable to the donor. Such gifts allow donors to have a positive impact on their community and the world, whether creating a permanent program, constructing a new building, or simply helping the charity to do good things for some length of time. This is very meaningful to many people. In addition, the donor might receive certain tax benefits or income from a gift. Those potential donors who understand the great value, to themselves or their loved ones, of creating a philanthropic legacy can hardly be stopped from doing so once they are aware of the concept. Those who do not see much value in it will never make such a gift no matter how much they are encouraged to do so by development professionals.

The primary task of major gifts and planned giving officers is not, as some people may think, the very unpleasant job of persuading prospective donors to make a large gift to the charity. Instead, development professionals have the very enjoyable role of making prospective planned gift donors aware of the great value to them of making a meaningful gift. For those prospective donors who recognize this value, development professionals are charged with stewarding them through the process so that they will realize their aspirations.

Good Things Come to Those Who Ask

If nonprofit organizations want planned gifts, they must ask for them. If nonprofit organizations want more planned gifts, they must ask more people and do so more effectively. However, a solid ask will only be effective if the development professional has identified the appropriate pool of prospects, understands what motivates planned giving prospects, knows how to work effectively with professional advisors, educates prospects, and cultivates their support. Once all of the other steps of the process have been carefully followed, the development professional is ready to proceed to an ask for support.

Interestingly, donors expect to be asked for planned gifts and are fine with it. In a survey conducted by Adrian Sargeant and Elaine Jay, 88.7 percent of donors to nonprofit organizations "indicated they believe it is appropriate for nonprofits to ask for legacy gifts."[1]

Ideally, every ask for major or planned giving support would occur during a face-to-face visit. However, with limited budget and staff resources, most development professionals cannot meet with all of their prospects. This usually means that the development professional will meet with and solicit her best prospects while all others are marketed to passively if at all. For example, a development professional might meet with his 120 best

What Fundraising Approach Method Works Best?

1. Person to person (team of two calling on one).
2. Person to person (team of one calling on one).
3. Telephone (after a personal letter).
4. Personal letter (without a telephone call).
5. Telephone call (then send a follow-up letter).
6. Telephone (without a letter for follow-up).
7. Special event benefit.
8. Direct mail (impersonal letter mass produced).
9. Door to door.
10. Impersonal telephone (to unaffiliated people).
11. Media advertising.

—Harold J. Seymour, *Designs for Fund-Raising* (Rockville, MD: Fundraising Institute, 1988).

prospects during the course of a year while letting the education and cultivation marketing effort stimulate "over-the-transom" gifts. However, an increasing number of organizations are beginning to treat planned giving just as they would any other type of fundraising. They are using direct mail and the telephone to effectively solicit gifts from second-tier prospects.

Using Direct Mail to Ask for Gifts

Direct mail appeals have long been the backbone of many successful annual fund campaigns. Now, they are beginning to be used more often in planned giving efforts as well. For example, in 2006, the American Civil Liberties Union (ACLU) Foundation ran the Legacy of Liberty Challenge Campaign. Through the generous commitment of an ACLU donor, the organization was able to promote a matching challenge grant. Donors who made a bequest or trust commitment or the donation of a charitable gift annuity (CGA) saw their contribution matched by the challenge grant up to $10,000 each in immediate cash support. The challenge grant magnified the impact of gifts and established a sense of urgency, something usually absent in gift planning.

A study of 15 years of bequest collection records at a large national non-profit organization with a mailing program of 1 million pieces discovered that donors who received a letter directly asking them for a bequest were 17 times more likely to give a bequest than donors who were not asked.[2] Direct mail works. It can inspire people to make a bequest commitment and it can uncover cases where donors have already made the commitment thereby giving development professionals the opportunity to properly recognize and steward these individuals.

Another direct mail example comes from the Natural Resources Defense Council (NRDC) which implemented a similar challenge grant program beginning in 2009. The NRDC Legacy Leaders Million-Dollar Challenge matches bequest commitments at a rate of 10 percent up to $10,000 per commitment. If a commitment is made, but the amount remains undisclosed, the commitment will be matched with a challenge gift of $150. The total value of the challenge grant is $1 million.

The NRDC, which has 1.3 million members and activists, chose to send the planned giving appeal to current members over the age of 55 or, if no age data was available even after an age-appending process, current members who have been members for at least five consecutive years. With some additional refinements, the prospect pool totaled approximately 50,000.

The NRDC sent two direct mail pieces in 2009 with another two scheduled for 2010. Each mailing will go to 25,000 people, meaning that some non-responding prospects will receive multiple appeals. The NRDC magazine, *On Earth*, carried an advertisement promoting the challenge program in an effort to educate prospects and reinforce the mailing.

The November 2009 direct mail package included a letter from John Adams, the NRDC Founding Director. The closed-face outer envelope featured a live postage stamp, a typed address, and the teaser: "An inspiring message from a longtime NRDC member in Wyoming." In his letter, Adams described the founding of the organization and its continuing vision. He also demonstrated his commitment to the organization by explaining that he and his wife have included a bequest provision in their estate plan. He then highlighted the challenge program and encouraged the reader to participate. He closed the two-page letter by mentioning that the individual can help safeguard the environment by making sure the NRDC is there for generations to come. The letter also referenced a lift note from a legacy donor (the one mentioned on the outer envelope) and a full-color brochure, *Guide to Bequests*, to help the donor understand how she can include the NRDC in her estate plans.

The lift note from Meredith Taylor, an NRDC planned gift donor, was a passionate testimonial. In her note, she explained why she and her husband have included the NRDC in their estate plans. She also encouraged the reader to follow her lead by making a commitment as well, "All you have to do is tell NRDC that you've included the Natural Resources Defense Council in your estate plans. There's no need to write a check; it's just a matter of saying that you've named NRDC in your Will."

While the NRDC *Guide to Bequests* brochure does not mention the challenge, it does review a number of charitable estate planning options and contains several lovely photographs of natural scenery and wildlife. The package also included a buckslip "Announcing the NRDC Legacy Leader Million-Dollar Challenge!" The buckslip briefly explained the terms of the challenge and, as the letter did, included the name and contact information of Michelle Quinones, Senior Gift Planning Specialist. The buckslip also outlined the benefits of being part of the Legacy Leader recognition society: lifetime NRDC subscriptions, invitations to special events, one gift membership and, unless the donor wished to remain anonymous, recognition in the NRDC annual report.

The final elements of the NRDC direct mail package were a "Confidential Reply Form" and business reply envelope. The reply form gave the recipient the option of disclosing that the NRDC is already part of her estate plans or indicating that she would like additional information. The form did not ask for the amount of the gift commitment. While that information would be needed for the challenge grant, NRDC did not want to create an obstacle to response. Instead, staff knew there would be plenty of time to seek that information once the form was received. In fact, this would give staff a terrific reason to follow up with those who responded to the direct mail appeal.[3]

When the NRDC receives a form, the organization sends appropriate follow-up information to those requesting it, and later calls those individuals. For those who indicate they have made a commitment, the NRDC sends a thank-you letter. The thank-you letter package contains a gift form confirming the commitment, confirming how the donor's recognition listing will appear in the annual report, and asking for the dollar amount of the commitment so that it can be matched. The package also contains information about how the donor can assign his one free gift membership. When the confirmation form is received, the donor is sent a certificate recognizing his membership in the Legacy Leader recognition group. The certificate mailing is followed by a friendly telephone call to thank the donor again and to make sure he received the certificate.

Because of the nature of the challenge grant, NRDC staff have a very positive and strong reason to follow up with donors to discover the actual gift amount. This leads to a variety of friendly telephone exchanges and face-to-face visits.

KEY CONCEPT

To create a sense of urgency with a direct mail appeal, secure a challenge grant. This will give prospects a reason to take immediate action while giving them a good feeling knowing that the value of their gifts will be magnified.

The results from two of the four planned mailings are in. The first two mailings generated 87 confirmed bequest commitments. Of those, 62 were willing to confirm the gift value. The value of the commitments from the first two mailings is $8.5 million with an average bequest value of approximately $137,000 and a typical bequest value of about $100,000. This has resulted in $330,000 in matching gift support so far, according to Michelle Mulia-Howell, Director of Gift Planning at the NRDC. In a typical year, the NRDC would receive approximately 60 bequest commitments. The organization now has more than 1,300 members of its Legacy Leader planned giving recognition group.

While the NRDC is using direct mail to generate inquiries and gifts, the organization is also relying on the telephone and face-to-face visits to follow up with people. The additional contacts provide additional cultivation and stewardship while giving staff the opportunity to learn more about prospects and donors. With a gift planning staff of one director, two officers, and an assistant, the NRDC could not have reached out personally to 50,000 individuals. The direct mail campaign, however, could do so.

Brian Sagrestano, President of Gift Planning Development, found when doing marketing to identified prospects with whom the charity has a limited relationship, planting the seed for a gift amount is important. A small New England college conducted an interesting experiment. The college first sent out a postcard asking people to consider increasing their income in retirement through a gift annuity with a $10,000 example. The college sent the same card to another group with a $25,000 example. The college found that the first card resulted in $10,000 gifts while the second card resulted in $25,000 gifts, even though both cards said the minimum gift amount was $10,000. The response rates to both cards were comparable. The power of suggestion is more powerful than we often realize.

When preparing a direct mail appeal, one should keep in mind many of the same points outlined in Chapter 4. In particular, one should keep the following points in mind:

- One should have a donor-centered reason for writing.

- Make sure the mailing is readable.

- Although the letter will go to many people, make it sound as though it is going to just one.

- Touch the reader's emotions by telling a story, providing a testimonial, or showing meaningful illustrations.

- Provide useful information and give prospects an easy way or, better yet, multiple easy ways to request additional information.

- Give people easy, confidential ways to commit.

- Be prepared with a solid follow-up regime.

Using the Telephone to Ask for Gifts

Just as the telephone is a powerful annual fund solicitation tool, it is also a strong tool for soliciting planned gifts, when used properly. One problem with direct mail is that it is easy to ignore. It is much harder for a prospect to ignore a telephone call. In addition, a telephone call can build rapport and answer questions in a way that direct mail will never be able to do. In a dynamic telephone conversation, the appeal can actually be tailored to each individual.

To be effective, calls must be made by intelligent, mature, well-trained professionals who can engage prospects in actual conversations. While the conversation will be structured and follow a designed flow, it should not involve the slavish reading of a script. Calls can be made to solicit planned gifts in general or specifically for bequests or CGAs. While volunteers can make calls, it will usually be more effective to have paid callers on the telephone, either employed and managed by the organization or by a professional telephone fundraising company. A planned giving telephone campaign is something that can benefit almost any nonprofit organization.

A university in Texas decided to use the telephone to encourage alumni to request a CGA proposal.[4] The university began by mailing 7,000 letters. The letters contained a response card so that alumni could request information. A total of 44 people (0.6 percent response rate) requested more information. The 6,956 nonresponders received a second mailing and response card. The second mailing generated 42 responses (0.6 percent). Student callers contacted the 86 individuals who requested more information. They explained the details of the CGA program and answered questions. Of the 86 alumni called, 40 requested a CGA proposal; the callers gathered the necessary information. Planned giving staff then prepared the CGA illustrations and sent them. The planned giving staff telephoned and, in some cases, visited the 40 prospects closing a total of eight CGAs worth $400,000. The minimum gift for establishing a CGA was $10,000. A $1,000 annual fund donor who was contacted established a $150,000 CGA and talked about doing another; her brother, not part of the initial prospect pool, gave $330,000 as a result of follow-up conversation inspired by his sister's gift. This one calling program was instrumental in generating at least $730,000 in support through CGAs.

The Texas-based university conducted another CGA test program with a much smaller prospect pool though it was similar in composition to the original. Instead of sending two letters, the university sent only one letter to 50 prospects. Callers followed up to all 50 prospects. Of those contacted, 20 were interested in receiving a proposal. The university planned giving staff prepared the proposals and anticipated closing at least four CGA gifts.

The planned giving staff at the Texas university discovered that they were able to close approximately 20 percent of the proposals they presented regardless of the test program. However, with the first test program, only 0.6 percent of the original prospect pool had requested a proposal. By contrast, after the calling was completed in the second test program, 40 percent were interested in receiving a proposal. While the first test produced $400,000 in gifts from the prospect pool, one can extrapolate the results of the second test to reveal that a potential to generate $19.6 million could exist with the original prospect pool. At the very least, these tests demonstrate that while direct mail can effectively support a telephone program, the telephone is a far more powerful medium when it comes to inspiring prospects to request a proposal. While the results in the second test might not have been so dramatic if more prospects had been included, the results would almost certainly still have been far, far greater than what was achieved in the first test. The streamlined process was more efficient and more productive. Neither approach generated any complaints from alumni.

Kent State University did a prospect screening and found it had approximately 27,000 planned giving prospects.[5] Recognizing that the university would never have a sufficient number of planned giving or major gift officers to see so many prospects, the university turned to the telephone. The university was already employing student callers to contact alumni for the annual fund. Staff created a simple tag to these calls when they were made to select prospects (i.e., those who were rated as planned giving prospects, over the age of 62, annual fund donors for 10 years, etc.). Regardless of the outcome of the annual fund call, provided that the prospect was in a positive mood, the student caller would ask if the prospect had ever considered doing something for the university beyond his lifetime, by remembering Kent State in his will. The results of the probe are categorized into "already in will," "considering/wants information/follow up," "considering/no information," and "not now."

While the use of student callers to qualify prospects was innovative, the postlead comprehensive follow-up program is what delivered the results, according to Mindy Aleman, Executive Director of Kent State University's Center for Gift and Estate Planning. Appropriate follow-up mail is sent depending on the response. Qualified prospects are then assigned to development staff for cultivation, visits, and, eventually, solicitation of a gift.

Center staff continue to monitor the progress made. The planned giving probe at the end of the annual fund call was designed to find the low-hanging fruit. As a result of the probes, the university has closed bequest commitments, trusts, CGAs, and current gifts when following up with the qualified planned giving prospects. In the five years since the effort began, Kent State has raised $1.3 million in new gifts and bequest commitments; during that time, only one complaint was received. The lead generation by telephone cost the center nothing since the planned giving probe was a simple, short piggyback onto the annual fund call.

A mid-Atlantic university recognized the potential of using the telephone for planned giving.[6] However, instead of adding a tag to an annual fund call, the university implemented an integrated direct-mail/telephone program to solicit bequest commitments and steward individuals who are willing to consider a commitment. The program was a stand-alone planned giving appeal and was not connected to the annual fund calls at all. In fact, the planned giving and annual fund staffs coordinated efforts to avoid either call being placed too soon following the other. The planned giving program involved personalized letters, a capsule planned giving case brochure, and will confirmation form and envelope. The precall packages were mailed to 18,161 alumni, retired staff, and retired faculty. While prospects who had already included the university in their will could have completed the form and sent it in, virtually no one did. So, nearly all prospects were assigned to receive a telephone call. When contacted, prospects were engaged in a conversation.

During the course of the conversation, callers asked open-ended questions instead of yes/no questions to engage the prospects. The average conversation lasted 10 to 15 minutes. Those who expressed a willingness to consider a bequest commitment received a thank-you letter, will confirmation form, and, if they requested it, additional information. Prospects were encouraged to complete the will confirmation form once they were ready to make a commitment so they could be recognized by the university's planned giving donor recognition society.

At the end of the first call, there were also those who said they had already included the university in their will. This group received a thank-you letter and then a call from a member of the gift planning staff. The staff member, either by telephone or in person, thanked the donor and tried to gather additional information and documentation of the gift in order to provide the donor with proper recognition.

Those who received the mailing following the first call but who did not send back the form were contacted again by telephone. This confirmation call identified questions the prospect might have, provided answers to questions, determined if the prospect had taken any action since the last call, and then reconfirmed where the prospect was on a decision-making continuum. Those contacted received a follow-up letter.

During the next three years, the university intends to follow up with those prospects who were receptive to the idea of bequest giving. Those prospects will receive two letters and two calls each year to move them closer to actually taking action to include the university in their estate plans. In addition, the university's development team will visit some of these prospects to further cultivate them.

For the mid-Atlantic university, 18,161 prospects were targeted. Eight prospects provided documentation to the university to demonstrate their bequest commitments. An additional 48 prospects verbally stated the university is in their will. An additional 13 have scheduled an appointment with an attorney. An additional 41 expressed serious interest and stated they would take action within the next three years. An additional 1,611 have some type of interest in bequest giving and, on some level, are willing to consider making such a gift at some time. Those who were willing to document their commitment, 13 at last count, had plans to make gifts valued at $1,000 to $50,000 each. After follow-up from the senior director of planned giving, one additional donor made a bequest commitment of $5 million. The university anticipates that the program will generate $13 million, and likely substantially more, at a cost of under, possibly far under, ten cents on the dollar raised.

The program for the university generated millions of dollars in a very cost-effective manner. However, only 1 percent of those contacted either had already included the university in their wills or had expressed a willingness to take action soon with another 14 percent willing to consider a bequest. The university could have achieved a higher response rate if it had narrowed its prospect pool. However, the staff realized that potential donors exist at every level of the university's prospect file. For example, though the response rates were even lower, some commitments were received from alumni nondonors. Other organizations might not make the same decision regarding the composition of the prospect pool. For example, some universities narrow their focus because of budgetary constraints or other factors and experience greater response rates. With a more narrowly defined prospect pool, some universities find 2.5 to 5 percent of those contacted have included the university in their wills or have expressed a willingness to take action soon with another 30 to 35 percent willing to consider a bequest. Response rates will also vary depending on the quality of the relationship that exists between prospects and the organization.

A symphony orchestra in the Pacific Northwest wanted to increase the number of bequest commitments generated by its marketing efforts. The orchestra's newsletter was generating a very low number of inquiries. So, the orchestra decided to implement a coordinated direct mail/telephone program. The organization mailed to 2,200 prospects who were identified by an electronic prospect screening and that remained highly-rated prospects following a manual review. Staff followed up the letters with telephone calls and reached 1,200 individuals. Of those reached, 13 (1 percent) stated that the orchestra was already in their will, 40 (3.3 percent) said they would put the orchestra in their will at a later time, 349 (29 percent) said they would consider a bequest gift. In addition, the program generated five current cash gifts. The orchestra estimates that deferred giving will total $2 million.[7] Staff was able to follow up with donors to confirm their commitment and appropriately recognize them. In addition, they were able to follow up with those who were considering a bequest commitment to make sure they had the information necessary to help them with their decision. Staff did not receive any complaints.

In the three bequest campaigns reviewed previously, callers were able to uncover existing bequest commitments that were previously unknown. While those gifts would likely have been fully realized without the telephone call, it was very valuable for the organizations to know about these commitments. Now that the organizations know about the commitments, they can appropriately recognize the donors thereby solidifying the commitments and bringing joy to the donors. In addition, by adding these individuals to the planned gift recognition societies, the organizations can inspire others. Finally, now that the organizations know about the commitments, they can talk with these donors further and determine whether a simple bequest is, in fact, the best gift for the donor or whether some other arrangement (i.e., CGA or trust) might make more sense.

An international Christian relief and development organization implemented a direct mail/telephone program to "enroll" prospects in an estate planning education series.[8] The program is described in Chapter 4. The relief organization was able to enroll 47 percent of those contacted. After receiving the education series by mail and after receiving the cultivation calls that were part of the series, prospects were asked to include the organization in their estate plans. Of the 6,300 original prospects, 282 made bequest commitments valued at $5.1 million. In addition, among those who received the educational series, annual giving numbers increased.

A telephone program is admittedly not the ideal way to solicit planned gifts. Doing so face-to-face is the best approach. However, as the old Bell System (AT&T) commercials used to say, "[The telephone] is the next best thing to being there." Leslie D. Bram, Associate Vice President/COO of the University of Florida Foundation, notes that even with a robust planned giving professional staff of six and 70 major gift officers, the Foundation still does not have sufficient staff, and never will, to visit with all of its planned giving prospects. When the state of Florida initiated the "Opportunity Scholarship Program," a challenge grant for the state's public universities, the Foundation looked for ways to broaden its outreach. The Foundation decided to implement a telephone program. The challenge grant created a sense of urgency and presented alumni with a great chance to have their gifts magnified by the matching grant from the state. The telephone program allowed the Foundation to reach out to 11,551 prospects resulting in 174 alumni who made bequest commitments or promises to take action soon and 769 alumni who are willing to consider a bequest commitment. The Foundation has not received any serious negative complaints, and the program is anticipated to possibly produce $6 million or perhaps significantly more, not including the state match. Most of this revenue would not have come in otherwise.[9]

There are many different telephone fundraising models in use for planned giving. Some organizations have implemented in-house efforts while others have contracted with telephone fundraising companies. No single model is correct. No single prospect focus is correct. Each organization must determine what is most appropriate given its unique set of circumstances. To further engage a marginally affiliated constituency, offering an estate planning education series might make sense to cultivate prospects prior to an ask. For an organization with a well-affiliated population, a coordinated mail and telephone appeal might be more appropriate. Some organizations might use a letter before the call while others, to conserve limited budget dollars, might send a precall postcard rather than a letter using its limited resources to make more calls. Some organizations will piggyback a planned giving probe onto an annual fund call. Some organizations will use the telephone to solicit stock gifts, or life insurance policies, while others will solicit CGAs as others solicit bequests. Some will offer all gift planning options to their prospects.

What we know is that the telephone medium can produce cost-effective planned giving results with little or no negative feedback if care is taken. The key steps for nonprofit organizations to remember are:

- Determine the objectives of an outreach program.

- Define the largest prospect pool possible given budgetary constraints, institutional priorities, and the limited ability to visit with all prospects.

- Consider the organization's capacity to handle the postcall follow-up work when determining the size of the prospect pool.

- Choose the calling model that can best achieve the objectives and that is most compatible with the prospect pool.

- Make sure that the callers are intelligent, mature, experienced, and articulate.

- Provide the callers with extensive training.

- Use a call outline rather than a hard script. Callers should stick to a structure and a call flow, but they should never actually read from a script.

- The letters and the calls used should be friendly and helpful in tone.

- Have a follow-up system in place to handle all responses, even from those who choose not to commit.

- Plan on visiting with those contacted, particularly those who commit.

Meeting Face-to-Face for the Ask

In an ideal world, a nonprofit organization would have the staff and funds required to develop and solicit every prospect for a planned gift of any kind through face-to-face visits. This is the most powerful way to accomplish planned giving goals. In reality, limited resources require the organization to focus face-to-face solicitation efforts on only the best prospects that will give the most immediate return on investment. As discussed earlier, all others can be cultivated and solicited through mail and the telephone.

Much of this section is informed by Bruce Makous, a consultant with Barnes & Roche, Inc.[10] This section incorporates a number of case studies and scripts to show how the process works. The techniques presented are based on Makous' 26 years of fundraising experience, and on more than 400 one-on-one donor meetings and tens of millions of dollars raised in major and planned gifts.

The techniques are appropriate not only for fundraising officers but also for volunteers, and these methods apply to nearly every type of nonprofit organization.[*]

Personal interaction with priority prospects is important to good cultivation and, eventually, solicitation. The best method for effective cultivation is a private, one-on-one visit. The goal of the development professional during the initial visit is to simply become better acquainted and earn the prospect's trust. Asking for a planned gift during an initial meeting will be ineffective, particularly if this is the first time that anyone from the charity has talked with the prospect. A prospective donor needs time to become familiar with the concept of philanthropic planning, and the idea itself needs time to grow and develop into an inspiration for the donor, which can require many months or even years.

The development professional needs to contact the prospect and set up a first visit. The goal of this meeting is to provide him with an update on all of the wonderful new developments at the organization, some of which have been made possible in part through his support. It is important for the organization to provide loyal supporters with a report on how their funds are being used, and to receive their feedback.

No matter how well-screened and selected the prospects are, only a small portion of them will be interested in the idea of a visit with a charity officer. This ratio can range from about one out of four for a highly cultivated donor base (i.e., some university alumni or religious congregations) to as low as one out of 40 for a charity with a less cultivated base. If it comes up while attempting to set up the first meeting, the development professional should make it clear that this visit will not involve a solicitation of any kind. The development professional must promise that there will be no request for a gift at this visit and, if the prospect agrees to the visit, that promise must be kept.

---

[*]Bruce Makous, CFRE, CAP, ChFC, a consultant with Barnes & Roche, Inc., graciously contributed extensive material throughout this entire chapter.

The prospects most likely to agree to a meeting are those with a program-matic affinity—those who benefit personally from the charity's programs or who are close to someone who has or will benefit. That is appropriate, since the main agenda of the visit is to cover relevant program information.

IN THE REAL WORLD

Setting up the Introductory Visit

In some communities and with some prospects, one may be able to simply drop in. This is what Roger Ellison, Vice President for Planned Giving at West Texas Rehabilitation Center Foundation, does with many of his prospects. He views such visits as a friend dropping by to thank a friend for a gift. However, such an approach will not work in all communities or with all prospects. Sometimes the best approach involves picking up the telephone, talking with the prospect, and asking for a meeting. It is important to do this in a friendly, nonthreatening way. The following is a fictionalized example of a telephone conversation between fundraiser Casey Goodman of The Hospital Foundation and long-time donor and planned giving prospect Mary Mann:

MARY: (answers the phone) Hello. This is Mary Mann.

CASEY: Hi, Mary. This is Casey Goodman from The Hospital Foundation. How are you? (Note: Never ask that of prospects in New York City. They will likely tell you that it is none of your business and then hang-up.)

MARY: I think I just gave something to you.

CASEY: I'm not calling to ask for a gift. We've appreciated your generous support over the years, and I actually just want to thank you for your contributions.

MARY: You're welcome. I don't think anyone has ever called to thank me.

CASEY: I'm glad to do it. You are among our most loyal supporters. Did you know that you have been contributing to the Hospital for eleven years?

MARY: Really? I guess I didn't realize it had been that long.

CASEY: Yes. You started in 1999. You have been very generous over the years, and we greatly appreciate it. If you don't mind my asking, how did you decide to start giving to us?

MARY: My husband Mark was diagnosed with prostate cancer about 14 years ago, I think. He stayed there for treatment, then we became involved with your community outreach programs. We found your health awareness events very helpful. And, they're still useful to me. My husband passed away last year. I think the Hospital sent a nice card.

CASEY: Yes. We were very sorry to hear about that. How are you doing?

MARY: I'm fine. What can I do for you today?

CASEY: One of my responsibilities is to provide updates to our VIPs like you. We have a number of exciting new developments here at the Hospital. I wonder if you might have perhaps a half-hour or so for a visit.

MARY: What would you want to come by to talk about?

CASEY: I want to update you on the many exciting things happening at the Hospital. I think you'll be amazed, and impressed at the impact of our public education programs.

MARY: Are you going to request another contribution?

CASEY: No. I will not be asking you for a gift. That's not what this is about. The purpose of this visit is to update you as a key investor and volunteer in our organization.

MARY: Okay. Actually, I would like to talk to you. I have some questions.

CASEY: What might be a good time to come by? Would next Tuesday or Wednesday be better for you?

The introductory visit provides the opportunity for the development professional to become acquainted with the prospect. The primary goal of this meeting is to lay the foundation for a friendly and trusting relationship between the individual donor and the development professional. To achieve this goal, it is best to have a long, one-on-one conversation. Learning about the prospect is the preeminent goal and listening is the best tool.

EXECUTIVE INSIGHT

Planned giving development is "purposeful conversation." It is purposeful because what I am looking to glean from the donor or potential donor is what makes them pound their fist on the table, what is it that turns their crank. In a word, it is identifying "passion." That is what I want to find out from every person I visit. It may not happen the first time or even the second, but development is a process of discovery.

—Mark R. Seeley, Director of Gift Planning, University of South Carolina

In preparing for this get-acquainted session, the development professional should learn as much as possible ahead of time about lifestyle, community interests, key accomplishments, and other notes of interest about this person. An informed web search can provide some of this valuable material as can a review of the organization's own database. This information supplements the broader screening process, and can actually provide the most valuable preparatory information. This is where the development professional can learn more about the prospect's community activities, areas of interest, family matters, and propensity for giving.

It is important to learn the donor's history and interests. Take, for example, a major prospect, we will call him James Hoeffel (see Case Study 1), on whom this principle was initially ignored. In order to solicit a gift, Hoeffel was treated to lunches with the president, PowerPoint presentations, and other persuasive methods for years, yet he would not make a gift commitment.

IN THE REAL WORLD

Case Study 1: James Hoeffel, the Wealthy Orphan

Very successful California businessman James Hoeffel, who built his wealth by developing a chemical method for extracting metals from recycled computer parts, has been courted by his alma mater, Falls Bridge University, for five years. His net worth is listed at $100 million. At first, he was given a presentation about creating a new chemistry center at Falls Bridge. Then, he was approached about funding a new technology transfer program. He was not interested in either concept. Gift officer Leo Mastrone visits him and hears his life story. Leo learns that James was an orphan whose foster parents adopted him, recognized his gifts, and sent him to college. His brother, who he says is equally brilliant, was not sent to college by his different foster parents and now lives very modestly. The difference in their lives has always troubled James. Leo talks to James about setting up a scholarship fund to provide full scholarships, all expenses paid, for brilliant but destitute high school graduates. James immediately agrees to contribute $2 million to endow that program.

1992–2003	Hoeffel gives annual stock contributions to Falls Bridge, increasing from $2,500 to $10,000 per year. Never attends alumni events.
6/1/2004	Hoeffel is brought to Falls Bridge campus and given a presentation, attended by the university president, about how important the new Center for Chemistry Innovation will be. They request $1 million to help fund it. Hoeffel says he's not interested.
12/2/2004	Hoeffel continues to give $10,000 in annual contributions, funded with company stock.
12/10/2005	Hoeffel continues to give $10,000 in annual contributions.
3/15/2006	Hoeffel is brought to campus and given a presentation, attended by three department heads, about the new Technology Transfer Program. Hoeffel says he's not interested.
12/2/2006	Hoeffel continues to give $10,000 in annual contributions.
12/10/2007	Hoeffel continues to give $10,000 in annual contributions.
12/12/2008	Hoeffel continues to give $10,000 in annual contributions.
3/2/2009	Fundraiser Leo Mastrone visits James Hoeffel. He learns his life history, and discusses the idea of a fund for scholarships for brilliant but destitute students. Hoeffel loves the idea.
3/15/2009	Hoeffel transfers $2 million in company stock to create the Hoeffel Scholarship Fund.

Note that in the case of Hoeffel, when a wiser gift officer inherited him as a prospect, the first thing he did was to learn Hoeffel's life story. He found that this very successful man was orphaned as a child, and his foster parents adopted him and sent him to college, which he felt was the sole reason for his success. The development professional proposed that Hoeffel establish a scholarship fund for brilliant but destitute students who would not otherwise be able to go to college. Hoeffel was immediately struck by this gift purpose, and he quickly made a seven-figure commitment for the Hoeffel Scholarship Fund. Understanding the donor's background is the key to finding the right gift purpose.

Getting the Introductory Visit off to a Good Start

The beginning of a face-to-face visit will set the tone for the entire visit. A development professional should not be officious. Instead, she should think of the meeting as a visit with a friend, while remaining appropriately professional. The following fictional conversation occurs at the start of a home visit between development professional Bobby Taggert of The Adams School and prospect Steven Berger, a long-time annual donor who gives $500 per year. The conversation begins:

STEVEN: Hi, there! Come on in!

BOBBY: Thank you! Thanks so much for seeing me today!

STEVEN: I'm glad you could come by.

STEVEN: [gestures toward the family room] We'll sit in here.

BOBBY: Thank you.

STEVEN: So. What's this about, again? I've never had a visit from you before.

BOBBY: Well, actually, you're one of our most loyal supporters.

STEVEN: Really? I don't give very much.

BOBBY: Actually, you're very generous. And loyal. You've been contributing to Adams for twenty-one years.

STEVEN: No kidding? I guess I didn't realize it had been that long.

BOBBY: You started in 1989 with a $25 gift to the library. You have been very supportive over the years, and we greatly appreciate it. In fact, I brought you a little gift. [Gives a school pen.]

STEVEN: Thank you. [Opening the box and admiring it.] Very nice!

BOBBY: Just a small token of our appreciation.

STEVEN: [Puts the pen away.] Yes, it's a great school. Obviously very close to my heart. Jane and I feel that the new president is doing a good job, too.

BOBBY: Tell me, if you don't mind my asking, how long have you and Jane been married?

STEVEN: Oh, goodness. Thirty-seven years this October, I believe. It was right out of law school. We were both interning at Fox Wallace, a large law firm here in town.

BOBBY: How interesting!

STEVEN: Yes, she was specializing in intellectual property. I was in litigation. We started dating, then had to disclose it to the HR department. They said it was okay, since we were in different departments. [He smiles.] It

was really embarrassing. But nowhere near as embarrassing as explaining it to our parents when we moved in together two months later. . . .
[. . . and so on, leading into an ongoing, detailed conversation about their life together—where they have lived, jobs, children, hobbies, vacations, and so on. One should try to remain as long as possible off of the focus on the charity. The objective is to learn about the prospect.]

Hearing the prospect's life story with emphasis on touch points related to the organization and the organization's mission is the best approach for a first meeting. Allow an hour or more, if available, for this part. Other approaches based on available time and circumstances can be workable. When scheduling appointments, it is best to allow extra time between visits so that one does not have to rush out the door at an inopportune moment.

Remember that philanthropic inspiration is usually a private matter of primary interest only to the single individual. Even a spouse will not necessarily share the inspiration. Take, for example, giving to the individual's college or university. Leaving a legacy with the donor's alma mater is meaningful to the individual, but not necessarily to the spouse. The same can apply to religious affiliation or to any kind of philanthropic mission. Therefore, at some point it is best to have a private, one-on-one visit with the interested party. Note that family philanthropy—the shared charitable inspirations of a couple or family—is also relevant, but it usually should be discussed only after understanding the interests of each individual involved and who that individual's influencers are.

After listening to the prospect's story, briefly update the prospect on program activities at the organization that will likely be of interest to the prospect. Include a brief report about other donor-established funds and show what other supporters have found inspiring. Do not suggest or request any commitment from the prospect. That is not the goal of this first meeting. If the donor brings up the idea of a gift commitment of some sort, it is best to postpone any discussion to give her time to contemplate options.

IN THE REAL WORLD

Beginning to Wrap up the Introductory Visit

Fundraiser Bobby Taggert and donor Steven Berger have now spent an hour or more of conversation focusing on the prospect's background and interests. And, they have just spent quite a while discussing Steven's and Jane's travels together in Europe and Asia. The conversation continues:

BOBBY: That's another wonderful story! You and Jane really have had an amazing life together!

STEVEN: Yes, I suppose so.

BOBBY: [Gestures toward the mantle.] And, your two beautiful children on top of that.

STEVEN: [Smiling.] We're very proud of them.

BOBBY: I can see why!

[. . . a pause in the conversation . . .]

STEVEN: Anyway, enough about me. So, what's happening at Adams? I know all about the new gym, and the library expansion.

BOBBY: President Chow is determined to make his mark. He has laid out his vision for the next decade, and it's very exciting and includes a new science building, a student activity center, and a major endowment fund.

STEVEN: [Frowning.] I see. And I suppose you're going to need some support for all of that.

BOBBY: True. And, I'll leave some information about it. But one of the most interesting new developments I wanted to tell you about is growth in the Legacy Society. This is a group of people who have decided to remember us in their wills or give us a planned gift.

STEVEN: Really?

BOBBY: The wonderful thing is that these individuals can establish a fund and determine how they would like to help other people like themselves. A recent supporter created the Jeri Baggins Scholarship Fund. She's pleased that, after she passes away, this is one way that she will be remembered.

Steven: It's nice. I know Jeri. I'm glad she's doing that. And, I've thought about that sort of thing. But even though it's a good thing to do, I need to be very careful with my money.

Bobby: Mrs. Baggins didn't have to give any money at all at this time. She simply made a commitment in her will.

Steven: Interesting.

Bobby: Anyway, I'm not asking you to do anything at all today. I just wanted to update you on our programs, and make you aware of activities that may be of interest.

Steven: You've certainly given me a few things to think about!

Bobby: Great. Yes. Exciting things are happening at the school. I'll just leave these materials for you.

Steven: Thank you. I'm very impressed with everything.

[. . . departure amenities, going to the door, etc . . . .]

Bobby: And, I was particularly pleased to become acquainted with you. Thanks for taking the time. It's really been a pleasure.

Steven: Good to meet you, too.

Bobby: Would you have any objection to me being in touch with you from time to time? Just to say hello and stay caught up?

Steven: Not at all. It would be my pleasure.

Note that in this scenario, although the opportunity arises, the fundraiser does not ask the donor to make any sort of commitment to a gift. Asking for a major commitment is very ineffective at this early stage, and can be viewed as a breach of trust, especially if the development officer has promised that there will be no solicitation at this visit. Since the donor has not really had time to contemplate the meaning of creating a legacy and how he may do so, it can result in a smaller, preemptive commitment, if any. On the other hand, the development professional may find that this is a sophisticated prospect who has similar commitments with other charities, may be well cultivated by the organization already, and may have already even given the idea of leaving a legacy with this organization some thought. Even so, it is still better to resist the temptation to ask for a commitment at this early stage.

What Do Journalism and Fundraising Have in Common?

All I ever needed to know about planned giving I learned in high school Journalism:

Who? Who is this person?

Why? Why are they inclined to give?

Where? Where will they give?

What? What assets work best?

How? What gift technique works best?

When? When will they make the gift?

"When" comes last for a reason. I am helping them write their legacy. My goal is to become their official biographer. That's a position of trust.

—John Gillon, Senior Director of Gift Planning, Wake Forest University Baptist Medical Center

As illustrated in the last conversation, the key takeaway for the charity representative from a first interaction is the prospect's consent to continue the conversation, which the prospect soon realizes will eventually become a discussion about a planned gift. This consent is essentially permission to ask him for a gift in the future, and with a positive response, it is already moving toward the intention to make a gift.

Waiting before explicitly outlining a gift proposal provides an opportunity for the donor to consider the concept in depth, and to learn more about the methods through which such a gift may be funded. It also opens the door for the development professional to provide information to the donor that can inspire and engender philanthropic interest, and other information about financial concepts in funding gifts. Finally, this gives the fundraiser time to learn more about the donor's areas of interest and financial situation. In the meantime, of course, the donor will continue annual giving and usually increase the amount and frequency of gifts as a result of the extra attention and information.

If a prospective major donor is going to share his personal philanthropic interests and financial matters with the charity's representative, there must be a sense of trust. When there is, the development professional may actually become an advisor on philanthropic matters, particularly those related to her organization, but also philanthropy in general. The officer may be the only one with whom the donor can discuss things such as the impact he wants to have in the world after death, what inspires him most, family interests, and general concerns about leaving a legacy gift. Much like in the purchase of a new home, there will be positive and emotional anticipation, as well as valid concerns that the purchase will be defective in some way.

After a successful first visit, the development professional has a basis on which to build a trusting and productive relationship. Contact the prospect frequently and find ongoing creative ways in which to continue to engage the individual over time. Case Study 2 illustrates how this might work over time. For example, one can send cards, letters, e-mail messages, and tokens of appreciation. Bring the prospect to the organization's offices and visit his home as often as possible. One should build a program that can support this kind of labor-intensive activity with a large group of prospects.

 **IN THE REAL WORLD**

Case Study 2: Jane Brassley, a Legacy of Science

Dr. Jane Brassley is a fictional alumna of an Ivy League school with a successful career as a chemist at a large pharmaceutical company for 36 years. Shortly after she retired, she attended an alumni dinner at which the president of the university spoke. During the dinner, she informed a friend, who happened to be on the university's Board, that she was thinking of leaving part of her estate to the university. The friend asked if she would like to speak with someone on the staff, and Jane agreed. The major gifts officer

(continued)

had several meetings at the donor's home and at the university's offices. The result was that Jane named the university as a 50 percent remainder beneficiary of a CRUT to fund a chair in science journalism. The CRUT was funded with her primary residence, a property worth $5 million.

1972–1999	Brassley attends the university's Annual Alumni Day almost every year; meets many university leaders.
05/01/2000	Brassley wins an alumni award and is a featured speaker at Alumni Day.
12/31/2000	Brassley retires from her position at the pharmaceutical company.
01/20/2001	Notice in alumni magazine about her retirement, award, career, with praise.
05/02/2001	At Alumni Dinner, Brassley mentions to a friend and fellow alum her interest in making a legacy gift; her friend, a university board member, introduces her to the university's major gifts officer.
05/03/2001	Major gifts officer speaks with Brassley; sets up meeting at her home.
06/24/2001	University president sends birthday gift: flowers and wine.
07/01/2001	Brassley sends warm letter to university president reiterating her interest in making a gift.
10/12/2001	Brassley makes annual contribution, $100.
10/24/2001	Thank-you letter to Brassley from president who again thanks her for legacy intent.
12/10/2001	Holiday card to Brassley from president.
05/02/2002	Brassley attends Annual Alumni Dinner.
10/10/2002	Brassley makes annual gift, $300.
10/29/2002	Brassley attends a special alumni event; sees major gifts officer; discusses CRT and intention; plans a follow-up meeting.
05/15/2003	Annual alumni event, dinner.
09/06/2003	Brassley visits campus for a special meeting; university department presentations and discussions.

10/15/2003	Staff sends follow-up proposal consolidating concepts from each department.
11/20/2003	Using info from follow-up letter, Brassley drafts letter of intent to name university beneficiary of a portion of CRT remainder. She chooses the science journalism proposal.
12/20/2003	Letter of intent finalized and cosigned.
01/25/2004	Notice that trust is funded and university is irrevocable remainder beneficiary.
04/12/2004	Special lunch meeting with president and board leadership to celebrate creation of the Jane Brassley Chair in Science Journalism.

The goal of cultivation is not only to develop a trusting relationship between the development professional and the planned giving prospect but also between the organization itself and the donor. The prospective major supporter must trust the leadership and must be convinced that the funds will be used wisely and as intended by the donor. Visits to the organization's offices, participation in program activities, volunteering, and attending events are excellent ways to engender the donor's trust with the charity.

The donor's philanthropic interest, combined with financial format, establishes the overall gift structure. As the planned giving professional becomes familiar with the individual prospect, the core inspiration for the gift will become apparent. It falls upon the development professional, more than anyone else, to translate those inspirations into gift concepts. To do this, the planned giving officer needs to understand not only areas of programmatic interest, but also personal motives for philanthropy.

For solicitation purposes, the planned giving officer can place donors into one of three main groups based on their philanthropic motivations: (1) *mission-only donors*, who are primarily interested in supporting the mission, not necessarily the specific charity itself; (2) *community-based donors*, who are connected with the charity itself through programs and activities, and want to give back and sustain the charity; and (3) *program-focused donors*, who are more or less connected with the charity, and are very inspired by the idea of supporting or creating a specific program concept.

The planned gift officer can recognize prospects or donors from these motivational groups by their relationships with the organization, primarily based on interest in the organization's activities and response to appreciation by the charity. The different motivations of these groups affect their interests in gift purpose. Mission-only donors are usually more interested in unrestricted gifts and have little interest in recognition. Community-based donors, for whom recognition is important, are more commonly interested in named funds and endowments and may be giving to meet some sort of community expectation, such as giving requirements for board members or capital campaign committee people. Program-focused donors have a vision about the use of their funds, and commonly create larger funds, with blended giving methods, and are interested in recognition for their accomplishments. There are several other less common motives, too, and the donor may have a combination of these primary motives, especially if it is a couple or family.

Understanding which motives are important to the prospect is key to creating the most appealing gift structure. This can result in a much larger gift. For example, those who have a strong vision regarding programmatic use of their funds will not be satisfied with a general unrestricted contribution. Those who wish to achieve lasting recognition for themselves or a loved one will prefer a named endowment or physical structure. And, the opposite is also true—some donors are opposed to any form of personal recognition for their gift.

As one becomes more familiar with an individual prospect, one will understand what types of program activities and gift structures are of greatest interest. In particular, the development professional should be aware of responses to the discussion of the concepts of program area, endowment, and named recognition. One should bring up these issues in the course of conversation when the occasion arises during ongoing interactions.

In the end, the donor's philanthropic interests will be combined with the financing to create the gift itself. From the start of the relationship, the development professional has information regarding the prospect's financial capability, which will determine the broad range of potential gift.

The planned giving officer needs to have one or more discussions with the prospect directed toward determining how the donor will fund the gift concepts that have been discussed. These topics should run parallel to discussions of gift purpose so that both have a sense of the range of gift.

One should always lead with philanthropic interest, however. It is not only the intention of charitable giving in general, but it is also good donor relations. No matter how a gift is structured, there will be some sacrifice required of the donor, so there must be a philanthropic motive for the donor to make the commitment. Remember, the economic appeal receives the economic answer: "No, thanks." Do not let financial goals overshadow the donor's philanthropic interests.

KEY CONCEPT

Donors give to things or causes that matter to them not to take advantage of all the benefits of some whiz-bang gift plan that we as fundraisers have come up with for them.

—Steven C. Greaves, Director of Planned Giving, Quinnipiac University

The use of special gift planning structures should be part of the ongoing education of the prospect about how other donors are making gifts. Since over 90 percent of all planned gifts are bequests or CGAs, one should make sure a donor knows about these two options early so that one can reference them in conversations. Spend time going over a CGA illustration without actually proposing one. Simply explain how they work to make sure the prospect knows about the option. Make sure that the prospect understands how named funds, multiyear pledge funding, and endowment structures work at the organization.

For complex gifts, the donor should get advice from one or more advisors, legal and financial, to determine the best method for funding a gift. Development professionals should encourage prospects to seek advice from legal and financial advisors. Working with an advisor allows both the planned gift officer and donor to get a firm sense of what type of gift plan may be the best fit for the donor. Gift planning will expand what the donor is able to accomplish compared to outright contributions and multiyear pledges alone.

When one determines the appropriate financial structure, create a financial proposal. If it is complex, work with the advisor or financial team to create the proposal.

IN THE REAL WORLD

How Much?

Determining how much to ask for is complex. One must factor in the prospect's income, net worth, his perceived financial security, the needs of loved ones, age of the prospect, and passion of the prospect for the organization or cause. There is no definitive rule for deciding how much to ask for.

While it is impossible to create a pat formula for the planned gift ask amount, some organizations have attempted to develop target guidelines. For example, a major university has developed an ask level based on 10 times the prospect's largest single gift. Some ask for 10 to 25 times an individual's annual giving. While that might be a fine formula for a major gift ask, planned gifts most often are associated with an individual's assets and net worth. Jerold Panas, CEO of Jerold Panas, Linzy & Partners, talks about a variety of formulae including taking an individual's net worth times age times a factor of .04.

By contrast, annual fund gifts are more associated with an individual's income. Bruce Makous, a consultant with Barnes & Roche, Inc., believes total legacy giving to all charities is often 10 percent of an individual's net worth. Giving to a single charity is often one-fifth of that, or 2 percent of net worth. This formula is based on actual patterns. Of course, an individual charity might get one-fourth, one-third, one-half, all, or none of the 10 percent.

The key is to inspire donors with mission, projects, and services that tap into their particular philanthropic passions.

By this time, months or years may have passed since the first visit, and those who are not interested will have certainly made the charity representative aware that a gift is unlikely. It is also likely that those who have continued to express an interest have probably already formed the intention to make a gift as a result of the ongoing discussions. There may be a few outstanding questions or financial details to be finalized, but there is frequently already agreement in principle that has evolved organically.

IN THE REAL WORLD

Asking for the Gift, Scenario 1

The planned gift conversation usually involves an ongoing dialogue that takes place over a period of time. Therefore, the concept of "The Ask" can be a bit of a misnomer. The following is a fictional conversation between development professional Parker Davis of the Foundation for Children and Youth and prospect Jane Legatin. It takes place at a cocktail party six months after the initial introductory visit. Parker has been sending Jane information about their endowment programs, and Jane has expressed an interest in creating an endowed fund.

JANE: I wondered when we could speak again about my little endowment fund.
PARKER: What exactly can I tell you?
JANE: I was wondering if I could make sure that only children who really need the help can receive the funding.

(continued)

PARKER: No problem. Would you want it to go only to help children in desperate situations? Those who have extreme financial need?

JANE: Exactly! I just want to make sure I am making a difference with my funding.

PARKER: Yes. That can be stated in the fund purposes. It's not a problem.

JANE: In that case, I think I want to go ahead with what we have discussed.

PARKER: This would be the bequest? A percentage of your net estate?

JANE: Yes. That's it. Let's go ahead with it. What's the next step?

The actual request for a commitment should be a comfortable experience for everyone. The donor should be prepared and should know what to expect. One planned gift officer reported that donors sometimes ask, "Is this the meeting when you will finally ask me for the gift?" They are frequently excited about closing this transformative arrangement.

By this time, the successful gift concept will be perceived as something of great value to the prospect, something she really wants to accomplish. Both parties should already know the likely answer to the request to make the commitment.

IN THE REAL WORLD

Asking for the Gift, Scenario 2

The following fictional conversation occurs between fundraiser Casey Goodman of The Greenville Hospital Foundation and prospect Mary Mann about 18 months after their first visit.

MARY: The Hospital is even busier than when Mark was here. Thanks for the tour.

CASEY: Glad you could come by. Don't let me forget to give you these revised CRUT illustrations you requested. We have the income going to you for your lifetime.

MARY: That's five percent, now, right?

CASEY: Exactly. It works out nicely for you. And there is a very significant remainder for the Foundation.

MARY: Thanks. I'll definitely take another look at it. My advisor told me, however, that I really don't need that income. He said he's going to have to rebalance the portfolio every time I get one of those CRUT payments.

CASEY: Well, maybe you should just give it outright, then. If you don't need the income.

MARY: True. How would that work?

CASEY: It depends on how you want to use the fund.

MARY: You would want it for unrestricted use, correct?

CASEY: That would be fine. But, let me suggest something. Can you come over here to the window?

MARY: That's the garden.

CASEY: It is really a beautiful spot.

MARY: [Contemplative.] I used to take refuge there frequently during Mark's illness. And I would bring him here in his wheelchair, too. It was very quiet and comforting.

CASEY: Would you consider using your gift to maintain the garden?

MARY: Hmmm. That would be a good purpose.

CASEY: And you know the garden remains unnamed after all these years. I thought you might want to name it for Mark. The Mark Mann Garden.

MARY: [She thinks about this for a moment.] Yes. How about the Mark Mann Garden of Hope?

CASEY: That would be lovely. I'll propose that name. I'm sure everyone will love it.

MARY: You know, that would be really nice. I'll give my lawyer a call in the morning so we can finalize this. I'm sure my financial advisor will be relieved!

A donor will delay the close if there is a mismatch in philanthropic purpose or financial structure. If everything fits well, donors will frequently set their own deadline to close the gift. Do not be surprised if it is sooner rather than later.

After the donor makes the formal commitment intention, the detailed understandings concerning gift purpose, program structure, amount, and finances must be put into writing before the funds are transferred. A gift agreement and other related legal documents should be drafted or reviewed by the donor's attorney.

The closing event should be much like closing on a house. All of the legal and financial arrangements are finalized ahead of time and the understandings are presented in the paperwork for signatures.

Ideally, a donor should never be disappointed about anything even for a moment. To reach this very high standard, the gift officer has to carefully manage expectations, starting with the first visit.

Once a gift is finalized and assets are transferred to the charity, follow-up is very important. One can prevent postgift dissatisfaction or remorse by being in touch with the donor frequently in the days and weeks following the close. Address any concerns quickly, and the donor will always be satisfied.

More than one representative of the organization should thank the donor many times over the years for her generosity to the charity. Surprisingly, however, since the donor has been transformed from an uninitiated prospect into a philanthropist who has created a meaningful charitable legacy, the donor will also thank the charity representatives for helping her experience this life-changing event.

Different Ask Scenarios When Meeting with a Prospective Donor

Generally, a planned gift will not be secured after just one contact with a prospect. It is most often not even appropriate to try to do so. Planned gifts often take a considerable amount of time to develop. A development professional must learn about a prospect's philanthropic interests and, current and future, economic circumstances and needs. When making the ask for support, the development professional must focus on the benefits to the donor, both economic and, most importantly, philanthropic. Conversations should be kept friendly and, to avoid confusion, should be devoid of technical jargon while being sure to carefully explain the details of the proposed gift arrangement, no matter how complex.

IN THE REAL WORLD

You Know You're Ready to Ask When . . .

You know you are close to an ask when you know the following:

- Gift target.
- Project target.
- Key solicitor.
- Key need.
- Ask vehicle and terms.

—Robert J. Crandall, President, Robert J. Crandall and Associates

Laura Fredricks, fundraising consultant and author, writes in her book *The Ask*:

We are now ready to go through three scenarios with specific language to ask for Bequest, Charitable Gift Annuity, or Charitable Remainder Trust. There are three questions that must be answered during the ask. I have found that if I get the answers to these questions incorporated into the ask [conversation or before], a planned gift will surely follow:

- What assets are the most logical to use to fund the gift?
- What gift vehicle is best suited for the donor and any other beneficiaries?
- When will the gift be made?

If you can get the answers to these questions during the ask [or before], there is no doubt you will close on the ask much more quickly than you will if you do not have these answers. Any asker needs to know upfront the assets that can fund the gift because the nature of the assets will largely determine the best gift vehicle. If the prospect wants to give a limited cash gift or a few appreciated securities, she may lean toward a gift annuity, whereas if she is considering real estate or a large amount of appreciated securities, she would lean in favor of a charitable remainder trust. Next, the asker needs to be sensitive to the donor's economic needs now and in the future. The asker needs to further explore the best planned gift vehicle for the donor. The donor may like a steady fixed income or may be attracted to the fluctuating investment. Lastly is the question of timing. When will the gift be made? One cannot assume just because a prospect is discussing a planned gift now the gift will be made soon. Planned giving prospects generally take their time and mull many things over before they commit pen to paper. . . . People asking for planned gifts need to be up to speed on how those personal circumstances can affect the original planned giving opportunity.[11]

The following are illustrations of three different ask conversations. Each conversation is focused on a different type of gift based on prior conversations with the prospect. Each are reprinted with permission from Fredricks' book, *The Ask*.

IN THE REAL WORLD

The Ask for a Bequest Gift

This first example of a planned gift ask is for an academy, a small organization that has one director of development, Ann, who is responsible for all aspects of fundraising, including building a bequest society. The donor, Trisha, 47 years old, has made steady gifts to the annual fund. Ann called Trisha to thank her for her most recent gift, and Trisha told Ann that she wished she "could do something more" but that she "needs to save" so she does not outlive her assets. Ann asked Trisha if she could stop by and chat with her about ways she could increase her support. Trisha agreed and the meeting was arranged. Here is what was said during that meeting:

ANN: Trisha, thank you for taking the time to meet with me today, and thank you for your wonderful and loyal gifts to the annual fund. Without loyal supporters like you we would not be able to give our students the best elementary school education they deserve.

TRISHA: You're welcome, and I'm happy to help. I'm sure that the cost for books, good teachers, and outside activities increases each year.

ANN: Absolutely, and thank you again. Trisha, you mentioned that you wanted some suggestions on how you could increase your support without decreasing your disposable assets.

TRISHA: Yes, I wish I could do it. It's just that you can never know how much you will need in the future for health care, to cover living expenses, and everything that may come up.

Ann: That's perfectly understandable. Your needs come first, and predicting as best you can, with the help of an attorney or financial planner, how much you need in the future should put your mind at ease. There is a way, however, to take care of your needs while you are living and also support the academy in a significant way.

Trisha: How does that work?

Ann: You can leave a set amount or percentage of your estate to the academy in your will.

Trisha: Too late; I've already done my will, and it is so costly to do another. I left some to my church, and the rest to my sister, niece, and nephew.

Ann: That's great that you have included your church in your will. That shows you believe in your church's mission, and your estate will reap tax benefits as well. You can still make this type of gift without creating another will. Simply ask your attorney to draft a codicil that will modify your will. I can provide the language for you to share with your attorney. How does that sound to you?

Trisha: I'll have to think about it, because I'm not very fond of these legal documents.

Ann: I can understand. When and if you are ready, this is just our suggestion of a way for you to do something really meaningful for the students of the academy without depleting your present-day income.

Trisha: Of course. When I return from a business trip, then the holidays with the family, I'll give it more thought.

Ann: Trisha, that would be great, and I'll make a note to call you after the holidays. In the meantime, thank you for all you do for the academy. We know how busy you are, but we would love to have you come back and, if you have the time, spend some time with the students. Give it some thought. In the meantime, we wish you and your family a wonderful holiday season.

Once a donor agrees to make a bequest commitment, it is important that she indicates this in writing. Having a signed bequest confirmation form will allow the organization to document the commitment, ensure that the donor's wishes are followed, and permit the donor to be appropriately recognized as part of the organization's planned giving society. The form will also encourage the donor to follow through on her commitment. (A sample bequest confirmation form is in the Appendix B.) Fredricks writes,

I strongly suggest that you give this form to them in person and have it filled out in your presence and returned to you. Too often these forms are mailed to donors and never returned to the organization. Then the fundraiser has the task of calling the donors to get the forms returned. If at all possible, hand-deliver the form to the donor right after she has stated that your group is in her will, so that you have accurate records in your files on your Bequest society members.[12]

IN THE REAL WORLD

The Ask for a Charitable Gift Annuity

This example is an illustration of how to ask for a CGA. Prospect Josh has just received a Jewish organization's CGA mailing. The organization did a targeted mailing to all its donors who had made an annual gift within the last two years and who were 60 years old and older but who had not made a planned gift to date. Josh fits these categories. His interest was piqued by the possible rate of income he could receive from a CGA, so he called the number on the brochure to find out more information. Planned giving officer Jerry received Josh's call, and Josh agreed to meet with Jerry at Josh's home to learn more about the benefits of a CGA. This is the first time that Josh has met with anyone from the organization.

JERRY: Josh, it's great to meet with you at your home. When we spoke you said that you just recently retired. Tell me, are you more busy now than you ever were?

JOSH: You know I heard that from a lot of people and never believed them until now. You can't believe the number of things I have going on.

JERRY: Well, good for you and congratulations on your retirement from all of us at our organization. We are very proud of you. You mentioned on the telephone that you received our brochure on Charitable Gift Annuities and had some questions. I'm here to help.

JOSH: Well, from the brochure it sounds like I could get a good rate of return, but I don't know how much that would be. A steady income now would surely help.

JERRY: Okay, Josh, I brought my laptop with me to show you exactly how this will work. If you want me to show you now I can; if not, I can send it to you or e-mail it to you in no less than two days from now.

JOSH: No, go right ahead.

JERRY: Okay, let me pull up [my software]. It's a software program that will calculate the exact annuity rate, payments, and tax deductions and exemptions that may apply. Ready. Josh, I'll need your full name and date of birth.

JOSH: Josh Appleton, June 19, 1936.

JERRY: For you, the rate would be 6.3 percent. The organization would pay you in quarterly installments for as long as you live. Part of that payment is tax free, and part is taxed as ordinary income. After you pass away (you know, I just hate to say those words), the organization would use the proceeds for a variety of purposes that we can discuss. I'd be happy to print out this illustration and send it to you so that you can think about it and review it with anyone you desire—family, attorney, financial advisor.

JOSH: No, it will be just my decision. And, I just want to give it to the Jewish organization. They can decide how best to use the money.

JERRY: That's terrific, Josh. Yes, you are absolutely right; the organization has a real need for unrestricted gifts so that we can maintain our programs while improving our outreach to serve our community. Permit me to explain how gift annuities work. Josh, our annuities begin at the $5,000 level and can be funded with cash or appreciated securities. You mentioned on the phone that you were considering something in the $5,000 to $10,000 range. Remember, if you make a $10,000 gift now, that will give you $630 a year, and you can take an immediate tax deduction of $3,578. Those numbers would be smaller with a $5,000 gift. And, the best part is that it is projected that your gift would ultimately give the organization [a substantial amount] which would be a fantastic and meaningful gift for so many of our beneficiaries.

JOSH: Well, I was prepared to write a check for $10,000 if I was convinced this was right for me.

JERRY: And, Josh, right now, how do you feel about this gift opportunity?

JOSH: It all looks good, and I like the amount of money each year, plus I could use the tax deduction this year. What do we do next?

JERRY: I will send you this illustration so that you will see the amount of your quarterly payments, how they are taxed, and the charitable deduction you would be eligible to claim on your taxes. I'll also send a gift annuity contract. You should have it in no less than two days. I'll give you a call then and follow up on any questions you may have.

JOSH: I need to do this before the end of the year, so please assure me this paperwork won't get in the way.

JERRY: You have my word. We have more than a month to process it, but let's say we will meet or speak next Monday, just so we keep this on track.

(continued)

In the previous example, the development professional showed the prospect how much he would be able to take as a tax deduction and how much he would receive each year. He was also reminded that the organization would ultimately receive a substantial benefit that will allow it to provide vital services to the community in the future. If the development professional had sufficient details in advance of the meeting, he would prepare the illustration and leave it with the prospect to review and discuss it with his advisors. Otherwise, once the information is gathered at the meeting, an illustration can be quickly prepared and sent to the prospect with a follow-up date scheduled at the meeting.

IN THE REAL WORLD

The Ask for a Charitable Remainder Uni-Trust

The final example features a couple, Matilda and Clyde Tucker, both 72 years old, who are in the midst of some financial planning with an attorney. The attorney has advised them to consider a charitable trust to lift appreciated assets out of their estate in order to avoid potentially high tax liabilities. The Tuckers have supported an African American organization for the past three years, making consistent gifts of $2,500 each year, so if they were going to do a charitable trust, this organization would be their first choice. Bill, a major gifts and planned giving officer for the organization, has met with the Tuckers on several occasions, the last being a trip to their Florida home. Each time, Bill introduced the idea of a major or planned gift, but the Tuckers were not ready to increase their gift level and were always going to do some financial planning but "things got in the way." After the Tuckers's meeting with the attorney, Clyde called Bill to set up an appointment to learn more about charitable trusts. They agreed to meet at Bill's office.

CLYDE: Hi, Bill, you remember meeting my wife, Matilda, late last year.

BILL: I sure do. Welcome back. Why don't we walk around the corner? I reserved us a conference room. I ordered coffee, water, and soda, but would either of you like something to eat?

MATILDA: Oh no, thank you, we just ate. What a great view of the river you have.

BILL: Thanks. Yes, our offices do have good views. So, how long will you be in town?

MATILDA: Oh, just two more days. We are going to visit with some friends, then we are flying back to Florida.

BILL: It's great that you are taking advantage of the city. Clyde, you said on the telephone that you and Matilda were considering a charitable trust.

CLYDE: That's right. We met a few months ago with our attorney to review our wills and our estate since I am worried that we may be hit with big taxes under the new tax laws. I still don't understand the estate tax that may go away in 2010 and then may come back, but either way our attorney knows we are charitably inclined and suggested we explore a charitable trust to protect our assets.

BILL: Well, we are honored that you both are thinking of our African American organization. Tell me, what size trust are you considering, and what assets will you use to fund this trust?

CLYDE: Well, we're not sure. We have an ocean-side property in Virginia that we bought back in 1954 for what was then a large amount. We decided that we no longer want to make the trips from up North to Virginia, and then we moved a few years ago to Florida. We put feelers out to several realtors, and they tell us we can get about $1.2 million, can you imagine!

BILL: Haven't real estate prices just gone over the top? Clyde and Matilda, I'm assuming that just the two of you own it and that no one else, family member or other relative, is expecting that this will be given to them at some time?

MATILDA: Oh, no. As you know, we don't have any children, and our family members, just my mother and Clyde's brother are well taken care of in our wills.

BILL: Okay, then, the timing could not be any better for you to consider making this gift of a highly appreciated and what sounds like a jewel of an oceanfront home work for you. I would suggest that you use this property to fund a charitable trust, and this is how it works. You transfer the property to the trust and designate both of you as beneficiaries of the trust. You will receive a fluctuating income for as long as either one of you is living. You will be able to deduct a portion of the value of your gift against income taxes and, since you are using an appreciated asset, you will escape a high amount of taxable capital gains. Let me stop here and ask you how you feel about making this type of gift.

CLYDE: Well, it sounds all right, but can we see how this works?

BILL: Absolutely, now that I know the approximate size of the trust and the assets that you would be using to fund the trust, I can draw up an illustration. The illustration will show you the exact amount of tax deduction you can take, the income you will receive for the first year, the amount of capital gains you will avoid, and the amount that is projected to come to the organization at the very end.

CLYDE: Let's see the paperwork for the fluctuating trust.

BILL: I'd be pleased. Why don't we step back into my office, and I can do this right away. Then, you can think it over, discuss it with your attorney, and I'll call in a week or so to answer additional questions.

In this example, the development professional could not prepare an illustration beforehand because he did not know the amount of the trust or the type of assets—cash or appreciated stock or real estate—that would be used to fund the trust. Once the development professional gathers the necessary information, he must expeditiously prepare an appropriate illustration and get it to the prospect.

In each of the three gift scenarios, the development professional answered the three key questions: (1) What assets will fund the gift? (2) What gift vehicle will be used? (3) When will the gift be made? The questions and answers were woven throughout each conversation in an organic way. Each conversation ended with the setting of a definitive date and time when the development professional would follow up with the prospect, ensuring that there will not be a gaping hole of time between this meeting and closing the gift.

With face-to-face visits involving an ask conversation, development professionals should remember the following:

- Keep meetings friendly but professional.
- Use the first meeting to cultivate and build trust, seldom asking for a gift at that time.
- Learn, in the normal course of conversation: (1) What assets will fund the gift? (2) What gift vehicle will be used? (3) When will the gift be made?
- Reinforce for the donor how the gift will affect the organization.
- Stay focused on the donor's philanthropic intent rather than any economic benefits.
- Recognize that prospects will make gifts when the time is right for them.
- Follow up all communications to advance the conversation to the next step.
- Keep promises.

Donors Make Marketing Recommendations

Sargeant and Jay asked supporters of nonprofit organizations to share their comments about planned gift marketing. Their results follow.[13] "The following comments are examples of the feedback we received when we asked respondents to suggest ways in which the promotion of legacy giving could be improved:"

- "Make it clearer that smaller amounts are useful, too."
- "Be specific as to the goals of the bequest. What gains are expected? How will the community gain?"

- "I think the nonprofit community can together inform people about bequest giving in general—and then solicit commitments from their own donors. I don't want an attorney or financial advisor suggesting which nonprofit I should bequest to."

- "It must be continuous—done in all the ways you have listed."

- "By publishing actual cases of how they have helped."

- "When you check that you have already made a bequest—don't keep sending promotions for it."

- "Explain what the organization does with its gifts."

- "Storytelling—reflecting future work, past work, spiritual legacy of work well done."

- "I think about changing my plans whenever I get appeals every month. Just too much is sent to those who already give support."

- "Make a named person available—it is hard to know who you should contact about a bequest."

Summary

Passive marketing will generate some over-the-transom gifts from time to time. However, to generate a strong flow of meaningful planned gifts will require development professionals to actually ask for such gifts. The most powerful method for approaching a prospect is a face-to-face visit. While development professionals should strive to meet with as many priority prospects as possible, most nonprofit organizations will not have sufficient staff to meet with all viable prospects. So, while face-to-face visits will be reserved for the very best prospects, second-tier prospects can be asked for gifts through direct mail or coordinated direct mail/telephone campaigns with personalized staff follow-up. Ignoring second-tier prospects should not be an option.

Regardless of the approach method utilized, the fundamentals of good communication are the same. Development professionals must focus on the interests and needs of the prospective donor. Their philanthropic desires are of paramount importance. All communications should be donor-centered and strive to be helpful to the prospect, answering questions and providing valuable information. As leads are generated and gifts are closed, timely follow-up will be essential. Organizations must factor this into the work plan before any major marketing effort is launched.

Nonprofit organizations that want more planned gifts to help secure their futures need to ask. If an organization does not ask, it will receive few if any planned gifts. If an organization asks for planned gifts, it might not always get them, but they will certainly get far more than they will by not asking at all. The best prospect identification, education, and cultivation efforts may yield virtually nothing unless followed by an ask.

Exercises

- It is important to be able to explain to prospects the various gift planning options and how each works without using jargon or confusing the prospect. Can you explain what the major gift planning options are in two or three sentences?

- It is important for prospects to understand the benefits to them of making a planned gift. Can you explain the major benefits of various planned giving options in just two or three sentences?

- After completing the first two exercises, try sharing your answers with your spouse, parents, or in-laws. Did they understand what you were describing?

- When writing to or speaking with prospective donors, it is important to relate the latest news from the organization, particularly things that have been made possible due to the support of other donors. List three things that your organization has accomplished within the past six months that it might not have been able to accomplish without donor support.

- Very often, it is useful to bring someone else from the organization to a meeting with a planned giving prospect. This individual might be a fellow development professional or volunteer member of the planned giving advisory council with particular expertise in handling a complex gift arrangement, someone from the service side of the organization who can better describe how a gift will be put to use, or a senior staff member who can express their appreciation to the donor. Make a list of the various people within your organization who can be part of your planned giving team.

- When communicating with prospective planned gift donors, it will be necessary to answer their questions and provide them with the information needed to make informed decisions. Anticipate what the common questions or objections might be and list them. Then, write down and memorize responses to these common questions. If you no longer need to worry about what you will say in response to these common issues, you will be able to focus more attention on the issues that are particularly distinct to the individual prospect.

CHAPTER 7

Stewardship

Thankfulness is the beginning of gratitude. Gratitude is the completion of thankfulness. Thankfulness may consist merely of words. Gratitude is shown in acts.

—Henri Frederic Amiel

After reading this chapter, you will be able to:

- Understand the importance of sound stewardship as part of the marketing cycle.
- Recognize the difference between external and internal stewardship.
- Identify the key elements of an effective, high-impact thank-you letter.
- Appreciate the value of creating and maintaining a legacy recognition society.
- Recognize the critical steps in securing a realized bequest.

When done correctly, marketing a gift planning program involves many steps. Prospective donors must be identified, their motivations must be understood, they must be educated about planned giving, they must be cultivated, and they must be asked to make a commitment. When a donor does make a commitment, it is certainly an important time for her. It is also an important time for the nonprofit organization that will be able to sustain its services or even initiate new programs due to the generosity of the donor. While the development

FIGURE 7.1

The Circular Planned Giving Process

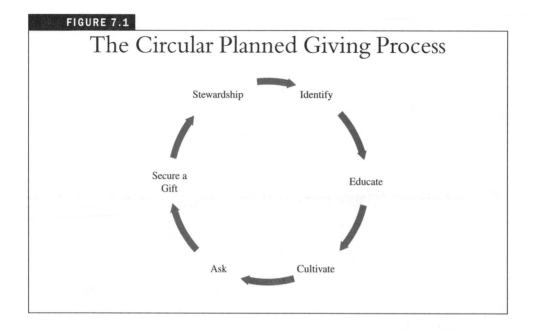

professional may feel like he has crossed the finish line, the reality is that the gift planning process continues. Obviously, it continues with other prospects. But, it also continues for the donor who has just completed a planned gift or planned gift pledge. When someone makes a planned gift commitment, it is not the end of the process. Instead, it is the beginning of the next phase of the process: stewardship.

Stewardship Closes the Circle

Stewardship is defined by the *AFP Fundraising Dictionary* as "a process whereby an organization seeks to be worthy of continued philanthropic support, including the acknowledgment of gifts, donor recognition, the honoring of donor intent, prudent investment of gifts, and the effective and efficient use of funds to further the mission of the organization."[1]

Stewardship will help the donor feel good about her commitment. It will ensure that revocable gifts (i.e., bequests) remain in force and, perhaps, increase in value over time. Good stewardship can also lead to another planned gift from the donor. For example, a donor who makes a bequest commitment may be impressed by the organization and a sufficient level of trust might have been developed through the process to allow the donor to feel comfortable making a donation to establish a charitable gift annuity (CGA). A donor who establishes a CGA may feel so comfortable having done so, he may decide to establish a second. Or, a CGA donor may make a bequest commitment; "some organizations show that 75 percent of the people who take out gift annuity contracts eventually make a bequest."[2]

IN THE REAL WORLD

Good Stewardship
Enhances Relationships

For the third time in my career, I am looking through the files of an organization's "planned gifts." Filled with copies of acknowledgment letters, these files lack the most important documents I hope to find. Where is the proof of a relationship? Where is the copy of the gift document or some type of confirmation that a gift even exists? Are these donors still alive? Do they feel that anyone appreciates their generosity?

Once again, I initiate the process of creating a donor-centered planned giving program. The first step is to make a list of every potential planned gift on file. Then, are the donors still alive? Can we track down updated address and telephone information? Is there a bank or trust company that might provide additional information?

Some donors have passed away. For the living donors, we mail a letter of introduction announcing a new and professional planned giving program. Included with the letter is a confirmation form that asks donors to reconfirm their commitment. The letter acknowledges the fact that many gifts change, and that we plan to change our effort to know our donors better and to involve them in our organization at whatever level they desire.

The results are what make my work so wonderful. A few respond that they changed their gift years ago when no one seemed to care. Most have simply been waiting for someone to ask. Now, my work is simple. I visit with each of these generous individuals making sure they know how important they are to our organization. Listening to their stories and turning those stories into wonderful documentation of a life well-lived ensures they will know their generosity is profound. These stories also serve as strong messages to others regarding the benefits of creating the "ultimate gift!"

—Susan Blair Brandt, Director of Planned Giving, Jupiter Medical Center Foundation

Good stewardship has two components. External stewardship involves thanking the donor, ensuring he is properly recognized, and reporting to the donor or his designees how the gift is utilized. Internal stewardship involves the efficient processing of donor gifts. It also involves, when appropriate, effectively investing those dollars and ensuring that the gift is used according to the donor's wishes.

IN THE REAL WORLD

Remembering to Put the Donor First

Using a donor-centered marketing approach will remind us to practice effective stewardship. Practicing effective stewardship will remind one to be donor-centered.

At the L.L. Bean Company, the successful mail order retailer, the customer is the center of their universe. One way the company has maintained its customer-first culture is that it has developed a list of statements about customers that are shared with each employee as a reminder. In the nonprofit world, it is a good idea to remind ourselves and our colleagues, from time to time, of the importance of the donor. Here is an adaption of the L.L. Bean list for the nonprofit sector:[3]

- The donor is the most important person ever in this office, in person, by mail, or on the telephone.

- The donor is not dependent on us; we are dependent on the donor.

- A donor is not an interruption of our work; she is the purpose of it. We are not doing a favor by serving her; she is doing us a favor by giving us the opportunity to do so.

- A donor is not someone to argue or match wits with. Nobody ever won an argument with a donor.

- A donor is a person who brings us his wants. It is our job to handle them in a way that is beneficial to him and our organization.

Thank Donors Quickly and Frequently

At every point of contact, planned giving prospects should be thanked. If a prospect is an annual fund donor, she should be thanked for that in the planned giving appeal before an ask is made. If one meets with a prospect, the prospect should receive a letter or note, preferably handwritten, thanking her for her time. Development professionals should actively search for reasons to thank prospects and donors. And, the ways in which appreciation is expressed should be diverse.

There are two powerful reasons to thank donors. First, it is quite simply the right thing to do. Second, not that another reason is needed, it can lead to additional giving.

A study of a large nonprofit organization's bequest donors found that donors who were asked and thanked gave twice as much as those who were not thanked. Those who were cultivated (notes, letters, visits, etc.) after the thank-you gave three to four times as much.[4]

Janet L. Hedrick, Senior Associate at Bentz Whaley Flessner and author of *Effective Donor Relations*, asserts that donors should be thanked seven times for each gift.[5] This does not mean one has to send seven thank-you letters. One should be much more creative than that. However, it does mean that one should look for multiple ways to express appreciation once a donor makes a gift. For example, here is a list of seven ways an organization can show its appreciation:

- The donor gets a written thank-you letter from the development professional within two business days of a gift or gift commitment being received.
- The organization's CEO or Board Chair sends a thank-you letter.
- A board member calls the donor within a week of receipt of the gift to express appreciation.
- The organization thanks planned gift donors by name, unless the gift was anonymous, in its newsletter.

- The organization thanks planned gift donors by name, unless the gift was anonymous, it its annual report.

- The donor gets thanked with an invitation to a donor recognition event.

- The donor gets thanked at other types of events throughout the year.

The formal thank-you letter from the organization should be sent within 48 hours of receipt of the gift or gift commitment, according to Hedrick. This will underscore that the organization both appreciates and needs the gift. A well-written thank-you letter will seldom begin with the words "thank you." Instead, the charity should exercise a bit of creativity and truly personalize the letter rather than just sending a form response. Penelope Burk, President of Cygnus Applies Research and Burk & Associates, is the author of *Donor-Centered Fundraising*. After completing a study of thank-you letters from nearly 200 charities, she outlined 20 attributes of a great thank-you letter:[6]

1. The letter is a real letter, not a preprinted card.

2. It is personally addressed.

3. It has a personal salutation (no "dear donor" or "dear friend").

4. It is personally signed.

5. It is personally signed by someone from the highest ranks of the organization.

6. It makes specific reference to the intended use of the funds.

7. It indicates approximately when the donor will receive an update on the program being funded.

8. It includes the name and phone number of a staff person whom the donor can contact at any time or an invitation to contact the letter writer directly.

9. It does not ask for another gift.

10. It does not ask the donor to do anything (like complete an enclosed survey, for example).

11. It acknowledges the donor's past giving, where applicable.

12. It contains no spelling or grammatical errors.

13. It has an overall "can do," positive tone as opposed to a handwringing one.

14. It communicates the excitement, gratitude, and inner warmth of the writer.

15. It grabs the reader's attention in the opening sentence.

16. It speaks directly to the donor.

17. It does not continue to "sell."

18. It is concise—no more than two short paragraphs.

19. It is received by the donor promptly.

20. Plus, in some circumstances, the letter is handwritten.

Burk also found that donors of every type, not necessarily planned gift donors, appreciate a personal touch from the organizations they support. She found that

> Ninety-five percent of all study donors said that they would be very appreciative if a member of the board of directors called them just to say thank you within a day or two of receiving their gifts. Eighty-five percent of individual donors . . . said that this would influence them to give again to the charities that made this gesture. Eighty-four percent of individual donors . . . would definitely or probably give a larger gift the next time under these circumstances.[7]

Given that most planned gifts are revocable and given that most planned gift donors are also annual fund contributors or members, it is essential to properly thank them. Appreciation should be expressed quickly, passionately, and personally.

KEY CONCEPT

When thanking donors, keep the focus on them by using the word *you* more often than the words *I* or *we*.

Recognize Planned Gift Donors

The *NCPG Survey of Donors* found that only 25 percent of planned gift donors who had informed a nonprofit organization of their bequest intention experienced being treated any differently as a result.[8] However, a majority of charity supporters believe that it is appropriate for an organization to provide recognition to donors who make a legacy pledge, according to research conducted by Adrian Sargeant and Elaine Jay.[9] Therefore, organizations that do provide such donors with special recognition will have a clear advantage over organizations that do not.

This does not mean that all planned giving donors will want a T-shirt that says, "I'm dying to give!" What it does mean is that the organization needs to develop a solid planned gift recognition program. For particularly special gifts, it might even involve actually asking the donor how he would like to be recognized.

Every organization should recognize planned gift pledgers and donors as members of a distinct legacy recognition group. Rachel Sisemore Crawford and Fred Hartwick wrote in the *Journal of Gift Planning* about the four benefits that a planned giving recognition society provides:[10]

- They are a forum for the organization to express appreciation to its planned gift donors.

- They serve as an incentive for nonmembers of the society to make similar gifts.

- They act as a regular reminder to donors of the importance of their future gifts (in the case of deferred gifts), which is particularly important since revocable pledges can be changed at any time before the donor dies.

- They can bring society members closer to the organization and may provide the opportunity to ask for current gifts or additional planned gifts.

When considering the membership composition of the legacy society, one should include those who have expressed a bequest intention. Most organizations will require the donor to provide some type of documentation of the commitment such as a completed will confirmation form. Although a donor may complete and sign such a form, the commitment remains revocable unless there is also a binding pledge agreement. Nevertheless, since only a tiny fraction of those who include a charity in their will ever remove the charity, it is important to recognize these individuals while they are still alive. Another group of donors to include are those who have made irrevocable life-income gifts such as CGAs. Rather than seeking to exclude people from the legacy society, organizations should strive to have such groups be as inclusive as possible while maintaining appropriate membership criteria.

IN THE REAL WORLD

Establish Criteria for Legacy Society Membership

It is important to define who is eligible for membership in an organization's legacy society. Each organization will develop its own particular policies that are consistent with the charity's culture and objectives. Adapted from a presentation at the 2006 National Conference on Planned Giving, the following are some actions that could qualify a donor for membership in a legacy society:

I. Donors commit to naming the organization in their estate plan through various planned gifts such as:

1. Charitable Gift Annuity (CGA).

2. Life estate.

3. Charitable remainder trust (CRT).

4. Charitable lead trust (CLT).

5. Beneficiary designations (i.e., retirement plan or life insurance).

6. Other options. For example, some organizations may choose to include as members of the legacy society those who establish an endowment fund with a minimum contribution amount for the benefit of the organization. The principal remains intact and is invested. It may be set up as a restricted endowment fund, which benefits a

(continued)

IN THE REAL WORLD (CONTINUED)

particular cause of the organization. An unrestricted endowment fund, on the other hand, can be established if the donor has no preference on where the funds are to be used.

II. Donors state that they have included the organization in their estate plan. It is important to establish a policy that membership is extended to individuals who disclose the commitment of a planned gift arrangement through written notification. It is not recommended that donors be asked to reveal the amount of a bequest commitment in order to become a member. Rather, first and foremost, the emphasis should simply be on just getting them to tell the organization that they have made a planned gift commitment.

—Elisa M. Smith, Vice President and Director of Financial Planning, STAR Wealth Management; from "Making Bequest Societies the 'Wow' of Your Planned Giving Program." National Conference on Planned Giving, October 2006, 8–9.

The legacy society should have its own brand identity while being consistent with the organization's overall brand. For example, the legacy society logo might incorporate the organization's logo. Before moving forward with a legacy society, it is a good idea to get organizational acceptance, perhaps even seeking board approval. Once approval has been granted and a brand identity has been created, prospects can be "invited" to be part of the legacy society.

Some donors may wish to remain anonymous, and those wishes should be respected. For example, "be cautious about offering opportunities for recognition. In some [Native American] cultures, this is an insult, saying to the donor that they give for glory rather than simply 'sharing the path.'"[11] Other cultures also frown upon recognition. Development professionals need to be sensitive to this. Donors should be asked how and even if they want to be recognized. While recognition is important to some, it is not valued by all. However, in lists of legacy society members, the organization should list "anonymous" to represent each such donor so that people know how many members of the legacy society there are including those who do not want their names used.

Crawford and Hartwick believe that legacy society members should receive certain benefits, tokens of appreciation that include:

- *A membership gift.* This should be a small item. It can be a coffee mug, lapel pin, pen, or other item imprinted with the legacy society logo.

- *An annual event.* This annual recognition event should be open only to members, and their guests, and should thank them. In addition, it should offer something of value. For example, if it is a luncheon event, it might also include a speaker who can speak about one of the organization's projects, or the speaker might be a service recipient talking about how she benefited from the organization.

- *Special newsletters and communications.* Periodically, the organization should share special information with legacy society members. This might involve a special newsletter or simply periodic letters. The information might be about new programs or services offered by the organization, recent news coverage about the organization, or changes in tax laws that might impact donors. The key is to offer timely information that donors will appreciate receiving.

- *Birthday and holiday cards.* Sending cards reminds donors that they are important to the organization. The development professional should add a short, handwritten note to the card to give it a personal touch. One should consider sending a card at Thanksgiving, a time when most people are not receiving greeting cards and a time uniquely appropriate for expressing appreciation to a donor. When sending holiday cards, be certain that the recipient observes the given holiday. Only send birthday cards if the recipient has elected to provide the date of birth information, not if you gleaned it from other sources.[12]

Some organizations recognize legacy society members in additional ways. For example, some charities will post a list of legacy society members on a special donor wall in the office lobby. Other organizations will provide legacy society members with a certificate of membership. Some

Executive Insight

Hosting an annual luncheon for planned gift contributors has multiple benefits for each participant. First, they are reengaged after the gift has been made. Second, they can share this special time with one or two family members and/or their financial advisor who they are encouraged to bring as their guests. Third, they can enhance their legacy by serving as a testimonial for gift planning by sharing their story, which can also be used for a newsletter, magazine, or annual report. Fourth, led by a volunteer member of the planned gifts committee, the luncheon program should feature the CEO and professional staff members' reports on current activities and future plans. It's a hit every year!

—James M. Greenfield, President, J.M. Greenfield & Associates

organizations will invite legacy society members to an annual meet-and-greet reception with the organization's board of directors. Some organizations will provide a special behind-the-scenes tour for legacy society members. The recognition options are limited only by the development professional's creativity and the organization's culture.

One powerful way to recognize planned gift donors is to invite them to share their story with others by posting it on the organization's web site. When a donor shares his story, including what inspired him to make the gift, and it is made public, the donor has established a tangible legacy that will inspire others.

When a member of the legacy society passes away, this individual should be publicly recognized, assuming they did not request to remain anonymous. It should be noted that some anonymous donors are willing to have the veil lifted upon their death; again, this is something to be discussed with donors. And, according to the donor's wishes, his spouse or children should be invited to continue to attend legacy society events and receive reports.

Reporting to Donors

Mostly what donors want from the organizations they support is regular information about how gifts are utilized. Even deferred gift donors want to know how effectively the organization is fulfilling its mission. For current planned gift donors, development professionals should discuss with the donor the organization's normal reporting procedures and determine if that will meet the individual donor's needs. If not, the development professional should determine what type of information the donor would like and how often.

The organization does not have to prepare elaborate and lengthy reports. A simple, one- or two-page letter will usually suffice. Renata J. Rafferty, in her book *Don't Just Give It Away*, advises philanthropists not to ask for detailed reports, "Let [the organization] know that you are not looking for a report. A report is a document of length and detail that is usually designed to obscure both the excitement and problems that are being encountered. You truly want the charity to view you as a partner in its work, and partnerships are successful only when all parties can be candid with one another."[13]

An organization's CEO can send an annual letter to donors to express appreciation for their support. The letter can provide service highlights from the preceding year; this might involve a story about someone served by the organization. The letter can also review how the legacy society has grown. If planned gifts are used to build the organization's endowment, the letter should discuss the investment performance of the endowment. The primary objectives of the report letter are to express appreciation, show donors how effectively the organization is fulfilling its mission, and review how fiscally responsible the organization is.

For deferred planned gift donors (i.e., bequest), the gifts may not be realized until the donors die. In these cases, it is still a good idea to update donors. This will give them a sense of satisfaction while reminding them that they are important and that the organization continues to need them. Development professionals should talk with deferred gift donors, particularly bequest donors, about who else they might like to have updates go to. For example, some organizations

Executive Insight

As a service each year to our trust income beneficiaries, we send out an annual letter at the beginning of the year to inform them of the value of the trust and, if possible, what the anticipated trust payments might be for the coming year. It also contrasts the trust value and payments by percentage over the previous year. Our letter is fairly concise and is more or less an opportunity to simply take the proactive measure of communicating with folks and thanking them for their support.

—David C. Troutman, Senior Major & Planned Gifts Officer, Wabash College

include the children of donors in recognition event invitations and reporting. Assuming it is the donor's wish to do this, such actions can reduce the likelihood of a will being contested and it can even inspire the children to make a gift of their own.

For many planned giving donors, it is important to involve their families. For many, part of the reason that they are making the extraordinary philanthropic gesture is to influence their children, either in how they remember their parents or to instill philanthropic values in them. This is a matter that should be explored with each donor; the organization should certainly not make any assumptions one way or the other.

Internal Stewardship

To earn and maintain the trust of donors, organizations must efficiently fulfill their missions. They must also safeguard donor privacy, ensure that the donor gifts are properly collected, process gifts efficiently, and use gifts for the purpose expressed by the donor. While the development professional may not be directly responsible for performing each of these activities, she is responsible for making sure that those who are actually follow through.

Part of internal stewardship involves making sure that gifts are actually received when the donor dies. The development professional is the donor's

IN THE REAL WORLD

Bait and Switch = Fraud

Many years ago, a mid-Atlantic museum launched a special project fundraising campaign. The executive director had plans for a new exhibition, and instructed the development staff to raise the funds for it. While not a full-blown capital campaign, it was nevertheless a major undertaking that involved current cash and planned gifts. As the campaign neared a successful conclusion, the executive director announced to the staff that she was indefinitely postponing the plans for the new exhibition. Instead, she wanted to use the newly acquired financial resources for another, completely unrelated project. The chief development officer protested, telling her that since the funds were explicitly raised for another purpose, donors would have to be contacted. During those contacts, each donor would have to be given the option of getting her money back or canceling her pledges, or allowing her gift to be used for the latest project. The executive director forbid the staff to approach donors in this manner for fear that some might actually ask for their money back or cancel pledges since the new project might be perceived as less attractive.

Recognizing that raising money for one purpose and then spending it on something completely different is unethical, the chief development officer took the matter to the board. When the board backed the executive director, the entire development and membership staff resigned in protest.

While an extreme case, this true story underscores the importance of being truthful with donors. It also underscores the fact that development professionals are responsible for making sure the wishes of donors are honored. In this case, the development staff did everything they could and, when they could do no more, they resigned rather than being a party to a bait-and-switch maneuver.

It is essential that organizations maintain the highest ethical standards to safeguard the public trust. It is the responsibility of development professionals to be the champions of ethical practice within their organizations. Nonprofit organizations can only raise money as long as they enjoy the trust and goodwill of the public.

advocate when it comes to the contribution. The nonprofit needs to make sure the donor's wishes are honored and that the bequest gift comes to the organization as the donor intended. Susan DameGreene, President of Bipster International, outlines the steps that organizations should take to secure their interests and honor the donor's wishes:[14]

- Write to the executor and/or the attorney. Throughout the process, you'll be amazed how much more efficiently the work will be done when you let the executor and/or attorney know you are watching. In your first communication: express condolences to the attorney and ask who else should receive condolences, request a copy of the will or document in which your nonprofit is named, send proof of 501(c)(3) status, ask the total amount of the bequest, ask about the timing of distributions and the amount of each distribution.

- When you get a copy of the document (will, trust, etc.), read it carefully to see where your nonprofit is named. It may be in several places. Is the name of your nonprofit correct? Can you accept what is being offered? Will it benefit your nonprofit more than your costs involved in accepting/administering? How can you gracefully turn it down?

- Set up the bequest in your bequest tickler file for handling. If you have a specific bequest and the amount is small, give your nonprofit's name and address to the executor, along with any reasonable information requested. If you have a specific and large amount, follow the previous step and also ask for an early distribution, if possible. If you have a percent of the estate or the residue, follow the previous two steps. Then, ask for a copy of the inventory (nine months from the date of the donor's death) and the final accounting (18 to 24 months later). Read the inventory and keep abreast of the estate expenses as the estate is being settled.

- Collect the assets due and determine how to handle.

- Close the bequest, but keep any remaining information. I would not recommend signing a receipt until you get your bequest. You can have an interested person or company hold the funds as agent if the executor objects.

From time to time, it may be necessary to engage your organization's legal counsel. In some states, the attorney general will intervene on behalf of a nonprofit organization. For example, an executor is entitled to collect a fee until the estate is settled. In some cases, the executor may not wish to expedite settlement since it would mean an end to administrative fees. In other cases, the executor might be guilty of insider dealing. For example, the executor might try to sell property at below market rates to a confederate. If a nonprofit organization has any suspicions about how a donor's estate is being handled, it should engage legal counsel. More often than not, when a wayward executor sees this action, he will correct his behavior.

IN THE REAL WORLD

Defend the Donor When They Are No Longer Able

After a bequest donor dies, they are no longer in a position to defend their interests. In most cases, family and the estate's executor will ensure that the donor's wishes are honored in all respects. However, for a variety of reasons, there will be times when this is not the case. Strong legal advice can help the organization deal with the situation to ensure that the donor's wishes are indeed honored.

A scholarship foundation in the Northeast learned of the passing of an elderly woman in the community. A member of the all-volunteer organization's board knew the woman and knew the foundation was in her will. The woman's attorney produced a copy of the will which included a nearly $1 million bequest for the foundation and nearly nothing for her two estranged children. The children produced another version of the will where the charitable provision was whited-out, literally. The attorney for the children approached the foundation to negotiate a settlement agreement. The foundation, under the advice of legal counsel, held firm and asked that the matter proceed to court as soon as possible. The attorney for the children initiated a series of delaying tactics hoping that the foundation would eventually negotiate rather than have

(continued)

IN THE REAL WORLD (CONTINUED)

the matter drag out. Under the advice of legal counsel, the foundation held firm. About one year later, surprisingly quickly given the circumstances, the court upheld the clean version of the will and the foundation received the full bequest.

When a donor passes away, his donative interests are generally in complete alignment with the charity's. It is up to the charity to ensure that the donor's interests are honored and, in the process, the organization will benefit.

Good internal stewardship will also ensure that good records are maintained. For example, one way to ensure that a donor's intent is honored is to know what that intent is. Carefully filing all correspondence, recording notes following each contact, and documenting gifts will be extremely helpful when the donor passes. Sophisticated fundraising software can assist with this but, even if the organization uses a card file and index cards, it is essential to keep good records. To ensure that good notes are routinely entered into the donor's record, one should record all information while it is still fresh. For example, after meeting with a donor, drive to the nearest coffee shop, get a cup of your favorite beverage, and start writing before you forget any important details. That way, one will be assured of having good, complete information.

IN THE REAL WORLD

Executive Insight

Make sure everyone in the development department is inputting data on all of your donors (e.g., their birthday, interests, family or close friends). Collecting important details will help you and the donor make a connection to your mission. Such details could also prove important after the donor passes, as well.

—Elizabeth Tice Eiesland Endowment and Planned Giving Director, Youth & Family Services Foundation

Summary

Once a planned gift is secured, good stewardship will close the process, further build the relationship between the organization and the donor, and set the stage for future current and planned giving. Donors recognize that their planned gifts are something truly special to them and to the nonprofit organizations they support. They expect development professionals to recognize this as well. One way to convey to donors that they are indeed greatly appreciated is to send them a thank-you letter promptly. In addition, to be effective, that letter will need to be personal and passionate. Development professionals will want to show their appreciation a minimum of seven times for each gift. Donors should also be publicly recognized in ways meaningful to the donors and inspirational to others.

Organizations will want to report to donors on a regular basis as a further act of sound external stewardship. This will build further trust with donors, increase their confidence in the organization, and make donors feel like the special people they are.

With effective, ethically-driven internal stewardship, organizations will ensure that the wishes of donors are honored. Development professionals will advocate for donors when they pass, both in shepherding the gift to the organization and in making sure the organization handles the gift according to donors' specifications.

Closing a gift is not the end of a process. Instead, it simply advances the relationship to a new stage. By exercising sound stewardship, organizations will strengthen the relationship with donors and inspire others to participate as well.

Exercises

- Good thank-you letters touch donors and enhance the relationship between donors and the organization. Review the thank-you letters your organization uses. Do they contain all of the elements discussed in this chapter? Identify any elements that are missing and resolve to write stronger letters in the future.

- Personal notes are an effective way to make someone feel special. Have you sent someone a handwritten thank-you note today? It could be for a donor's gift, a prospect's time, an advisor's advice. If you have not, take a moment and send someone a personal note now.

- Maintaining the privacy of donor records is critically important and ethically required. Does your organization have a privacy policy? If so, take a moment to review it. If not, talk to colleagues about developing one.

- Providing donors with small tokens of appreciation is an excellent way to thank them for their support, assuming they value the gift. Does your organization offer small gifts of appreciation? Do donors appreciate them? Ask a few donors how they feel about the gift.

- Having board members call donors immediately after a gift is received is a meaningful way to thank them. It is also an excellent way to help your board understand the value of planned giving. Recruit and train some board members to call donors to thank them. In addition to thanking donors and hearing them sing the praises of the organization, board members can gather useful information such as finding out what inspired the donors to make such generous gifts.

CHAPTER 8

Getting Started

Luck is a matter of preparation meeting opportunity.

—*Oprah Winfrey*

After reading this chapter, you will be able to:

- Understand the need for gaining board and senior management acceptance of the planned gift marketing plan.
- Secure organizational acceptance through the development of an Internal Case for Donor-Centered Philanthropic Planning.
- Garner cooperation from development colleagues.
- Recognize the common elements of a marketing plan.
- Understand some of the many measures of planned gift marketing performance.
- Launch your new or enhanced donor-centered planned gift marketing program.

The end of this book is your beginning. Your organization may already have a planned gift marketing effort. Or, you may be looking to start one. Either way, it is now time to begin your new or enhanced donor-centered planned gift marketing endeavor.

We have examined what it means to be donor-centered. We have carefully studied the five stages of a donor-centered marketing effort: Prospect Identification, Education, Cultivation, Solicitation, and Stewardship.

Now, you are ready to get started. As you begin, there is much that must be accomplished.

Is Your Organization Ready?

The following is a guide prepared by the Partnership for Philanthropic Planning to help development professionals determine if their organization is ready for serious planned gift marketing and, if so, what level of program is appropriate.

Before you begin, try to look at your organization from the donor's perspective by conducting a mission-effectiveness survey. If the answers to any of the following points are not affirmative, you must address those areas first, before beginning a gift planning program:

How visible is the organization? Does the public know the organization's name? Is the public aware of the organization's activities? Is there evidence the organization is a legitimate charitable organization? Does it have a well-communicated, future-oriented mission statement? A vision statement? A strategic plan which is publicized? Is the volunteer Board of Directors representative of a cross-section of the organization's constituency? Do they have limited terms of office and are they elected or appointed to office? Can you be certain that volunteers, benefactors and employees are receiving appropriate compensation and/or benefits from the organization? Is the organization financially well-managed and able to professionally administer large contributions? Does the organization have a long-term mission? Is the organization perceived as stable, with constituents who are confident that the organization will be around for a while? Does the organization follow government regulations? Does it hold 501(c)(3) nonprofit status and 170 charitable status with the Internal Revenue Service? Does it hold any required state or city licenses to solicit funds? Does it publish and/or make available upon request an annual report or current financial statement? What percentage of contributions is used for fund raising? How does this compare to similar charitable organizations?

When your organization has established a strong foundation for development activities, take a gradual approach to adding gift planning to your other fundraising strategies. This guide suggests three distinct, but interrelated phases in the development of an effective gift planning program:

I. Phase One, the Bequest and Beneficiary Designation Program, is quite basic, but the results can be very rewarding. It requires a thorough understanding and implementation of a practical wills and bequests program for which effective educational efforts and marketing and public relations programs are critical elements. Many times outright gifts of appreciated securities and real estate are also included as part of a phase one program. For many charitable organizations, it may *not* be necessary, prudent, or affordable to progress beyond this stage of the gift planning process.

II. Phase Two, the Life Income Gifts Program. The nonprofit organization which has successfully initiated Phase One may be ready to proceed with a life income gifts program. This phase assumes an advanced understanding of gift planning options and commitment of the resources necessary to move successfully into a fully developed gift planning program. It builds on the successes achieved in the development of a strong Phase One foundation by continuing educational, marketing and public relations efforts.

III. Phase Three, the Charitable Gift and Estate Planning phase, is the most proactive option. This is the level at which organizations engage in professional gift planning and counseling with prospective donors. It involves well-trained third parties, such as attorneys, accountants, financial planners and other members of the planning team in the dialogue with prospective donors. It requires the retention of a level of professional expertise and training which many nonprofits may not have available on a full-time basis. In many cases, the donor will actually engage the services of a professional who will help tailor the gift to ensure that it meets the donor's needs and protects the donor's interests.[1]

If the organization is ready to pursue some type of gift planning program—either a Phase I, II, or III program—then the next step is to ensure that there is organizational support for the planned giving program.

Getting Organizational Acceptance

Before a development professional can launch a donor-centered planned gift marketing effort, there must be broad support within the organization for the gift planning program, in general, and the concept of the donor-centered approach, specifically. This means engaging the organization's board and senior management as well as colleagues. There must be organizational acceptance from the top down, from those who are responsible for approving the budget to those responsible for implementation.

Gaining board approval is essential for three reasons: (1) at most organizations, the board will approve the budget; (2) board members should be expected to make planned gifts; and (3) board members should encourage others to make planned gifts. Laura Hansen Dean, and Pamela J. Davidson, in the *Journal of Gift Planning*, elaborate on these points:

> Boards have a key role in development for their charity, but few seem to know this or embrace it. Many boards mistakenly take the approach that fundraising is a staff function, and they simply want to know how it all turns out. This approach will be ineffectual in a comprehensive effort to increase planned gift awareness because it will omit key individuals: the charity's board.
>
> Board members are the charity's leadership, its best prospects and key volunteers who can carry its message, and should always be considered and approached in those multiple roles. The board has many critical roles in a proactive gift planning program, but often is not expressly told that its roles include fundraising. Fundraising responsibilities should be part of a board member's job description to be shared with a prospective member before he or she accepts the board position. Board members must also be told that they must make planned gifts to the charity, with appropriate size and method for each, for if insiders don't give, why should outsiders ever consider it? This message should be shared with incoming and returning board members, even if it means a change in the organization's paradigm of its board's leadership and other roles.[2]

Dean and Davidson also compiled a list of questions one should ask about the board to gauge its fundraising readiness and to identify areas that need attention. They write,

> [A]s you evaluate your board leadership and involvement, consider the following:
>
> • Do your board members know that they should be planned gift donors? Are they willing to let you use their gift stories as testimonials? Do they understand their participatory and ongoing role in the success of the gift planning program? Do they know any planned gift techniques other than bequests?

- Is your board leadership willing to commit staff, time and budget to a proactive gift planning effort? Does the board realize that such an effort will take time and cannot be an added responsibility to an already overloaded staff member? Do they realize that once they start to promote gift planning that they must continue to do so, on a continuous and sustained basis?

- Are any of your board members willing to act as volunteers, cultivators and perhaps even solicitors of planned gifts? Are they willing to undergo some technical training so they can be effective listeners and learn how to leave ideas and suggestions with potential donors? Are they influential? Can they talk about the charity with passion and conviction? Do they know its success stories and that gifts matter? How does your board provide technical assistance in promoting and administering planned gifts? Are members willing to devote budget to such services, or do they know of opportunities to collaborate with other charities, such as a community foundation?

- Does your board understand restricted gifts and endowments? Is it willing to honor donor restrictions in perpetuity for certain types of gifts? Is it willing to create the structure administratively to support these obligations?[3]

By answering the questions posed by Dean and Davidson, development professionals will understand what issues must be addressed in order to ensure full buy-in from the organization's board.

Case for Support

Most development professionals are familiar with what an organizational Case for Support is. It is a comprehensive document that enshrines the organization's mission statement. The Case outlines the organization's goals and objectives and describes the reasons why prospective donors might want to contribute. The Case broadly describes the organization's various programs and explains the role of philanthropy in being able to provide those programs and achieve the indicated goals and objectives. The Case for Support should describe:

- Organization's needs.

- Strategies, tasks, and plans.

- Staff.

- The cause.

- Budget.

- Governance.

- Goals.

- Financial history.

- Facilities.

- Mission.

- Objectives.

From the one sweeping Case document, multiple Case Statements can be developed for specific constituencies or campaigns. For example, an organization might develop different Case Statements for its annual fund, capital, and planned giving campaigns. Case Statements might be tailored for different audiences such as individuals, corporations, and foundations. Case Statements should include the following elements:

- The institution's services, programs, and objectives.

- How the goals of the fundraising program support the institution.

- Ways in which the institution will remain significantly productive in the next decade.

- The difference it would make if a donor supported the cause.

- What the institution must do to improve or change its activities and aims, and why the institution is valuable to society.[4]

IN THE REAL WORLD

Executive Insight

The Case is a centralization or documentation of all information describing the organization's cause and why it deserves philanthropic support. The Case Statement is a shorter, campaign-specific or constituency-specific document.

—*CFRE Review Course* (AFP 2004)

The Case for Support and the individual Case Statements are primarily designed for external consumption. They are typically organization focused. While these can be useful documents, Brian M. Sagrestano and Robert E. Wahlers suggest the development of an additional type of Case document. The Internal Case for Donor-Centered Philanthropic Planning (see Appendix C for a sample document) is a document designed primarily for, as the name suggests, an internal rather than external audience. The purposes of the Internal Case are to:

- Invoke the highest purpose of the organization's existence—its mission, and demonstrate how the fulfillment of your long-term mission will be strengthened through future and endowment gifts.

- Focus on the needs of your donors—how through future and endowment gifts your donors can be assured that their support will enhance the part of your mission that is most important to them, and that they can establish a meaningful and permanent legacy that meets your needs while also meeting their needs.

- Provide the rationale behind the request for future and endowment gifts.

- Identify a range of long-term resource needs and objectives.

- Serve as the springboard for creating a variety of communication and marketing efforts in support of your future and endowment giving program.[5]

In short, the Internal Case is designed to secure staff and board acceptance of a donor-centered gift planning program. The process of developing the document and the document itself will help educate internal stakeholders about gift planning, the importance of planned giving to the organization, and the value and appropriateness of a donor-centered approach. Once the document is approved, it will enshrine institutional memory in the face of staff and volunteer leadership turnover. Without internal buy-in, it will be difficult, if not impossible, to secure external acceptance.

According to Sagrestano and Wahlers, the Internal Case should include the following ten elements:

- Description of the long-term mission and historic significance of your organization.

- Definitions of future and endowment gifts.

- Stories of donors who have made significant future and endowment gifts in the past that are supporting your organization today, including the impact those gifts have had on those you serve and the long-term outcomes those gifts have created for your organization.

- How future and endowment gifts will help your donors create their own legacies with your organization to ensure its long-term future.

- How future and endowment gifts will fit with your donors' overall plans for the present and future generations of their families, to ensure a meaningful legacy beyond your charity.

- Organization's values and philosophy about long-term resource management, including legacy and endowment policies.

- Information about specific tools that will help donors achieve their long-term objectives for the charity, for themselves, and their families.

- Information about donor recognition and stewardship, to ensure that the charity maintains the legacy for all time.

- The name and position of the person at the charity who will coordinate the effort to encourage future and endowment gifts.

- A clear commitment to donor-centered service and confidentiality.[6]

As with any case document, the Internal Case development and approval process offers a number of benefits. The document can help shift or solidify the organizational culture through consensus with all stakeholders, which ensures that they take ownership of the initiative. For many, a donor-centered philosophy may be new. Gaining acceptance of this orientation is critical. Reminding stakeholders of the long-term impact that planned giving can have for the organization and, when possible, relating stories about such gifts and how they have been used already, will also underscore the importance of planned giving. The process of developing the Internal Case will also give one the opportunity to obtain feedback from stakeholders. This will provide an opportunity to respond to objections and provide additional relevant information. This feedback will also allow the development professional to evaluate the organization's readiness to implement a donor-centered planned gift marketing program. The Internal Case will also outline themes and, perhaps, stories that can be used in the marketing materials that are subsequently developed. Finally, the Internal Case development and approval process provides a terrific opportunity to educate the organization's volunteer leaders about the importance of gift planning. Along the way, some will be inspired to make their own planned gift and serve as volunteers in the gift planning effort.

IN THE REAL WORLD

The Case Development Process Offers Many Benefits

Imagine writing a foundation proposal requesting "lots of money for a big building to support our good work." The most sympathetic foundation executive wouldn't tolerate such a vague and lazy request for a minute.

Yet, most planned giving programs tell donors little more than that.

The typical planned giving brochure, crammed with information on the joys of charitable remainder trusts, gift annuities and pooled income funds, usually has a picture that illustrates the mission of the organization and a wan plea that "gifts from estates are vital to our future."

I've had donors, particularly older people who are prime targets of planned giving appeals, tell me they can't throw away stuff like that fast enough. And, why shouldn't they? It's the same old message about tax and income benefits from yet another organization that feels it doesn't have to bother to say why it needs and deserves planned gifts.

This brochure-driven, tax-and-income-centered approach to planned giving violates basic fundraising principles. It presents no compelling case, shows no commitment from key volunteers, and relies on impersonal methods. Worse, it makes beleaguered development directors think they have to become tax and legal experts before they can start a planned giving program.

(continued)

Let me suggest another approach: put fundraising back in planned giving. Sure, you will need to find technical help if someone wants information on a charitable trust. But most planned gifts will be simple bequests.

Five Things You Can Do

1. Write a case statement that appeals both to the head (specific objectives) and heart (the benefits to those your organization serves as a result of planned gifts).

2. Work the case statement draft through your volunteer committees—planned giving, finance, development—revising the statement as you go along. View each of these meetings as an opportunity to encourage planned gifts from those around the table.

3. Refuse to move the case statement to the next committee unless you have a volunteer from your current committee who has made his or her planned giving commitment. (That's what I do, and it works.) By the time you reach the board, you should have two or three volunteers saying why they have included your organization in their estate plan.

4. Have the board of directors sign off on the case statement by formal board resolution. By now it should have a specific dollar goal, time table, and agreed upon objectives. Again, the case statement should be presented to the board by you and at least one volunteer—preferably a board member—who has made a planned gift commitment. The volunteer should encourage his or her fellow board members to consider making their own planned gift arrangements, with technical support offered to them as needed.

5. Now that your volunteers have something they can communicate comfortably—the case for planned gifts and their own planned gift commitments—set up appointments for them and you to talk with long-time supporters about including your organization in their estate plan.

I find that case-centered planned giving develops planned gift commitments fairly quickly—especially from volunteer leaders—provides personal stories for your newsletter that will, at minimum, be read by those who know the individual planned giver you are profiling, and makes the planned giving program something your organization considers a serious board responsibility, rather than seeing it as "(YOUR NAME HERE)'s project."

The case-centered approach is seldom as tidy as I've presented it. Its only virtue is that it works better than using mailings, seminars, and newsletter articles—all useful tools—without having a fully developed and institutionally approved case statement to back them up.

But there is a lot you can do on your own. Applying basic fundraising principles to planned giving is a good place to start.

—Philip J. Murphy, Planned Giving Specialist, Zimmerman Lehman

Enlisting board support is critical to a successful donor-centered marketing initiative. Kathryn W. Miree, President of Kathryn W. Miree & Associates, advises in the *Journal of Gift Planning* that one should approach board members on an individual basis. Bequest marketing programs should always begin with an organization's board for several reasons:

- The board must understand the importance of bequests to the future funding and viability of the organization. This group funds the marketing program and is responsible for reviewing its effectiveness. This is easier when the board member has personally considered a bequest.

- The board should be the most committed to the long-term viability of the organization and, therefore, the most likely to make a bequest. They volunteer time, have detailed insight into the operation and finances of the organization and have high personal contact with the organization and its staff.

- The board's commitment is important when recruiting other bequest donors. They can accompany staff on calls, serve as the subject of newsletter articles, be publicly listed (with permission) in the annual report and special tributes for donors.[7]

Gaining Staff Acceptance

Once board and senior management approval have been obtained, it will be easier to garner the support of other staff members at the organization. However, such support will not come automatically. The planned giving professional will have to work with colleagues to educate them about gift planning so that they will understand their role in the philanthropic planning process, feel comfortable discussing gift planning concepts with their prospects, and feel supported.

A mid-Atlantic university found that its major gift officers, representing various academic units, seldom discussed planned giving with their prospects. To change this dynamic, the planned giving staff presented an educational program to the entire university development team during one of its periodic gatherings. The program discussed some of the fundamentals of gift planning while focusing on feedback provided by alumni. The educational program was designed to give major gift officers valuable insight and new ways to help meet the needs of their prospects.

A university in New England found that many of its major gift officers were not entirely comfortable with the wide range of planned giving instruments. To deal with this, the planned giving staff met individually with the major gift officers to determine how they could be of assistance. Some of the major gift officers requested a planned giving "cheat-sheet" that simply and succinctly explained how various common planned giving vehicles work. And, they customized each "cheat-sheet" to the specifications of the individual major gifts officer to ensure that it would be user-friendly. Some major gift officers wanted a leaflet that described various situations a donor might find herself in, the corresponding gift vehicle that would work best, and the benefits to the donor. In addition, the leaflet contained a listing of the common gift planning vehicles along with an outline of the features of each. By contrast, other major gifts officers wanted simply to know the primary gift planning options along with an outline of their features and the benefits to the donor. Accompanying charts helped the major gifts officers visualize how each gift mechanism would work. All leaflets contained the names and contact information for the gift planning team.

Planned giving professionals should try to work effectively with all development colleagues while recognizing that this might not always be possible to achieve. However, by personally engaging colleagues, providing useful assistance to them, and by tailoring one's actions to the needs of the individual, relationships will be enhanced and success will come more often than not.

By helping to meet the needs of colleagues, planned giving professionals can earn their trust and confidence. This will foster more gift planning conversations and ultimately help more donors. In other words, this benefits the organization and its prospective supporters.

Developing prospect clearance protocols will keep major gift officers and planned giving officers from bumping into each other, and such protocols will better serve prospects and donors. If a prospect receives a call from a major gifts officer and a planned giving officer on the same day from the same organization, for example, she is liable to think that the organization does not know what it is doing, and she is likely to be annoyed by the duplicate contact. In addition, it is also a good idea to coordinate marketing activity with colleagues to ensure that the planned giving message is heard without directly competing with the organization's other development messages. For example, gift planning mailings should be coordinated with annual fund mailings to ensure that they do not end up in the prospect's mailbox at the same time. Again, this better serves donors while keeping colleagues happy. Happy colleagues will be infinitely more cooperative.

Building the Marketing Plan

Once one has created and obtained approval of the Internal Case for Donor-Centered Philanthropic Planning, it is time to create the planned gift marketing plan. Such plans will be unique to each organization given its distinctive objectives, prospect pool, staffing levels, and budget resources among other factors. The plan will be informed by the Internal Case. For example, a small organization with limited staff and budget may decide to only market bequest giving while a much larger organization may choose to market the full array of gift planning options. Once drafted and implemented, development professionals will need to remain flexible. Plans never unfold exactly as intended. It is important to adapt to changing circumstances.

Executive Insight

While marketing involves creativity, the most powerful marketing tool is strategy. No one knows an organization's donors like its development staff. Sometimes, staff simply does not realize how to use what they know. Begin with an analysis of donors. Use that knowledge to craft a [planned gift] marketing plan that focuses on the organization's best donors in a way that can be accommodated by staff and fits the charity's budget. Work smart. Do only those things that can be done well. And constantly analyze the results. If you approach a [planned gift] marketing plan in this way; your program is guaranteed success.

—Kathryn W. Miree, President, Kathryn W. Miree & Associates

While each marketing plan will be unique, they will all have many elements in common:

- *Mission.* The plan should refer to the organization's mission and highlight those services or programs that are unique to the organization or that are particularly performed well by the organization. The emphasis should be on those items and the most acute needs that will be most meaningful and attractive to prospective donors.

- *Key Goals.* The plan should outline the primary goals for the planned giving program. For example, does the organization want to reach out to new audiences? Does the organization want to close more bequest commitments? Does the organization want to close more CGAs? Does the organization want to educate more prospects about gift planning? Where possible, reasonable, quantifiable, measurable goals should be identified.

- *Target Markets.* The target markets must be identified relative to the goals that have been set. There are any number of ways that the target markets can be described. Some individuals may also be in multiple target groupings. For example, a consistent annual fund donor who is age 65 may be a prospect for bequest communications and may also be part of the target market for CGAs. Someone who is 80 may only be in the target pool for CGA promotion.

- *Key Objectives.* The plan should identify the primary objectives associated with each target market. For example, the goal might be to secure more bequest commitments. The target markets might be: (1) consistent annual fund donors over the age of 60, and (2) consistent annual fund donors from age 40 to 59. An objective for the first group might be to solicit more bequest commitments. An objective for the second group might be to provide more estate planning education.

- *Strategies and Tactics.* With each objective, one should outline the strategies and tactics that will be used to achieve the objective. For example, if an objective is to cultivate 200 more prospects, the strategy might be to offer educational programs. The tactics might include offering will clinics, estate planning seminars, and direct mail-based estate planning courses. For each strategy and tactic, the plan should identify the person responsible for execution. Figure 8.1 provides a schematic of how goals, target market, key objectives, strategies, and tactics fit together.

FIGURE 8.1

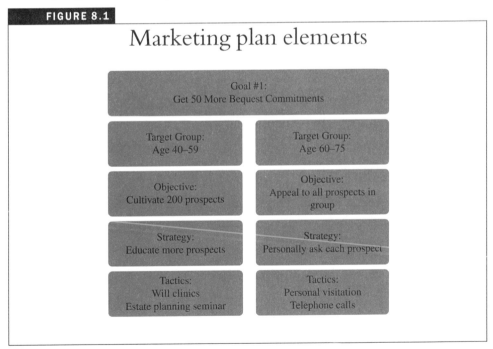

Marketing plan elements

Goal #1:
Get 50 More Bequest Commitments

Target Group:
Age 40–59

Target Group:
Age 60–75

Objective:
Cultivate 200 prospects

Objective:
Appeal to all prospects in group

Strategy:
Educate more prospects

Strategy:
Personally ask each prospect

Tactics:
Will clinics
Estate planning seminar

Tactics:
Personal visitation
Telephone calls

- *Budget.* The marketing plan should include a detailed budget. The expense of each of the tactics deployed should be outlined. "According to the top 10 percent of the *Chronicle of Philanthropy's* 'Philanthropy 400,' fundraisers spend, on average, half of their total planned giving budget on marketing," writes Michael Kateman, Executive Director, Development, Alumni & Public Relations at Columbia College.[8]

- *Outcomes.* The plan should also define anticipated outcomes relative to the goals and objectives. While it is important to project closed gifts, effective planned giving involves important long-term cultivation. Therefore, there are vital outcomes that do not involve the number or value of gifts. For example, if one is planning to offer educational programs, it is important to have an attendance goal. It might also be helpful to measure how useful the audiences think the educational seminars are. There are many facets of a planned giving program that should be measured. The performance of each tactic should be evaluated. The outcome measurements should all relate back to the goals and objectives and, when important milestones are reached, help achieve those goals and objectives. The more completely and accurately one projects outcomes, the more likely one is to have his budget approved. A worksheet for calculating the cost to raise a planned gift dollar can be found in Appendix D.

- *Calendar.* The plan should include a comprehensive marketing calendar for the year. This will help keep the marketing effort on track and avoid scheduling conflicts. In addition to a calendar, a Gant chart or other project management tool can be particularly helpful with managing complex marketing efforts. Table 8.1 is a sample calendar. A similar calendar would be used for each target market. Response rates will depend on the organization's relationship with the target group, the organization's historic results, and the quality of the marketing program. Obtaining results from similar organizations could help one develop reasonable benchmarking targets.

TABLE 8.1

Sample Calendar

Target Group	Medium	Type	Quantity	Response Rate	Number of Responses	Jan	Feb	March	April	May	June	July	August	Sept	Oct	Nov	Dec
Consistent Annual Fund Donors, Age 60–75	Direct Mail	Letters	1,000							X						X	
	E-mail	Newsletter	500				X		X		X		X		X		X
	Newsletter		1,000			X				X				X			
	Seminar	Will Clinic	500				X							X			

SUBTOTAL

Executive Insight

My perspective is that nothing will put a planned giving program into the toilet quicker than a decision to pause or cease marketing. The longer the pause, the worse the situation and the longer it takes to get back up to speed. It may take a while for the effects to show, but gifts will dry up if you do not market effectively.

—Roger Ellison, Vice President for Planned Giving, West Texas Rehabilitation Center Foundation

Evaluating the Marketing Effort

Planned gift marketing is an extraordinarily complex business. As such, it can be difficult to measure outcomes. The first thing a development professional needs to do is define what outcomes are important. This will, in part, be defined broadly by the goals and objectives. For example, a small organization focused on bequest marketing might measure inquiries, number of attendees to seminars, and bequest commitments for which a confirmation form has been received. In others, one will want to measure the effectiveness of planned gift marketing in ways beyond how many gifts were closed and how much revenue that represents. While counting the money is certainly important, other factors are also important and, therefore, should be measured.

Evaluating the performance of a planned giving program will involve an analysis of many factors and a comparison of actual performance to the original marketing plan. Tom Cullinan, in the *Journal of Gift Planning*, outlines a number of areas for measure:

- *Current and Deferred Gift Commitments.* Organizations should track how many gift commitments are documented each month, quarter, and year. In addition to tracking the number of commitments, the dollar value should also be tracked when possible.

- *Personal Meetings and Proposals.* Planned giving is a complex process that may involve years of cultivation before a gift is closed. To measure an important part of that process involves tracking how many face-to-face visits are made and how many proposals are presented. By itself, this level of activity will not indicate much. However, it will help present a more complete picture of the marketing effort.

- *Prospect Identification.* To ensure that the planned gift pipeline is always flowing, it is important for the development professional to continually uncover newly qualified prospects. Therefore, this is an activity worth measuring.

- *Communications and Marketing.* Keeping track of response rates to various marketing communications will allow the planned giving professional to know what is working and what is not. This will allow one to modify strategy and tactics to ensure the greatest return for the organization and the greatest value to the donor.

- *Seminars, Workshops, and Presentations.* These are effective ways to educate prospects and cultivate their support. There are a number of ways to measure this area of activity. One can measure the number of seminars conducted, the number of participants, the personal meetings that result, and so on.[9]

One must also measure the tangible outcomes of the planned giving program that will impact the organization's bottom line:

- *Realized Net Gift Income.* This is the ultimate bottom line. How much did the planned giving effort cost, and how much came in the door? For a new gift planning effort, the net income will be quite small. However, over time, one should expect it to grow significantly. A survey of 1,540 non-profit organizations found that the average amount raised for every $1 spent on planned giving was $20.

- *Expectancies Discovered.* Not all planned gifts will be quickly realized. While some gifts (i.e., CGAs) will involve an immediate transfer of cash or assets, many planned gifts are deferred (i.e., bequests). Since these commitments will likely result in future revenue for the organization, it is important to track these. While it might not always be possible to accurately track the dollars attached to each expectancy, an effort should be made to gather this information whenever possible.

- *Irrevocable Gift Commitments Secured.* Some deferred planned gifts (i.e., bequests, certain types of trusts) are revocable. Others are not. Charities should track irrevocable gift commitments.

- *Other Numbers and Dollars.* A variety of other numbers might be useful to track and could help with future budgeting efforts. It is important to track the results from all marketing tactics. It could be useful to track whether a planned giving officer is at least covering her salary. Some organizations expect the gift planner to bring in gift commitments valued at four times her salary, plus benefits, within the first three years on the job; the ability to accomplish this depends, in part, on the maturity of the gift planning effort. Some organizations expect a new gift planner to be fully effective within 12 to 18 months while others permit three to five years. There are a number of Return-on-Investment figures that can be studied. What is reviewed will depend on the marketing plan and the requirements of management.[10]

Because planned giving efforts take time to produce results, sometimes years, maintaining a strong process is essential. Therefore, it is important to measure process activity as well:

- Response to marketing and communications.
- Appointments with prospects.
- Proposals delivered.
- Advisor contacts.
- Presentations made.
- Coached contacts (i.e., contacts supported by the planned giving officer but made by a major gifts officer, board member, volunteer, etc.).
- Prospect research developed.

- Cold calls.
- Call reports and contact management.
- Moves.
- Budget considerations.[11]

Because planned giving is a complex practice, it is important that development professionals be on the same page as management when it comes to evaluating performance. Management and the development professional need to agree on what will be measured, how, and when. Then, reasonable standards of performance can be set relative to the organization's goals and objectives.

At a minimum, Larry Stelter, President of The Stelter Company, advises tracking and measuring the following items:

- The number of new members added to your legacy society each year.
- The number of donors you contact each year via:

  - Letters.
  - Telephone calls.
  - Personal visits.

- The number of active prospects in your giving pipeline, along with where they are in the cultivation process.
- The number of planned gift proposals personally delivered to donors.
- The number of new planned gifts completed this year.

KEY CONCEPT

An organization must tally the number of gifts and gift commitments it receives and, when possible, the value of those gifts and commitments. In addition, it is important to measure process activity to encourage the tangible results that those efforts produce since they will one day lead to planned gifts.

- The number of planned giving direct mail pieces you send and the response rates for each—whether by reply card, letter, phone call or otherwise.

- Your ability to increase traffic on your web site through promotions in your gift planning publications.

- To measure professional advisor relationships, track:

  - How many educational lunches you host.

  - How many direct mail pieces you send and the responses for each.

  - The number of e-mails and telephone calls you make and receive.

  - The number of referred prospects or donors you receive.

By effectively and appropriately measuring performance, development professionals will be able to report how effective they have been, and they will recognize the areas for improvement. By demonstrating success, year to year, development professionals will be better positioned to lobby for more resources to expand the planned giving program. A successful program that goes unmeasured is not likely to inspire as much confidence with an organization's leadership.

Successful planned giving helps to secure an organization's future. Once planned gifts account for an ever-increasing percentage of philanthropy directed at the organization, then staff, volunteers, and donors will take notice. Success will inspire greater success.

Summary

With an approved Internal Case for Donor-Centered Philanthropic Planning, a solid planned gift marketing plan, and an understanding of the marketing process, you are now ready to implement a donor-centered planned gift marketing program.

It will not be easy. Some marketing efforts will underperform relative to projection. Other marketing efforts will do fine or pleasantly surprise you.

Circumstances will change. The economy will falter. The economy will soar. Your organization will achieve great things. Your organization will embarrass itself, sometimes in small ways, sometimes in big ways. Sometimes the boss will be patient. Sometimes the boss will want to know when the next big gift will be closed.

Through all of the ups and downs, surprises, and pressures, stay the course. You have a plan. You know what to do. You know to stay focused on the donor.

Planned gift marketing is a process. It is an endeavor not commonly known for immediate gratification. Relationships and the resulting gifts take time to develop. But, if you are patient and maintain a donor-centered approach, your donors will take excellent care of your organization.

Ours is a noble profession. We help people realize their philanthropic aspirations, protect their loved ones, and take care of themselves. As a result, we do our share to help make the world a better place. Thank you.

Exercises

- A solid planned gift marketing plan is built on a solid case for support. If your organization has a Case, review it. Then, begin to develop an Internal Case using the sample in Appendix C as a guideline.

- The planned gift marketing plan should begin with your organization's mission statement. Identify the mission statement and begin your marketing plan with it.

- It is important to understand what you would like to achieve. Begin to consider what your planned giving goals are. You will need to outline your overall goals so that you can begin to develop the plan for achieving those goals.

- Getting the support of your colleagues is essential to planned giving success. Make a list of your development colleagues. What can you do for them to help them better engage prospects in the gift planning process? Could they benefit from training? Could they benefit from a summary sheet defining planned giving vehicles? How can you help them help you?

Executive Insight

The composition of this book has been for the author a long struggle of escape, and so must the reading of it be for most readers if the author's assault upon them is to be successful, a struggle of escape from habitual modes of thought and expression. The ideas, which are here expressed so laboriously are extremely simple and should be obvious. The difficulty lies, not in the new ideas, but in escaping from the old ones, which ramify, for those brought up as most of us have been, into every corner of our minds.

—John Maynard Keynes, economist and author of *General Theory of Employment, Interest and Money*

Planned Gift Program Potential Worksheet

To truly project how much a planned giving program can produce, one must understand as many of the variables as possible including the nature of the prospect pool, the wealth of prospects, the passion of prospects, the history of the organization, past performance, the purpose of the fundraising effort, the nature of the cause, the community, past philanthropic performance, the marketing effort, and so on. Collectively, this makes it difficult to forecast planned giving results. However, one can fairly easily gauge an organization's potential given a mythical, ideal set of circumstances. The following worksheet is meant to provide development professionals with an understanding of the broad potential impact of planned giving for their organizations. While this is not a scientific forecasting tool, it can help with forecasting by outlining aspirational targets. The worksheet looks at two common, easy-to-market types of planned gifts.

Bequests

Step 1: Size of database = _____ Records

Since the core prospect market for a bequest program is frequent annual donors, you should count the number of donors to your organization. However, depending on your organization, you might want to include other loyal supporters such as volunteers.

Step 2: Number of records × 5.3% = _____, Low-end number of Potential Donors

Take the number of records you have and multiply that figure by 5.3 percent,[1] which is the percentage of Americans over the age of 50 that have made a bequest commitment. If your donor file skews younger, you might want to back off that number a bit.

Step 3: Number of records × 33% = _____, High-end number of potential donors

Take the original number of records you recorded in Step 1 and multiply that figure by 33 percent,[2] which is the percentage of Americans that are willing to consider a bequest gift.

Step 4: Low-end number of potential donors/3 = _____ the revised low-end number of potential donors

Unfortunately, not every potential bequest donor will choose to support your organization. Some donors will support other organizations. Some who will be willing to consider a commitment will ultimately decide not to do so. The formula assumes that your organization can secure bequest gifts from one-third of its potential market. If you are feeling conservative, increase the denominator. If you are more ambitious, lower it. The outcome will be the estimated low-end number of potential donors that you can secure over time with an effective marketing effort.

Step 5: High-end number of potential donors/3 = _____ the revised high-end number of potential donors

This follows the same process as Step 4 except it is applied to the high-end number of potential donors. Unfortunately, not every potential bequest donor will choose to support your organization. Some donors will support other organizations. Some who may be willing to consider a commitment will ultimately decide not to do so. The formula assumes that your organization can secure bequest gifts from one-third of its potential market. If you are feeling conservative, increase the denominator. If you are more ambitious, lower it. The outcome will be the estimated high-end number of potential donors that you can secure over time with an effective marketing effort.

Step 6: Estimated number of low-end potential donors ×$_____ = $_____, potential dollars

Take the estimated number of low-end potential donors (Step 4) and multiply by $35,000, which is what some believe to be at or near the average bequest value in the United States. Alternatively, you can multiply the number of potential donors by your organization's average bequest gift value, being sure to deduct any unusually large gifts when calculating the average. The result is the gross potential dollars that could come from future bequest gifts at the low-end. Of course, this does not take into account the growth of the donor base (Step 1) over time.

Step 7: Estimated number of high-end potential donors ×$_____ = $_____, potential dollars

This step follows the same process as Step 6 except it is applied to the high-end number of potential donors. Take the estimated number of high-end potential donors (Step 5) and multiply by $35,000, which is what some believe to be at or near the average bequest value in the United States. Alternatively, you can multiply the number of potential donors by your organization's average bequest gift value, being sure to deduct any unusually large gifts when calculating the average. The result is the gross potential dollars that could come from future bequest gifts at the high-end. Of course, this does not take into account the growth of the donor base (Step 1) over time.

Step 8: Summary

Low-end potential donors (Step 4):   _____
Low-end potential dollars (Step 6): $_____
High-end potential donors (Step 5):   _____
High-end potential dollars (Step 7): $_____

After completing all eight steps, you will have a low-end to high-end gauge of your organization's potential for bequest giving over time.

While this is not a forecast, it does provide some indication of the potential results for your organization. How does your organization's current bequest marketing performance compare?

Charitable Gift Annuity

Step 1: Size of database = _____ Records

Since the core prospect market for a CGA program is people over the age of 65, you should count or estimate the number of donors to your organization who are 65 or older. Depending on your organization, you might want to include other loyal supporters such as volunteers.

Step 2: Number of records × 8.3% = _____, number of potential donors

There are an estimated 400,000 CGAs in the United States. However, this does not mean that there are that many CGA donors. Many such donors make multiple CGA donations. No one really knows how many CGA donors there are in the United States. For the sake of this exercise, we will estimate the number at 300,000. Presently, there are approximately 36.3 million Americans over the age of 65. That means 8.3 percent of older Americans are CGA donors. If you feel the number is lower, use a lower factor. If you feel the number is greater, use a larger factor. This will give you the potential number of donors for your organization given the current market penetration of CGAs in general. This does not include those who would be willing to consider, but who have yet to take action. How does your organization compare?

Step 3: _____, of potential donors × $_____ = $_____ potential dollars

Take the number of potential donors and multiply it by your organization's minimum CGA value or current average CGA value to calculate the dollar potential that exists. How does that compare with your current program?

Step 4: Summary

Number of potential donors = _____

Potential dollars = $_____

Bequest Confirmation Form

The following sample Bequest Confirmation Form is somewhat comprehensive. Different organizations may wish to request less information or additional information depending on their needs and the uses for the form. This sample is for a school. The last line of the form reminds the donor that her gift will be valued because of the impact it will have on the next generation.

Today's date: _____

Name: _____

Home address: _____

Work address: _____

Home phone: _____ Work phone: _____

Date of Birth: _____ Social Security Number: _____

Bequest is in: ____Will____Revocable Trust   Other: _____

Please check appropriate box:

[   ] Outright bequest

[   ] Contingent bequest

Approximate value of gift: $ _____

Purpose of gift, if not for the general purposes of the charity:

_____

_____

Execution date of will/trust: _____

Attorney of record: _____ Phone: _____

Address: _____

Executor of estate: _____

Phone: _____

Relation to you: _____

[   ] I have attached a photocopy of the relevant portion of my will or revocable trust.

Please return to: [Title]

                    [Charity name]

                    [Address]

                    [Phone number]

                    [E-mail]

Future gifts will allow us to educate the next great generation of Academy alumni.*

*The Bequest Confirmation Form is reprinted with kind permission. Laura Fredricks, *The Ask* (San Francisco: Jossey-Bass, 2006).

Sample Internal Case for Donor-Centered Philanthropic Planning: GPD Academy

Statement of Purpose, Mission, and History

Founded in 1898, GPD Academy (the "Academy") is an independent school located in the heart of Boston, and a leader in preparing students for higher education. The Academy integrates rigorous classroom studies with experiential learning opportunities—to prepare students for the rigors of top-flight colleges and universities and a lifetime of achievement. Under the able leadership of Head Master Christian James, the Academy has grown dramatically in the last twenty years, adding three hundred additional students, two new buildings and updated labs and athletic facilities. At the same time, the Academy has maintained small class sizes and added many nationally known faculty. The original funding for the Academy was provided by a gift under the will of Gavin P. Darcy, an immigrant who felt that too often education focused on books and not enough on experience. His vision for the school remains our focus today, with both academic and practical education required of every student.

What Is Donor-Centered Philanthropic Planning?

Philanthropic planning is a powerful and meaningful way for individuals to give to the Academy to ensure our long-term future, while also meeting personal planning objectives. Future gifts (also called planned gifts, legacy gifts or deferred gifts) are constructed in the present by donors, but usually do not benefit the Academy until some future date. Future gifts generally take two forms, revocable and irrevocable. Revocable future gifts allow donors to make commitments now but reserve the right to alter their plans up until death. The most common types of revocable future gifts include naming the Academy as the beneficiary of a will, living trust, life insurance policy, payable on death account, pension plan or retirement account. Irrevocable future gifts are binding commitments now that provide for the Academy in the future. Most often they take the form of life-income gifts including charitable gift annuities, pooled income funds, and charitable remainder trusts.

Donor-centered philanthropy is an emerging model for raising funds. Instead of asking what donors can do for the Academy, it asks what donors need to accomplish for themselves, their families and their future using a values-based approach. It seeks out what is really important to them in their lives. It then asks how the Academy and other charities they support can be integrated into their tax, estate and financial planning to help meet these goals. The tools of donor-centered philanthropic planning provide donors with the ability to meet both their personal planning objectives and their philanthropic goals to leave a more meaningful and lasting legacy.

The Important Roles of Endowments at the Academy

In order to maximize impact and long-term outcomes, the majority of future gifts are designated for endowments. Endowments funds are invested to provide future cash flow for the Academy. Some endowments provide the net income earned by the fund each year, while others use a trustee-determined draw rate. The most famous endowment gift came from our founder Gavin P. Darcy. His estate gift of $400,000 provided that $200,000 should be used to create the school and an additional $200,000 should be used to endow its operations. GPD recently received a gift of $5 million from the estate of Bob and Jane Fellows, the effects of which will be seen for generations to come. The Fellows gift was inspired by their deep belief in experiential learning and will completely endow the hands-on learning component of our educational program. These gifts illustrate one of two important ways that GPD uses endowments, to ensure the long-term future and viability of the Academy. There are no more important gifts, as without these gifts the Academy would have to rely solely on tuition and current gifts, both of which can drop dramatically when the economy is uncertain.

In 1980, Yolanda Seri used a current gift to create the Seri Endowment for Writing, which paid to create our Writer-In-Residence Program. When she passed on last year, we received the proceeds of her retirement plan, worth more than $2 million, which were added to the endowment to ensure this program for the future. This type of gift illustrates the second use of endowments, to fund and pursue new programs that it could not otherwise offer due to limited financial resources. Without the Seri Endowment, Justine Bellini '89 would likely not have pursued a literary career and written her best-selling novel, *Our Own Worst Enemy*.

Properly designed, constructed, managed and stewarded endowments strengthen the long-term well-being of the Academy by assuring a base of support. More importantly, they provide the means for our donors to impact future generations of Academy students who will change the world.

Why Should the Academy Seek Future Gifts Now?

In 1998, John J. Havens and Paul G. Schervish, of the Boston College Center on Wealth and Philanthropy published a study projecting an astonishing $41 trillion transfer of wealth between 1998 and 2052, with over $6 trillion to benefit charities through estates during that time (Schervish, Paul G. and Havens, John J., "Why the $41 Trillion Wealth Transfer Estimate is Still Valid," www.bc.edu/research/cwp/features/wealth.html). Even if this amount is reduced by the current economic downturn, a significant number of charitable bequest dollars have been, and will continue, to be transferred to charities in both the short- and long-terms. In 2008, seven of the ten largest gifts to charity were in the form of bequests (http://blogs.wsj.com/wealth/2009/01/26/the-dead-more-generous-than-the-living-in-2008/). Because this wealth is transferred when the donor no longer needs it to live on, bequest gifts are the largest gifts that donors can and do make.

Gifts That Continue, Even in a Down Economy

Future gifts continue to be planned and mature regardless of the economy. During difficult economic times, people are more likely to update their wills. Concerns about current income, the value of investments and decreasing retirement savings cause individuals to postpone philanthropy or consider future gifts, since they do not impact the donor until death. The Giving USA Foundation recently completed an analysis of giving patterns since 1966, using data from *Giving USA*. They found that while giving from individuals, foundations and corporations either remained static or declined during recession years, future gifts actually grew by 5% during recession years. This allows future gift revenue to serve as a "lifeboat" for the Academy when all other forms of revenue, including endowment spending amounts, are going down.

Broad Appeal—Everyone Is a Legacy Giving Prospect

Recent studies have debunked several myths about future gift prospects. The 2007 study, "Bequest Donors: Demographics and Motivations of Potential and Actual Donors" (the Bequest Study) conducted by the Center on Philanthropy at Indiana University (CPIU), found that the majority of individuals still do not have a will. Of those who do, only 7.5% have included a charitable provision. When asked why, the number one response in the 2000 National Committee on Planned Giving (now Partnership for Philanthropic Planning) study of donor behavior indicated that donors did not include a charitable bequest because it had never occurred to them. The Bequest Study also showed that donors age 40 to 60 are significantly more likely to consider a charitable bequest than donors over age 60, and that wealth level is not a factor in whether a donor considers a charitable bequest. Individuals who are engaged in the Academy's mission and focused on what it can accomplish in the future are the best future gift prospects, regardless of age or wealth (Sargeant, Adrian and Shang, Jen. "Identification, Death and Bequest Giving." Association of Fundraising Professionals, September 2008).

The Bequest Study showed that donors who had included a charitable bequest in their plans made annual gifts more than double in size than their counterparts who had not included charity in their estate plans. There are many reasons for this including: the donor has elevated the charity to the status of a family member and has a much greater investment in the charity's success; and the donor is providing greater lifetime support to a program that will be endowed later by a bequest. Future gifts will increase not only long-term support, but also current support from the Academy's most loyal and engaged donors.

We Are Ready

The Board of Trustees, together with the President, recently completed a five-year strategic plan. To implement the plan, the Academy will need to increase current revenue as well as endowment. With clearly articulated immediate and long-term goals, we are prepared to share with prospects the impact they can have today and the outcomes they can create for tomorrow. We have a robust group of regular consistent donors, the type of people who are the most likely to consider and create future gifts. The Academy is committed to a long-term approach, with endowment and gift policies that ensure confidentiality and that donor wishes will be fulfilled. We have developed a stewardship program to share successes with donors and their families, illustrating the immediate impact and long-term outcomes created by their gifts. The President has committed resources to building a robust future gift program, designating Katherine Prinzi,

Vice President of Advancement and Elizabeth Cornish, Director of Development, to lead our future giving effort.

Most importantly, we have a compelling mission, to help deserving kids from our communities to reach their full potential through classroom and experiential learning. A student like Barry Goldberg '74, who received a full scholarship to come here, but now provides scholarships to needy kids from his old neighborhood. Or, a student like Debra Johnston '88, who later came back to run the writing center. GPD Academy alumni are changing Boston and the world, and future gifts will allow us to educate the next great generation of Academy alumni.[*]

---

[*]This "Sample Internal Case for Donor-Centered Philanthropic Planning: GPD Academy" (2010) was written by Brian M. Sagrestano, President and CEO, Gift Planning Development, LLC. It is reprinted here with his kind permission.

Cost to Raise a Planned Gift Dollar Worksheet

P artnership for Philanthropic Planning has published guidelines for the accounting of planned gifts including the *Valuation Standards for Charitable Planned Gifts*[1] and *Guidelines for Reporting and Counting Charitable Gifts*.[2] However, there are differences between accounting measures and marketing measures. The former affects the financial statements and how gifts are reported while the latter can provide additional useful information to marketers.

The following is a sample planned giving evaluation worksheet that has been used at the University of Colorado Foundation[3] and allows one to calculate the cost to raise a planned gift dollar. Though it does not include a variety of marketing process measures, it does encourage the collection of other vital information that can be used to evaluate and justify the gift planning program:

*State Annual Goal = $*_____

In stating your annual goal, you may choose to not include realized bequests, realized CRTs, realized annuities, realized life insurance policies, realized retirement plan assets, etc., to avoid any issues of double counting. You would include the identification of any new revocable gifts (including bequests) by your current staff.

Divide Annual Goal by Gift Type.

The following are some examples. New CRTs for which your institution serves as trustee, including the amount of any additions to existing CRTs. New trusts identified for which your organization does not serve as trustee, and for which your organization (as charitable beneficiary) is listed irrevocably, including the amount of any additions to previously identified external trusts. New gift annuities (including deferred) outright gifts, including cash, stock, tangible property, irrevocable pledges, lead trust distributions, business interests, real estate, gift portion of bargain sales, IRA gifts under the Pension Protection Act of 2006, ownership of life insurance (cash value), and other outright gifts that were brought in with the assistance of gift planning professionals in your department. All revocable gifts (bequest intentions as specific, percentage and residual, IRA beneficiary designations, insurance beneficiary designations, external trusts for which you are a revocable charitable remainderman, and commitments from living trusts). This will likely be your largest category. New pooled income fund gifts. (CUF did not consider new PIF gifts in its stated goal, as we do not anticipate getting any in the coming fiscal year. These gifts have tapered off tremendously.)

Set Assumptions.

CUF values are shown; these values should be replaced by values appropriate to the experience of the organization using this worksheet. In the *Valuation Standards for Charitable Planned Gifts*, PPP provides default values for some assumptions. PPP defaults are evaluated annually and updated as necessary.

Gift Type Average Horizons:

Trusts, both internal and external (20 years)

Gift annuities (12 years)

All bequest intentions and other revocable gifts (10 years)

Pooled income fund gifts (CUF did not include in annual goal)

Average Payout Rate per Gift Type:

Trusts (7%)

Gift annuities (7%)

Discount Rate (9.5%)

(CUF used the endowment return over the previous three years.)

Investment Assumptions:

Trusts (9%)

Annuities (9%)

Residual and percentage bequest intentions (3%)

Specific bequests (not applicable)

Outright gifts (not applicable)

Calculate the net present value of the current goal for each gift type using the PPP *Valuation Standards for Charitable Planned Gifts***, or a method of your choice. Total the net present values of each goal by gift type to arrive at your "Net Present Value Total Goal."**

List direct and indirect "costs" of your program. The following are some examples:

Staff salaries and benefits

External and internal costs of trust and annuity management (if you serve as trustee). This may be fees paid to an outside services provider and/or salaries of internal staff in your finance department, costs for preparation of tax returns, mailing costs, and so on.

Marketing costs.

Registration and other fees (for gift annuities).

Office overhead (including travel and other costs incurred in raising new gifts).

All other costs identified in your budget.

List any department "revenue" (aside from new gifts). The following are some examples:

Fees charged directly to trusts.

Fees charged directly to annuity pools or PIF trust.

Fees charged to outright gifts brought in by members of your department.

Fees on new endowments created by outright gifts brought in by members of your department.

Tax on constituency (e.g., contributions from schools, colleges or the university that are "earmarked" for a gift planning effort).

Any unrestricted dollars raised for your program.

Other.

Determine Cost to Raise New Gifts.

Costs − Revenue = _____ ("Net Departmental Costs")

Net Departmental Costs − Costs to Maintain Current Portfolio through Depletion (if you manage one or more gift annuity pools or serve as trustee of a current trust program) = _____ ("Cost to Raise New Gifts")

Divide "Cost to Raise New Gifts" by "Net Present Value Total Goal" to arrive at "Cost to Raise a Planned Gift Dollar."

Notes

Chapter 1

1. Tony Alessandra, "The Platinum Rule," adapted from the book *The Platinum Rule* (Warner Books, 1996), www.alessandra.com/dobusiness.htm (accessed May 26, 2010).

2. Penelope Burk, *Donor Centered Fundraising* (Chicago: Burk & Associates, Ltd./Cygnus Applied Research, Inc., 2003), 22.

3. Emily Krauser, "Executive Summary Bequest Donors: Demographics and Motivations of Potential and Actual Donors" (Indianapolis: Center on Philanthropy at Indiana University for Campbell and Company, 2007), 3.

4. Kathryn W. Miree, "Tailored to Fit: Designing a Comprehensive Bequest Marketing Plan," *Journal of Gift Planning* 5, no. 4 (2001): 13.

5. Russell N. James III, "The Myth of the Coming Charitable Estate Windfall," *The American Review of Public Administration* 39 (2009): 661–674.

6. *Planned Giving in the United States 2000: A Survey of Donors* (Indianapolis: National Committee on Planned Giving [now Partnership for Philanthropic Planning], 2001), www.pppnet.org/resource/donors-survey.html (accessed May 26, 2010).

7. Krauser, "Executive Summary Bequest Donors," 2.

8. "2009 Stelter Donor Insight Report: Donors on the Move," Report, (Des Moines: The Stelter Company, 2009), 3.

9. Ibid.

10. U.S. Census Bureau, www.census.gov/newsroom/releases/pdf/cb06-ff05.pdf (accessed June 29, 2010), 1.

11. The Center on Philanthropy at Indiana University. *Giving USA 2010: Executive Summary* (Glenview, IL: Giving USA Foundation, 2010), 10.

12. Ibid.

13. "Single Word Costs Charities Billions Each Year," 2010, www.remember-acharity.org.uk/news_release_list.jsp?newsID=29 (accessed May 26, 2010).

14. NCPG Strategic Directions Task Force, "The Future of Charitable Gift Planning," *Journal of Gift Planning* 11, no. 2 (2007): 16.

15. Philip J. Murphy, "Get Wild with Planned Giving: Think of It as Fund-raising!" (San Francisco: Zimmerman Lehman, 2007), www.zimmerman-lehman.com/plannedgiving.htm (accessed May 26, 2010).

16. Brian Sagrestano, "Marketing Planned Gifts" in *The Planned Giving Course* (Partnership for Philanthropic Planning of Greater Philadelphia, December 5, 2008).

Chapter 2

1. "2009 Stelter Donor Insight Report," 9.

2. Michael J. Rosen, "The Planned Giving Donor Profile" in *The Planned Giving Course* (Partnership for Philanthropic Planning of Greater Philadelphia, December 5, 2008).

3. Laura Fredricks, *The Ask* (San Francisco: Jossey-Bass, 2006), 144.

4. Russell N. James III, "Health, Wealth, and Charitable Estate Planning: A Longitudinal Examination of Testamentary Charitable Giving Plans." *Nonprofit and Voluntary Sector Quarterly*, 38, no. 6 (2008): 1026–1043.

5. Russell N. James III, "The Presence and Timing of Charitable Estate Planning: New Research Findings." New Orleans: AFP International Conference, March 2009.

6. Ibid.

7. U.S. Census Bureau, www.census.gov/newsroom/releases/pdf/cb06-ff05.pdf (accessed June 29, 2010), 2.

8. "Equity Ownership in America," Investment Company Institute and Securities Industry Association, Fall 1999, www.census.gov/compendia/statab/2009/tables/09s1171.pdf (accessed July 6, 2010), 1.

9. David B. Moore, e-mail message to author, Feb. 10, 2010.

10. Russell N. James III, "Causes and Correlates of Charitable Giving in Estate Planning: A Cross-Sectional and Longitudinal Examination of Older Adults" Report. Association of Fundraising Professionals, July 2008, 2.

11. Ibid.

12. Krauser, "Executive Summary Bequest Donors," 3.

13. "2009 Stelter Donor Insight Report," 3.

14. Scott R.P. Janney, e-mail message to author, Feb. 15, 2010.

15. David Hare, "From the Playwright," (Philadelphia: Lantern Theater Company, February 2010).

16. James, "Causes and Correlates of Charitable Giving in Estate Planning: A Cross-Sectional and Longitudinal Examination of Older Adults," 3.

17. Thomas T. Perls and Ruth C. Fretts. "Why Women Live Longer than Men." *Scientific American*. 100, no. 7 (1998), http://healthfully.org/lgev/id2.html (accessed July 6, 2010).

18. Margaret May Damen. "Women as Philanthropists: Gender and Generational Synergy for Effective Gift Planning." *Journal of Gift Planning* 11, no. 4 (December 2007): 5–9, 27–36.

19. Fidelity Charitable Gift Fund. "Gender Differences in Charitable Giving 2009: Executive Summary." Spring 2009, www.charitablegift.org/docs/Gender-Study-Executive-Summary.pdf.

20. Robert D. Putnam. *Bowling Alone* (New York: Simon and Schuster, 2000) 18–19.

21. Putnam, *Bowling Alone*, 119.

22. Adrian Sargeant and S. Lee, "Improving Public Trust in the Voluntary Sector: An Empirical Analysis," *International Journal of Nonprofit and Voluntary Sector Marketing* 7, no. 1 (2002): 68–83.

23. Ibid.

24. C. Toppe and A. Kirsch, "Keeping the Trust: Confidence in Charitable Organizations in an Age of Scrutiny" (Washington, DC: Independent Sector, 2002).

25. Andrew Watt, "Ethical Fundraising: What Are the Challenges Facing an Individual in Developing an Organizational Ethical Policy?" Seattle: AFP International Conference, 2004.

26. Roger Ellison, "Generosity–Passion Chart," www.rogerellison.com/articles (2010; accessed May 29, 2010).

27. Brian Sagrestano, e-mail message to author, April 6, 2010.

Chapter 3

1. Jay Conrad Levinson, *Guerilla Marketing Excellence* (New York: Houghton Mifflin Company, 1993), 11–12.

2. "Yul Brynner Antismoking Commercial," www.youtube.com/watch?v=JNjunlWUJJI (accessed July 6, 2010).

3. Peter Benoliel, "Donor Roundtable," Philadelphia: Partnership for Philanthropic Planning of Greater Philadelphia Planned Giving Day, October 2009.

4. Center on Philanthropy at Indiana University, "Generational Differences in Charitable Giving and in Motivations for Giving" Report. (Indianapolis: Center on Philanthropy at Indiana University for Campbell and Company, 2008).

5. Brian Sagrestano, "The Impact of Changing Generational Cohorts on Individual Giving and Gift Planning" (Philadelphia: Partnership for Philanthropic Planning of Greater Philadelphia, September 2009).

6. Judith E. Nichols, *Global Demographics: Fundraising for a New World* (Chicago: Bonus Books, 1995), 128.

7. Arthur Brooks, *Who Really Cares* (New York: Basic Books, 2006), 50.

8. Patrick Rooney, "Research Unveiled: What Every Fundraiser Needs to Know about Bequest Giving," New Orleans: AFP International Conference, March 2009.

9. Ibid.

10. Adrian Sargeant and Jen Shang, "Identification, Death and Bequest Giving," Report. Association of Fundraising Professionals, September 2008, 34–39.

11. *Planned Giving in the United States 2000: A Survey of Donors* (Indianapolis: National Committee on Planned Giving [now Partnership for Philanthropic Planning], 2001), www.pppnet.org/resource/donors-survey.html (accessed May 31, 2010).

12. Paul G. Schervish and John J. Havens, "The New Physics of Philanthropy: The Supply Side Vectors of Charitable Giving—Part 1: The Material Side of the Supply Side," *The CASE International Journal of Educational Advancement* 2 no. 2 (2001): 95–113.

13. Paul G. Schervish and John J. Havens, "The New Physics of Philanthropy: The Supply Side Vectors of Charitable Giving—Part 2: The Spiritual Side of the Supply Side," *The CASE International Journal of Educational Advancement* 2, no. 3(2002): 221–41.

14. Sargeant and Shang, "Identification, Death and Bequest Giving," 35.

15. Legacy Leaders, "The George Washington University: Alumni Relations Strategy Research" (Washington, DC: The George Washington University, 2008). Used with permission.

16. Sargeant and Shang, "Identification, Death and Bequest Giving," 35.

17. Sargeant and Shang, "Identification, Death and Bequest Giving," 36.

18. Sargeant and Shang, "Identification, Death and Bequest Giving," 37.

19. Legacy Leaders, "The George Washington University: Alumni Relations Strategy Research."

20. Sargeant and Shang, "Identification, Death and Bequest Giving," 38.

21. Rob Cope, e-mail message to author, June 17, 2010.

22. Sargeant and Shang, "Identification, Death and Bequest Giving," 40.

23. Sargeant and Shang, "Identification, Death and Bequest Giving," 41.

24. Sargeant and Shang, "Identification, Death and Bequest Giving," 41–42.

25. Sargeant and Shang, "Identification, Death and Bequest Giving," 42.

26. Legacy Leaders, "The George Washington University: Alumni Relations Strategy Research."

27. Remember a Charity. www.rememberacharity.org.uk (accessed July 6, 2010)

Chapter 4

1. "2009 Stelter Donor Insight Report," 6.

2. "2009 Stelter Donor Insight Report," 7.

3. Frank Luntz, *Words That Work: It's Not What You Say, It's What People Hear* (New York: Hyperion, 2007), 126.

4. Luntz, *Words That Work: It's Not What You Say, It's What People Hear* (New York: Hyperion, 2007), 241–264.

5. Chip Heath and Dan Heath, *Made to Stick: Why Some Ideas Survive and Others Die* (New York: Random House, 2007), 16–18.

6. Margaret Holman, "Improving Your Solicitation Skills: How to Really Ask for a Gift . . . and Get It!" Parsippany: New Jersey AFP Conference on Philanthropy, 2009.

7. Sargeant and Shang, "Identification, Death and Bequest Giving," 28–29.

8. Save the Children, www.savethechildren.org (accessed May 10, 2010)

9. Sargeant and Shang, "Identification, Death and Bequest Giving," 43–44.

10. Sargeant and Shang, "Identification, Death and Bequest Giving," 44.

11. Sargeant and Shang, "Identification, Death and Bequest Giving," 46.

12. Robert Cialdini, "The Power of Persuasion: Putting the Science of Influence to Work in Fundraising," *Stanford Social Innovation Review*, Summer 2003. www.ssireview.org/images/articles/2003SU_feature_cialdini.pdf (accessed June 15, 2010).

13. Sagrestano, "Marketing Planned Gifts."

14. Larry Stelter, *A Mercifully Brief, Real World Guide: How to Raise Planned Gifts by Mail* (Medfield, MA: Emerson and Church Publishers, 2008).

15. Ibid.

16. Robert F. Sharpe Jr., "Marketing Success in Today's Environment" in *Give and Take* (Memphis: The Sharpe Group, November 2006).

17. "Facebook Fact Sheet," www.facebook.com/press/info.php?statistics (accessed March 27, 2010).

18. Erick Schonfeld, "Twitter Hits 50 Million Tweets Per Day." *The Washington Post* (February 23, 2010), www.washingtonpost.com/wp-dyn/content/article/2010/02/23/AR2010022300133.html (accessed May 31, 2010).

19. Guy Kawasaki, *Rules for Revolutionaries* (New York: Harper Business, 1999), 68–69.

20. Levinson, *Geurrilla Marketing Excellence*, 118.

Chapter 5

1. Robin R. Ganzert, Tracy A. Mack, Joseph Fortuna, William L. Sutton Jr., "High-Impact Philanthropy: Strategies for Partnering with Professional Advisers," *Advancing Philanthropy* (March/April 2009): 33–35.

2. Scott R.P. Janney, "Get Donor Advisors onto Your Team: The Planned Giving Advisory Council and Other Strategies." Univest Foundation Planned Giving and Development Spring Seminar, May 9, 2007.

3. Ibid.

4. Ganzert et al., "High-Impact Philanthropy."

5. James M. Kouzes and Barry Z. Posner, *The Leadership Challenge* (New York: Jossey-Bass, 2003).

Chapter 6

1. Adrian Sargeant and Elaine Jay, "Determinants of U.S. Donor Behaviour: The Case of Bequests, Part 1," Report. Association of Fundraising Professionals, June 2004, 11.

2. Susan DameGreene, "How to Develop a Successful Bequest Program: A Simple, Easy-to-Follow Plan for Starting, Increasing and Collecting Bequests at Your Nonprofit," *The Journal of Gift Planning* 7 no. 22 (2003): 48.

3. A sample copy of the NRDC November 2009 planned giving direct mail appeal can be found at: http://malwarwicknews.com/2010/01/sample-nrdc (accessed July 6, 2010).

4. Michael J. Rosen, "Dialing Delivers for Planned Giving, Too," Philadelphia: Planned Giving Council of Greater Philadelphia.

5. Mindy Aleman, e-mail messages to author, Feb. 12 and 22, 2010.

6. Mid-Atlantic university, e-mail messages to author, March 4, 16, 22, and 23, 2010.

7. Janet Aldrich Jacobs, "A New Model for Marketing." *Planned Giving Today*, January 2004: 5–6.

8. Rosen, "Dialing Delivers for Planned Giving, Too."

9. Leslie D. Bram, e-mail messages to author, March 29, 2010.

10. Bruce Makous, "Solicitation: The Art of the Ask," White paper, 2010.

11. Fredricks, *The Ask*, 158–159.

12. Fredricks, *The Ask*, 161.

13. Adrian Sargeant and Elaine Jay, "Determinants of U.S. Donor Behaviour: The Case of Bequests, Part 2," Report. Association of Fundraising Professionals, June 2004, 1.

Chapter 7

1. "AFP Fundraising Dictionary" (Arlington: Association of Fundraising Professionals, 2003), www.afpnet.org/files/ContentDocuments/AFP_Dictionary_A-Z_final_6-9-03.pdf.

2. *CFRE Review Course Participants Manual* (Arlington: Association of Fundraising Professionals, 2004), G–17.

3. Levinson, *Guerilla Marketing Excellence*, 20–21.

4. DameGreene, "How to Develop a Successful Bequest Program," 48.

5. Janet L. Hedrick, *Effective Donor Relations*. (Hoboken: John Wiley & Sons, 2008), 63.

6. Burk, *Donor-Centered Fundraising*, 36.

7. Burk, *Donor-Centered Fundraising*, 57.

8. *Planned Giving in the United States 2000: A Survey of Donors*.

9. Sargeant and Jay, "Determinants of U.S. Donor Behaviour, Part 1," 11.

10. Rachel Sisemore Crawford and Fred Hartwick, "Creating and Maintaining a Planned Giving Society," *Journal of Gift Planning* 5, no. 4 (2001): 20.

11. Kayt C. Peck, "A Planned Gift Is a Planned Gift, Right?" Baltimore: AFP International Conference, 2010.

12. Crawford and Hartwick, "Creating and Maintaining," 51.

13. Renata J. Rafferty, *Don't Just Give It Away*, (Worcester: Chandler House Press, 1999) 125.

14. DameGreene, "How to Develop a Successful Bequest Program," 49–50.

Chapter 8

1. "Are You Ready for Planned Giving?" Partnership for Philanthropic Planning, 2010, www.pppnet.org/resource/ready-gg.html.

2. Laura Hansen Dean, and Pamela J. Davidson, "How to Evaluate Your Gift Planning Program," *Journal of Gift Planning* 6(1) (March 2002): 14.

3. Dean and Davidson, "How to Evaluate Your Gift Planning Program," 14–15.

4. *CFRE Review Course Participants Manual* (Arlington: Association of Fundraising Professionals, 2004), C3, C5–6.

5. Brian M. Sagrestano and Robert E. Wahlers, "Making the Case Using Donor-Centered Philanthropic Planning," Baltimore: AFP International Conference, 2010.

6. Ibid.

7. Kathryn Miree, "Tailored to Fit: Designing a Comprehensive Bequest Marketing Plan," *Journal of Gift Planning* 5, no. 4 (December 2001): 47.

8. Michael Kateman, "A Strategic Look at Marketing," *Journal of Gift Planning* 6, no. 4 (December 2002): 45.

9. Tom Cullinan, "Evaluating Gift Planner Performance: A Guide for Charity Managers," *Journal of Gift Planning* 12, no. 1 (March 2008): 24.

10. Cullinan, "Evaluating Gift Planner Performance," 25.

11. Cullinan, "Evaluating Gift Planner Performance," 35–40.

Appendix A

1. Russell N. James III, "The Myth of the Coming Charitable Estate Windfall," *The American Review of Public Administration* vol. 39 (December 2009): 661–74.

2. Krauser, "Executive Summary Bequest Donors," 2.

Appendix D

1. *Valuation Standards for Charitable Planned Gifts* (Indianapolis: Partnership for Philanthropic Planning, 2009), www.pppnet.org/pdf/2009_valuation_standards.pdf.

2. *Guidelines for Reporting and Counting Charitable Gifts* (Indianapolis: Partnership for Philanthropic Planning, 2009), www.pppnet.org/pdf/PPP_counting_guidelines_%282009%29.pdf.

3. Kristen Dugdale, "The Case for Gift Planning: Analyzing the Cost to Raise a Planned Gift Dollar," *Journal of Gift Planning*, vol. 11, no. 1 (March 2007): 5–28.

Glossary

1. The terms and definitions in the Glossary are from "23 Planned Giving Terms You Should Know: a Glossary of Common Terms" (2008) written by Katherine Swank, JD, Consultant, Target Analytics, a Blackbaud Company (www.afpnet.org/files/secure/index.cfm?FileID=23838). The material is used here with the kind permission of the author and Target Analytics. Additional terms and definitions have been added from: "AFP Fundraising Dictionary" (2003) by the Association of Fundraising Professionals (www.afpnet.org/files/ContentDocuments/AFP_Dictionary_A-Z_final_6-9-03.pdf).

Glossary

Bequest expectancy or planned gift expectancy Term commonly used within planned giving programs to unofficially report the value or approximate value of gifts to be received in the future. Some organizations use an expectancy value of $1 for gifts until a more appropriate value can be determined. Other organizations choose to use an average gift expectancy value. This is often arrived at by using a five- or 10-year rolling average of actual planned or bequest gifts received by the organization. Be careful not to inflate that value by including unusually large gifts. Because some planned gifts may not be received for months or years from a complex estate or where an asset must first be sold, having an expectancy amount helps to provide a picture to organizational leadership and other staff members of the importance that bequest gifts have on future revenue.

Bequest intention or planned gift intention A donor's indication of his or her intent to leave a future gift. An intention is neither a legal nor binding commitment upon the donor's estate. Rather, it is a courtesy notification of the donor's desire to make a future gift. With the average bequest gift hovering at around $35,000, many organizations treat these donors as they would a major donor and include them in a legacy recognition club. Because of the nonbinding nature of the intention, however, it is most wise to provide benefits that are either of no cost or low cost, such as listing donors in acknowledgment publications, sending them special invitations or advance notices for organizational activities, or perhaps giving them a token thank-you gift.

Bequest notification or planned gift notification The estate representative's official notification that a bequest or other estate gift has come to realization. If the gift is a percentage of an estate, a remainder gift, or a gift of personal property, it may not be possible to determine the value of the gift immediately. In this case, a gift expectancy value may be used.

Capital gains   When investment (or capital) assets are held for longer than a year and then sold to another person or given to a charity, the gain or appreciation in the value of the asset is subject to government taxation on the gain (or profit). If the price of the asset has declined instead of appreciated, this is called a capital loss. Capital gains occur in both real assets, such as property, as well as financial assets, such as stocks or bonds.

Charitable bequest   A provision in a will, trust, or estate plan that allocates a gift to a designated charity. The most common gifts to nonprofit beneficiaries are cash, securities, and real property including homes and personal property (things). Many wills and trusts are still written with quite formal language and might be similar to this example: "I give, bequeath, and devise the sum of fifty-thousand dollars ($50,000) to St. Mark's Church, located at 123 Main Street, Middletown, Alabama."

The most common gift amounts are usually stated in one of the following three ways:

1. A *specific amount*, such as the example just given.

2. A *percentage amount*, such as " . . . Ten percent (10%) of my estate to St. Mark's Church . . ."

3. A *remainder amount* also called "residue," such as After all specific bequests have been paid, "I give, bequeath, and devise the remainder of my estate, including real and personal property, to St. Mark's Church . . ."

Charitable gift annuity (CGA)   An irrevocable transfer of property (e.g., cash, securities) in exchange for a contract to pay the donor or the donor's designee an annuity for life. Depending on state law, payments could begin immediately or may be allowed to be deferred until a future date. Because the value of the property exceeds the value of the annuity, it is partially a gift to the institution. While most charitable gift annuity contracts are established between the donor and the organization to receive the remainder gift amount, community foundations have been given permission from the IRS to issue such gift annuity contracts on behalf of other qualifying charitable organizations. Additionally, there are different types of charitable gift annuities, and not all states permit the use of each type:

- When all of the annuitants have passed away, the residuum, or remains of the initial gift plus any interest income, is distributed to the charity to be used according to the contract's directions. Usually, this is for general use by the charity but may be restricted by the donor for a particular use, such as student scholarships or biomedical research.

- A college tuition annuity allows a donor to create a single-life annuity that defers payments until a child or grandchild is expected to enter college. The child has the option of accepting the annuity payments for his or her lifetime or to receive much larger payments over a shorter period of time, usually four to five years.

Charitable lead trust (CLT) Similar to a charitable remainder trust, the CLT is different in that the annual payments are given to a charitable organization and the principal reverts to the donor or to his or her designated beneficiaries at the end of the trust term. If the principal reverts to the donor, he or she gets a charitable income tax deduction; if to another, that person gets a charitable gift tax deduction.

Charitable remainder trust (CRT) An irrevocable trust that pays a specified annual amount to one or more people for a fixed period of years (often the life of the individual). At the end of the term of the trust, the remaining trust assets are distributed to the charity.

- A *charitable remainder annuity trust* provides a fixed payment as determined and stated in the trust document.

- A *charitable remainder uni-trust* pays out a fixed percentage of the trust value each year as determined and stated in the trust document. The value of the uni-trust is recalculated annually to determine the current payout.

Contingent bequest A provision in a will, trust, or estate plan that allocates a gift to a designated charity as an alternative to a higher priority bequest or condition to be met. Contingent bequests can also incorporate specific amounts, percentage amounts, or remainder amounts, such as the previous examples under the definition of "Charitable Bequest." For instance: "In the event that (named individual) predeceases me, I give Marcus University Foundation, 2345 East Street, Centerville, Texas, 25% of the residue of my estate to be used wherever the needs and opportunities are greatest."

Cost basis This term generally means the purchase price of an asset or property. An asset's value will change over time and can therefore appreciate or depreciate from its original cost basis. Its value at the time of gifting would be classified as appreciated if it was worth more than was paid for it. Conversely, it would have depreciated value if it was worth less than was originally paid.

Cost per dollar raised Usually presented in dollars and cents, the "cost per dollar raised" attempts to calculate the effectiveness of a fundraising effort or campaign. The cost per dollar raised concept can be applied to a specific solicitation piece such as the May 2008 Gift Annuity Solicitation Appeal, or it can be applied to an entire campaign or program such as the Bequest Marketing and Solicitation Effort. There is no standard method between organizations, so costs per dollar raised can vary widely depending on what expense items are being included. Typically for planned giving solicitation efforts, costs are limited to the printing, mailing, and postage expenses that may or may not include mail house and data processing expenses. To assess the cost per dollar raised for a comprehensive planned giving program, staff salary and benefits, office expenses, outside vendor and legal/financial management, as well as other larger budgetary expenses, might be considered in the cost.

Donor–advised fund A fund in which the donor exercises the privilege of making nonbinding recommendations to the governing body as to which public charity or charities should receive grant money from this fund.

Estate tax   A federal tax on the net value of an estate before it is distributed to beneficiaries.

Fair market value   An estimate of what a willing buyer would pay to a willing seller, in a free market, for an asset or a piece of property.

Gift tax   This is a tax imposed on the lifetime transfer of property as a gift to a noncharitable beneficiary. The tax, paid by the donor, is based on the fair market value of the property on the date of the gift.

Gross estate   All the property, including life insurance and any transfers, owned by a decedent, or in which a decedent held any financial interest, or both.

Income or current beneficiary   The person(s) or entity(ies) that receive(s) the current income or distributions from a trust according to its terms.

Legacy   This term is often synonymous with *bequest*.

Life estate   A gift where the donor retains the right of use for life.

Life-income gifts   A generic term used to describe a variety of charitable gift vehicles that provide an income, usually for life, to a donor and/or his or her designated beneficiaries. Life-income gifts include, among other things, charitable gift annuities, charitable remainder trusts, both uni-trust and annuity trusts, and charitable lead trusts.

Noncash asset   When related to an outright gift or a planned gift, this term usually refers to an asset such as securities, life insurance policies, CDs, retirement accounts, real property, and the like. Conversely, gifts of currency and checks, as well as gifts using credit cards, are considered cash or cash-equivalent assets.

Personal property or tangible personal property   Think of this as things that can be touched or things that are tangible. Examples of gifts of tangible personal property to charities include book collections, art, and jewelry. It does not include, however, cash or cash equivalents such as checking accounts.

Planned gift or planned giving   Once called *deferred giving*, "planned giving" or "planned gift" refers to any charitable gift that requires more thought and planning to execute than the average donation. Planned giving has traditionally been defined as the gift that an individual makes near the end of his or her lifetime. There are many kinds of planned gifts, including, but not limited to: simple bequests in a will or an estate plan, charitable gift annuities, charitable remainder trusts, charitable lead trusts, and noncash assets.

Present value   The value that a gift expected in the future would be worth today. A future gift of $100,000 is not as valuable as a gift of $100,000 today due to factors such as inflation, currency fluctuations, and investment risk. Financial advisors may use the phrase *time value of money*, referring to the way the value of money changes over time. The present value of a gift of $100,000 to be received five years from now, given a 5 percent discount, would have a present value of only $78,352.62.

Probate   This is a court-supervised process of settling an estate in which all expenses are paid and all property is distributed in accordance with the terms of a will.

Real property   A general term that encompasses land, land improvements such as buildings and machinery sited on the land, as well as the various property rights associated with owning the land, buildings, and machinery. Real property that is mortgaged or otherwise is subject to another person's preceding claim is known as encumbered. Charitable gifts of encumbered property have their own sets of challenges and tax consequences.

Remainder beneficiary   The person(s) or entity(ies) that receive(s) the remaining assets from a trust when its controlling terms have been met or its term of years for existence has come to an end.

Return on investment (ROI)   This term is used by some organizations in place of the term *cost per dollar raised* and means essentially the same. In a more global setting, however, ROI has nonmonetary objectives such as public awareness of a product or new sales leads. In the financial world it means the ratio of money gained or lost on an investment relative to the amount of money invested.

Securities   Used for planned gift purposes, *securities* is a general term that includes the following: shares of corporate stock or mutual funds, bonds issued by corporations or governmental agencies, stock options or other options, limited partnership units, and various other formal investment instruments that can be exchanged for money.

Split interest gifts These gifts, usually involving property or business interests, start with the idea of making a partial gift of an asset to charity while still retaining a partial interest in it. Because the donor retains some portion of the assets or the income from the assets, the term *split interest gift* is derived. The "split" refers to the fact that ownership is now divided between the original owner and in our case, a charity. Splitting the interest creates a problem in determining the value of the portion given to charity (gift portion) and the value of the portion which was kept (retained interest).

Testate This involves having made and left a legal will at time of death.

Will This is a legally executed statement of a person's wishes about what is to be done with the person's property after his or her death.[1]

References

Alessandra, Tony. "The Platinum Rule," adapted from the book *The Platinum Rule*.: Warner Books, 1996, www.alessandra.com/dobusiness.htm (accessed on May 26, 2010).

Association of Fundraising Professionals. *AFP Fundraising Dictionary*. Arlington: Association of Fundraising Professionals, 2003, www.afpnet.org/files/ ContentDocuments/AFP_Dictionary_A–Z_final_6-9-03.pdf.

Association of Fundraising Professionals. *CFRE Review Course Participants Manual*. Arlington: Association of Fundraising Professionals, 2004.

Benoliel, Peter. "Donor Roundtable." Partnership for Philanthropic Planning of Greater Philadelphia Planned Giving Day, October 2009.

Brooks, Arthur C. *Who Really Cares*. New York: Basic Books, 2006.

Burk, Penelope. *Donor-Centered Fundraising*. Chicago: Burk & Associates, Ltd./Cygnus Applied Research, Inc., 2003.

Center on Philanthropy at Indiana University. *Giving USA 2010: Executive Summary*. Glenview, IL: Giving USA Foundation, 2010.

Center on Philanthropy at Indiana University. "Generational Differences in Charitable Giving and in Motivations for Giving." Indianapolis: Center on Philanthropy at Indiana University for Campbell and Company, 2008.

Cialdini, Robert B. "The Power of Persuasion: Putting the Science of Influence to Work in Fundraising." *Stanford Social Innovation Review*, Summer 2003. www.ssireview.org/images/articles/2003SU_feature_cialdini.pdf (accessed June 15, 2010).

Crawford, Rachel Sisemore, and Fred Hartwick. "Creating and Maintaining a Planned Giving Society." *Journal of Gift Planning* 5(4) (2001): 19–52.

Cullinan, Tom. "Evaluating Gift Planner Performance: A Guide for Charity Managers." *Journal of Gift Planning* 12(1) (March 2008): 18–43.

DameGreene, Susan. "How to Develop a Successful Bequest Program: A Simple, Easy-to-Follow Plan for Starting, Increasing and Collecting Bequests at Your Nonprofit." *Journal of Gift Planning* 7(22) (2003): 17–52.

Damen, Margaret May. "Women as Philanthropists: Gender and Generational Synergy for Effective Gift Planning." *Journal of Gift Planning* 11(4) (December 2007): 5–9, 27–36.

Dean, Laura, and Pamela Davidson. "How to Evaluate Your Gift Planning Program." *Journal of Gift Planning* 6(1) (March 2002): 13–43.

Dugdale, Kristen. "The Case for Gift Planning: Analyzing the Cost to Raise a Planned Gift Dollar." *Journal of Gift Planning* 11(1) (March 2007): 5–28.

Ellison, Roger. "Generosity-Passion Chart." www.rogerellison.com/articles, 2010.

Fidelity Charitable Gift Fund. "Gender Differences in Charitable Giving 2009: Executive Summary." Spring 2009, www.charitablegift.org/docs/Gender-Study-Executive-Summary.pdf.

Fredricks, Laura. *The Ask*. San Francisco: Jossey-Bass, 2006.

Ganzert, Robin R., Tracy A. Mack, Joseph Fortuna, William L. Sutton Jr. "High-Impact Philanthropy: Strategies for Partnering with Professional Advisers." *Advancing Philanthropy* (March/April 2009): 33–35.

Hare, David. "From the Playwright." Lantern Theater Company (*The Breath of Life*). February 2010.

Heath, Chip, and Dan Heath. *Made to Stick: Why Some Ideas Survive and Others Die*. New York: Random House, 2007.

Hedrick, Janet L. *Effective Donor Relations*. Hoboken: John Wiley & Sons, 2008.

Holman, Margaret. "Improving Your Solicitation Skills: How to Really Ask for a Gift . . . and Get It!" New Jersey AFP Conference on Philanthropy, 2009.

Investment Company Institute and Securities Industry Association, "Equity Ownership in America." Fall 1999, www.census.gov/compendia/statab/2009/tables/09s1171.pdf.

Jacobs, Janet Aldrich. "A New Model for Marketing." *Planned Giving Today*, January 2004: 5–6.

James III, Russell N. "The Myth of the Coming Charitable Estate Windfall." *The American Review of Public Administration*, 39 (2009): 661–674.

James III, Russell N. "Causes and Correlates of Charitable Giving in Estate Planning: A Cross-Sectional and Longitudinal Examination of Older Adults." Arlington: Association of Fundraising Professionals, 2008.

James III, Russell N. "Health, Wealth, and Charitable Estate Planning: A Longitudinal Examination of Testamentary Charitable Giving Plans." *Nonprofit and Voluntary Sector Quarterly*, 38(6) (2008): 1026–1043.

James III, Russell N. "The Presence and Timing of Charitable Estate Planning: New Research Findings." New Orleans: AFP International Conference, March 2009.

Janney, Scott R.P. "Get Donor Advisors onto Your Team: The Planned Giving Advisory Council and Other Strategies." Univest Foundation Planned Giving and Development Spring Seminar, May 9, 2007.

Kateman, Michael. "A Strategic Look at Marketing." *Journal of Gift Planning* 6 (4) (December 2002): 11–46.

Kawasaki, Guy. *Rules for Revolutionaries*. New York: Harper Business, 1999.

Kouzes, James M., and Barry Z. Posner. *The Leadership Challenge*. New York: Jossey-Bass, 2003.

Krauser, Emily. "Executive Summary Bequest Donors: Demographics and Motivations of Potential and Actual Donors." Indianapolis: Center on Philanthropy at Indiana University for Campbell and Company, 2007.

Legacy Leaders. "The George Washington University: Alumni Relations Strategy Research." Presentation to The George Washington University, 2008.

Levinson, Jay Conrad. *Guerilla Marketing Excellence*. New York: Houghton Mifflin Company, 1993.

Luntz, Frank. *What Americans Really Want . . . Really.* New York: Hyperion, 2009.

Luntz, Frank. *Words That Work: It's Not What You Say, It's What People Hear.* New York: Hyperion, 2007.

Makous, Bruce. "Solicitation: The Art of the Ask." White Paper. Philadelphia, PA. 2010.

Miree, Kathryn W. "Nonprofit Marketing Strategies to Reach Donor Advisors." *Journal of Gift Planning* 7(4) (December 2003): 9–38.

Miree, Kathryn W. "Tailored to Fit: Designing a Comprehensive Bequest Marketing Plan." *Journal of Gift Planning* 5(4) (2001): 13–50.

Murphy, Philip J. *"Get Wild with Planned Giving: Think of It as Fundraising!"* Zimmerman Lehman, 2007, www.zimmerman-lehman.com/planned giving.htm.

NCPG Strategic Directions Task Force. "The Future of Charitable Gift Planning." *Journal of Gift Planning* 11(2): 16–26.

Nichols, Judith E. *Global Demographics: Fundraising for a New World.* Chicago: Bonus Books, 1995.

NRDC November Planned Giving Direct Mail Appeal, 2009, http://malwarwicknews.com/2010/01/sample-nrdc.

Oseola McCarty Memorial Page at The University of Southern Mississippi. www.usm.edu/pr/oolamain.htm.

Partnership for Philanthropic Planning. *Are You Ready for Planned Giving?* Indianapolis: Partnership for Philanthropic Planning, 2010, www.pppnet.org/resource/ready-gg.html.

Partnership for Philanthropic Planning. *Planned Giving in the United States 2000: A Survey of Donors.* Indianapolis: National Committee on Planned Giving (now Partnership for Philanthropic Planning), 2001, www.pppnet.org/resource/donors-survey.html.

Peck, Kayt C. "A Planned Gift Is a Planned Gift, Right?" Baltimore: AFP International Conference, 2010.

Perls, Thomas and Fretts, Ruth. "Why Women Live Longer than Men." *Scientific American*. 100(7) (1998): online at www.cmu.edu/CSR/case_studies/women_live_longer.html.

Putnam, Robert D. *Bowling Alone*. New York: Simon and Schuster, 2000.

Rafferty, Renata J. *Don't Just Give It Away*. Worcester: Chandler House Press, 1999.

Rooney, Patrick. "Research Unveiled: What Every Fundraiser Needs to Know about Bequest Giving." Baltimore: AFP International Conference, March 2009.

Rosen, Michael J. "The Planned Giving Donor Profile." *The Planned Giving Course* (Partnership for Philanthropic Planning of Greater Philadelphia), December 5, 2008.

Rosen, Michael J. "Dialing Delivers for Planned Giving, Too." Planned Giving Council of Greater Philadelphia (now the Partnership for Philanthropic Planning of Greater Philadelphia).

Sagrestano, Brian M. "The Impact of Changing Generational Cohorts on Individual Giving and Gift Planning." Partnership for Philanthropic Planning of Greater Philadelphia, September 2009.

Sagrestano, Brian M. "Marketing Planned Gifts." *The Planned Giving Course* (Partnership for Philanthropic Planning of Greater Philadelphia), December 5, 2008.

Sagrestano, Brian M., and Robert E. Wahlers. "Making the Case Using Donor-Centered Philanthropic Planning." Baltimore: AFP International Conference, 2010.

Sargeant, Adrian, and Elaine Jay. "Determinants of U.S. Donor Behaviour: The Case of Bequests." Report. Arlington: Association of Fundraising Professionals, 2004.

Sargeant, Adrian, and S. Lee. "Improving Public Trust in the Voluntary Sector: An Empirical Analysis." *International Journal of Nonprofit and Voluntary Sector Marketing*, 7(1) (2002): 68–83.

Sargeant, Adrian, and Jen Shang. "Identification, Death and Bequest Giving." Report. Arlington: Association of Fundraising Professionals, 2008.

Schervish, Paul G., and John J. Havens. "Why the $41 Trillion Wealth Transfer Estimate Is Still Valid." *Journal of Gift Planning*, 7(1) (January 2003): 11–15.

Schervish, Paul G., and John J. Havens. "The New Physics of Philanthropy: The Supply Side Vectors of Charitable Giving—Part 1: The Material Side of the Supply Side." *The CASE International Journal of Educational Advancement* 2(2) (2001): 95–113.

Schervish, Paul G., and John J. Havens. "The New Physics of Philanthropy: The Supply Side Vectors of Charitable Giving—Part 2: The Spiritual Side of the Supply Side." *The CASE International Journal of Educational Advancement* 2(3) (2002): 221–41.

Schonfeld, Erick. "Twitter Hits 50 Million Tweets Per Day." *The Washington Post*, February 23, 2010, www.washingtonpost.com/wp-dyn/content/article/2010/02/23/AR2010022300133.html.

Seymour, Harold J. *Designs for Fund-Raising*. Fundraising Institute, 1988.

Sharpe Jr., Robert F. "Marketing Success in Today's Environment" *Give and Take*. Newsletter. Nashville: The Sharpe Group, November 2006.

"Single Word Costs Charities Billions Each Year," 2010, www.remembera-charity.org.uk/news_release_list.jsp?newsID=29.

Smith, Elisa M. "Making Bequest Societies the 'Wow' of Your Planned Giving Program."National Conference on Planned Giving (October 2006): 8–9.

Stelter, Larry. *A Mercifully Brief, Real World Guide: How to Raise Planned Gifts by Mail*. Medfield, MA: Emerson and Church Publishers, 2008.

The Stelter Company. "2009 Stelter Donor Insight Report: Donors on the Move." Report. Des Moines: The Stelter Company, 2009, www.stelter.com.

The Stelter Company. "Stelter Donor Insight Report: Discovering the Secret Giver." Report. Des Moines: The Stelter Company, 2008, www.stelter.com.

The Stelter Company. "Stelter Donor Insight Report: Profile of a Bequest Giver." Report. Des Moines: The Stelter Company, 2008, www.stelter.com.

Toppe, C., and A. Kirsch. "Keeping the Trust: Confidence in Charitable Organizations in an Age of Scrutiny." Report. Washington: Independent Sector, 2002.

United Way Worldwide. *Of Legacy Builders and Planned Givers: United Way's Toolkit to Increase Endowed and Planned Gifts.* Alexandria: United Way Worldwide. www.brattleboromuseum.org/pdfs/epg_toolkit.pdf.

Watt, Andrew. "Ethical Fundraising: What Are the Challenges Facing an Individual in Developing an Organizational Ethical Policy?" Seattle: AFP International Conference, 2004.

"Yul Brynner Anti-smoking Commercial," www.youtube.com/watch?v= JNjunlWUJJI. (accessed July 6, 2010).

About the Author

Michael J. Rosen, CFRE is President of ML Innovations, Inc., a fundraising and marketing consulting firm in Philadelphia. The firm serves nonprofit organizations and the for-profit companies that work with them including Canadian-based Legacy Leaders for whom MLI developed and launched a U.S. market expansion. Prior to MLI, Michael cofounded The Development Center, a pioneering direct mail/telephone fundraising company established in 1982 and sold in 1997.

Michael is an alumnus of Temple University where he majored in journalism. He served as the Editor of *The Yardley News* before transitioning to the development profession.

Michael has contributed chapters to the book *Membership Development: An Action Plan for Results* (Aspen Publishers), written by Dana Hines and Patricia Rich, ACFRE. He wrote the Foreword for the book *Effective Telephone Fundraising* by Stephen F. Schatz, CFRE. In addition, his articles have been published in *Advancing Philanthropy*, *AFP Fundline*, *Donor Developer*, *Fund Raising Management Magazine*, *Membership Matters*, *Nonprofit Nuts & Bolts*, *International Journal of Nonprofit and Voluntary Sector Marketing*, *The Nonprofit Executive*, *Planned Giving Today*, and *The Pulse of Planned Giving*. He has served as the Consulting Editor to The Taft Group's *Donor Developer* newsletter. He has been quoted in *Association Trends*, *CASE Currents*, *The Chronicle of Philanthropy*, *Inbound/Outbound Magazine*, *The Nonprofit Times*, *The Wall Street Journal*, and a number of regional newspapers.

In addition to his writing, Michael lectures internationally at a variety of conferences and seminars. He is certified as a Master Trainer by the Association of Fundraising Professionals (AFP), and frequently speaks at AFP conferences internationally and regionally. He is also a regular continuing education faculty member at Villanova University where he teaches fundraising ethics. In addition, Michael has been a lecturer for the Institute of Fundraising (UK), the Association of Zoos and Aquariums, a number of Planned Giving Councils (PPP), the 2009 Partnership for Philanthropic Planning National Conference on Philanthropic Planning, and a number of universities. He has represented AFP in testimony before the Federal Trade Commission.

Michael serves as President of the Partnership for Philanthropic Planning of Greater Philadelphia and as a member of the Editorial Board of the *International Journal of Nonprofit and Voluntary Sector Marketing* (John Wiley & Sons). He served as Vice President for Ethics Education, Association and Government Relations for the AFP Greater Philadelphia Chapter. He has also served as a member of the Board of Directors of the AFP Foundation for Philanthropy and as Board Chair of the AFP Political Action Committee. Michael also served as a member of the AFP Research Council where he reviewed research relevant to planned giving. He was a founding member of the Philadelphia Direct Marketing Association's (PDMA) Telemarketing Council.

Active in the community, Michael serves on the Executive Committee of the Board of the Philadelphia Children's Alliance. He also serves as a member of the Advisory Board of the Ark Theatre of Los Angeles. Michael is a former member of the Board of the Pennsbury Scholarship Foundation, a past president of the Board of the Philadelphia Area Repertory Theatre, a former member of the Jewish Federation of Greater Philadelphia Board of Trustees, and a former member of the Board of the Friends of the Silver Lake Nature Center.

Michael has earned the PDMA Circle of Friends Award, and has received special volunteer recognition from the AFP Foundation for Philanthropy, Friends of the Silver Lake Nature Center, and Pennsbury Scholarship Foundation. A member of Alpha Lamda Delta Honor Society, he has been listed in Who's Who in the East and Who's Who of Leading American Businessmen.

An avid, award-winning photographer, Michael resides in an historic house on a cobblestone alley in Philadelphia with fellow fundraiser and wordsmith, his wife, Lisa.

To learn more about MLI, visit: www.mlinnovations.com.

To share your thoughts with Michael, send an e-mail to mrosen@ mlinnovations.com.

AFP Code of Ethical Principles and Standards

ETHICAL PRINCIPLES • Adopted 1964; amended Sept. 2007

The Association of Fundraising Professionals (AFP) exists to foster the development and growth of fundraising professionals and the profession, to promote high ethical behavior in the fundraising profession and to preserve and enhance philanthropy and volunteerism. Members of AFP are motivated by an inner drive to improve the quality of life through the causes they serve. They serve the ideal of philanthropy, are committed to the preservation and enhancement of volunteerism; and hold stewardship of these concepts as the overriding direction of their professional life. They recognize their responsibility to ensure that needed resources are vigorously and ethically sought and that the intent of the donor is honestly fulfilled. To these ends, AFP members, both individual and business, embrace certain values that they strive to uphold in performing their responsibilities for generating philanthropic support. AFP business members strive to promote and protect the work and mission of their client organizations.

AFP members both individual and business aspire to:

- practice their profession with integrity, honesty, truthfulness and adherence to the absolute obligation to safeguard the public trust
- act according to the highest goals and visions of their organizations, professions, clients and consciences
- put philanthropic mission above personal gain;
- inspire others through their own sense of dedication and high purpose
- improve their professional knowledge and skills, so that their performance will better serve others
- demonstrate concern for the interests and well-being of individuals affected by their actions
- value the privacy, freedom of choice and interests of all those affected by their actions
- foster cultural diversity and pluralistic values and treat all people with dignity and respect
- affirm, through personal giving, a commitment to philanthropy and its role in society
- adhere to the spirit as well as the letter of all applicable laws and regulations
- advocate within their organizations adherence to all applicable laws and regulations
- avoid even the appearance of any criminal offense or professional misconduct
- bring credit to the fundraising profession by their public demeanor
- encourage colleagues to embrace and practice these ethical principles and standards
- be aware of the codes of ethics promulgated by other professional organizations that serve philanthropy

ETHICAL STANDARDS

Furthermore, while striving to act according to the above values, AFP members, both individual and business, agree to abide (and to ensure, to the best of their ability, that all members of their staff abide) by the AFP standards. Violation of the standards may subject the member to disciplinary sanctions, including expulsion, as provided in the AFP Ethics Enforcement Procedures.

MEMBER OBLIGATIONS

1. Members shall not engage in activities that harm the members' organizations, clients or profession.
2. Members shall not engage in activities that conflict with their fiduciary, ethical and legal obligations to their organizations, clients or profession.
3. Members shall effectively disclose all potential and actual conflicts of interest; such disclosure does not preclude or imply ethical impropriety.
4. Members shall not exploit any relationship with a donor, prospect, volunteer, client or employee for the benefit of the members or the members' organizations.
5. Members shall comply with all applicable local, state, provincial and federal civil and criminal laws.
6. Members recognize their individual boundaries of competence and are forthcoming and truthful about their professional experience and qualifications and will represent their achievements accurately and without exaggeration.
7. Members shall present and supply products and/or services honestly and without misrepresentation and will clearly identify the details of those products, such as availability of the products and/or services and other factors that may affect the suitability of the products and/or services for donors, clients or nonprofit organizations.
8. Members shall establish the nature and purpose of any contractual relationship at the outset and will be responsive and available to organizations and their employing organizations before, during and after any sale of materials and/or services. Members will comply with all fair and reasonable obligations created by the contract.

9. Members shall refrain from knowingly infringing the intellectual property rights of other parties at all times. Members shall address and rectify any inadvertent infringement that may occur.
10. Members shall protect the confidentiality of all privileged information relating to the provider/client relationships.
11. Members shall refrain from any activity designed to disparage competitors untruthfully.

SOLICITATION AND USE OF PHILANTHROPIC FUNDS

12. Members shall take care to ensure that all solicitation and communication materials are accurate and correctly reflect their organizations' mission and use of solicited funds.
13. Members shall take care to ensure that donors receive informed, accurate and ethical advice about the value and tax implications of contributions.
14. Members shall take care to ensure that contributions are used in accordance with donors' intentions.
15. Members shall take care to ensure proper stewardship of all revenue sources, including timely reports on the use and management of such funds.
16. Members shall obtain explicit consent by donors before altering the conditions of financial transactions.

PRESENTATION OF INFORMATION

17. Members shall not disclose privileged or confidential information to unauthorized parties.
18. Members shall adhere to the principle that all donor and prospect information created by, or on behalf of, an organization or a client is the property of that organization or client and shall not be transferred or utilized except on behalf of that organization or client.
19. Members shall give donors and clients the opportunity to have their names removed from lists that are sold to, rented to or exchanged with other organizations.
20. Members shall, when stating fundraising results, use accurate and consistent accounting methods that conform to the appropriate guidelines adopted by the American Institute of Certified Public Accountants (AICPA)* for the type of organization involved. (* In countries outside of the United States, comparable authority should be utilized.)

COMPENSATION AND CONTRACTS

21. Members shall not accept compensation or enter into a contract that is based on a percentage of contributions; nor shall members accept finder's fees or contingent fees. Business members must refrain from receiving compensation from third parties derived from products or services for a client without disclosing that third-party compensation to the client (for example, volume rebates from vendors to business members).
22. Members may accept performance-based compensation, such as bonuses, provided such bonuses are in accord with prevailing practices within the members' own organizations and are not based on a percentage of contributions.
23. Members shall neither offer nor accept payments or special considerations for the purpose of influencing the selection of products or services.
24. Members shall not pay finder's fees, commissions or percentage compensation based on contributions, and shall take care to discourage their organizations from making such payments.
25. Any member receiving funds on behalf of a donor or client must meet the legal requirements for the disbursement of those funds. Any interest or income earned on the funds should be fully disclosed.

A Donor Bill of Rights

PHILANTHROPY is based on voluntary action for the common good. It is a tradition of giving and sharing that is primary to the quality of life. To assure that philanthropy merits the respect and trust of the general public, and that donors and prospective donors can have full confidence in the not-for-profit organizations and causes they are asked to support, we declare that all donors have these rights:

I.

To be informed of the organization's mission, of the way the organization intends to use donated resources, and of its capacity to use donations effectively for their intended purposes.

II.

To be informed of the identity of those serving on the organization's governing board, and to expect the board to exercise prudent judgement in its stewardship responsibilities.

III.

To have access to the organization's most recent financial statements.

IV.

To be assured their gifts will be used for the purposes for which they were given.

V.

To receive appropriate acknowledgement and recognition.

VI.

To be assured that information about their donations is handled with respect and with confidentiality to the extent provided by law.

VII.

To expect that all relationships with individuals representing organizations of interest to the donor will be professional in nature.

VIII.

To be informed whether those seeking donations are volunteers, employees of the organization or hired solicitors.

IX.

To have the opportunity for their names to be deleted from mailing lists that an organization may intend to share.

X.

To feel free to ask questions when making a donation and to receive prompt, truthful and forthright answers.

DEVELOPED BY
Association for Healthcare Philanthropy (AHP)
Association of Fundraising Professionals (AFP)
Council for Advancement and Support of Education (CASE)
Giving Institute: Leading Consultants to Non-Profits

ENDORSED BY
(in formation)
Independent Sector
National Catholic Development Conference (NCDC)
National Committee on Planned Giving (NCPG)
Council for Resource Development (CRD)
United Way of America

Model Standards of Practice for the Charitable Gift Planner

Preamble

The purpose of this statement is to encourage responsible gift planning by urging the adoption of the following Standards of Practice by all individuals who work in the charitable gift planning process, gift planning officers, fund raising consultants, attorneys, accountants, financial planners, life insurance agents and other financial services professionals (collectively referred to hereafter as "Gift Planners"), and by the institutions that these persons represent.

This statement recognizes that the solicitation, planning and administration of a charitable gift is a complex process involving philanthropic, personal, financial, and tax considerations, and often involves professionals from various disciplines whose goals should include working together to structure a gift that achieves a fair and proper balance between the interests of the donor and the purposes of the charitable institution.

I. Primacy of Philanthropic Motivation

The principal basis for making a charitable gift should be a desire on the part of the donor to support the work of charitable institutions.

II. Explanation of Tax Implications

Congress has provided tax incentives for charitable giving, and the emphasis in this statement on philanthropic motivation in no way minimizes the necessity and appropriateness of a full and accurate explanation by the Gift Planner of those incentives and their implications.

III. Full Disclosure

It is essential to the gift planning process that the role and relationships of all parties involved, including how and by whom each is compensated, be fully disclosed to the donor. A Gift Planner shall not act or purport to act as a representative of any charity without the express knowledge and approval of the charity, and shall not, while employed by the charity, act or purport to act as a representative of the donor, without the express consent of both the charity and the donor.

IV. Compensation

Compensation paid to Gift Planners shall be reasonable and proportionate to the services provided. Payment of finder's fees, commissions or other fees by a donee organization to an independent Gift Planner as a condition for the delivery of a gift is never appropriate. Such payments lead to abusive practices and may violate certain state and federal regulations. Likewise, commission-based compensation for Gift Planners who are employed by a charitable institution is never appropriate.

V. Competence and Professionalism

The Gift Planner should strive to achieve and maintain a high degree of competence in his or her chosen area, and shall advise donors only in areas in which he or she is professionally qualified. It is a hallmark of professionalism for Gift Planners that they realize when they have reached the limits of their knowledge and expertise, and as a result, should include other professionals in the process. Such relationships should be characterized by courtesy, tact and mutual respect.

VI. Consultation with Independent Advisers

A Gift Planner acting on behalf of a charity shall in all cases strongly encourage the donor to discuss the proposed gift with competent independent legal and tax advisers of the donor's choice.

VII. Consultation with Charities

Although Gift Planners frequently and properly counsel donors concerning specific charitable gifts without the prior knowledge or approval of the donee organization, the Gift Planner, in order to insure that the gift will accomplish the donor's objectives, should encourage the donor early in the gift planning process, to discuss the proposed gift with the charity to whom the gift is to be made. In cases where the donor desires anonymity, the Gift Planner shall endeavor, on behalf of the undisclosed donor, to obtain the charity's input in the gift planning process.

VIII. Description and Representation of Gift

The Gift Planner shall make every effort to assure that the donor receives a full description and an accurate representation of all aspects of any proposed charitable gift plan. The consequences for the charity, the donor and, where applicable, the donor's family, should be apparent, and the assumptions underlying any financial illustrations should be realistic.

IX. Full Compliance

A Gift Planner shall fully comply with and shall encourage other parties in the gift planning process to fully comply with both the letter and spirit of all applicable federal and state laws and regulations.

X. Public Trust

Gift Planners shall, in all dealings with donors, institutions and other professionals, act with fairness, honesty, integrity and openness. Except for compensation received for services, the terms of which have been disclosed to the donor, they shall have no vested interest that could result in personal gain.

Adopted and subscribed to by the National Committee on Planned Giving (now the Partnership for Philanthropic Planning) and the American Council on Gift Annuities, May 7, 1991. Revised April 1999. Reprinted with permission.

Index

A

Ability
estate size and, 34, 37
factors impacting, 33–37
Academy, 222
Acceptance
organizational, 255–57
staff, 263–65
Access, to donors, 162
Accounting, of planned gifts, 291–94
Advertising, 151–53
cost-effective, 152
in external media, 151–52
headlines, writing, 152
print, 152–53
Advice, free, 165–66
Advisory group, envisioning, 172
AFP Code of Ethical Principles and Standards, 28
African Americans
charitable bequests by, 31
fraternities and sororities, 77
motivation of, 72

philanthropy of, 73
Age
charitable gift annuity and, 42
propensity and, 41–43
Aging population
charitable bequest and, 6
charitable gift annuity and, 8
Aleman, Mindy, 194
American Cancer Society, 68, 158, 159
American Civil Liberties Union (ACLU), 187
Annual fund, 27
donors, 54
Annual funds
donations to, 4
Annual giving, estate giving to, 34
Annual letter, 245, 246
Annual report, listing donors in, 238
Appreciated stock, 35
taxes and, 64
Appreciation
showing donors, 237–39
tokens of, 243

Ask, 185–232
  amount, 216–17
  for bequest gift, 222–23
  for charitable gift annuity, 224–26
  for charitable remainder uni-trust, 226–28
  closing, 221
  conversations, 222–28
  with direct mail, 187–92
  through face-to-face visits, 186, 200–220
  follow-up, 220
  marketing recommendations from donors, 228–29
  necessity of, 186–87
  scenario for, 217–19, 220–26
  using telephone, 192–200
Association of Fundraising Professionals, 18
Attorneys, planned giving and, 30–31
Authority, in messaging, 107, 108
Average bequest value (ABV), 56

B
Baby Boomer generation, 70, 71
  marketing to, 72
  nonprofit organizations and, 71
  philanthropic values of, 13
  women, 44
Background marketing, 17
Bait and switch, 247
Barden, Ann, 143–144
Behind-the-scenes tours, 244

Benchmarking targets, 268
Bequest confirmation form, 283–84
Bequest giving, gender and, 44
Bequests
  ask for, 222–23
  planned gift program potential worksheet for, 277–80
Bequest-specific motives, 75, 81–84
Bequest tickler file, 248
Board, governing
  enlisting support of, 263
  gaining approval of, 256
Bottom line, increasing, 166–67
  relationships and, 168
Bram, Leslie D., 198
Brand identity
  creating, 92–95
  of legacy society membership, 242
Brand name, of organizations, 65
Brandt, Susan Blair, 235
Brassley, Jane, 211–13
Brozo, Jim, 92, 112
Budget, for marketing plan, 268
Budget limits, for organizations, 150–51

C
Calendar, marketing, 268, 269
Case for Support, 257–63
  defined, 258
  development process for, 261–63
  Internal Case for Donor-Centered Philanthropic Planning, 259

Case studies
  Brassley, Jane, 211–13
  Hoeffel, James, 204–5
Charitable bequests, 5, 6, 26
  actual *versus* considering, 7
  by African Americans, 31
  aging population and, 6
  by Hispanics, 31
  inflation and, 13
Charitable estate planning, predicting, 39
Charitable gift annuity (CGA), 5, 10, 13, 25, 26, 30, 32, 43, 62, 72, 73, 82, 95, 104, 168, 188, 192, 193, 195, 215, 241, 266
  age and, 42
  aging population and, 8
  ask for, 224–26
  brand identity and, 93
  direct mail and, 111
  establishment of, 235
  legacy society membership and, 241
  planned gift program potential worksheet for, 280–81
  safety of, 112
  target market for, 266–67
Charitable lead annuity trusts (CLAT), 11, 42
  taxes and, 42
Charitable remainder annuity trusts, 11
Charitable remainder trust (CRT)
  legacy society membership and, 241

Charitable remainder trusts (CRT), 7, 12, 32, 66, 213
Charitable remainder uni-trusts (CRUT), 42, 67, 212
  ask for, 226–28
Charitable testamentary provision, 39
Charities
  generational cohorts and, 71
  trust in, 48
Charity officer, visit with, 201
Children, propensity and, 40
Circular planned giving process, 30, 234
Closing, ask, 221
Coca-Cola, 103
Cold calls, 273
Colleges, giving back to, 78
Comfort zone, of planned gift donors, 68
Commitment
  formal, 219
  request for, 218
  writing, importance of, 223
Committee, 173
  council *versus,* 172
  planned giving, 173
  time commitment of, 175
Communication, 96–102
  materials, 109–11
  open, 167
Communications
  evaluating, 271
  gift giving and, 80, 81

Community, sense of, 77

Community-based donors, 213

Community foundations, 5

Community life, nonprofit organizations and, 33

Community service, 163

Confidentiality, commitment to, 260

Consistency, in messaging, 107

Continuing education credits, 161

Conversations, ask, 222–28

Corporate citizenship, 163

Council, 173–74
    building robust, 171–72
    committee *versus,* 172
    credibility of, 179
    development of, 169
    professional advisory, 172
    recruiting members, 179
    reinventing, 169

Crandall, Robert J., 221

Creativity, in marketing, 266

Credibility
    of council, 179
    of donor advisors, 164
    in messages, 104
    of organizations, 61

Cullinan, Tom, 169–170

Cultivation
    advertising, 151–53
    communication channel for, 96–102
    through direct mail, 111–16
    through e-mail, 134–38
    through events, 142–45
    existing materials, 109–11
    through face-to-face visits, 145–51
    fundamental strategic approach, 95–96
    goal of, 213
    messages about, 103–9
    need for, 90–91
    through newsletters, 120–26, 159
    of planned gift prospects, 89–156
    of professional advisors, 157–84
    social networking technology, 139–42
    through telephone communication, 116–20
    through websites, 126–34

D

Damen, Margaret May, 44

Deferred gifts, 106, 272
    evaluating commitments, 270
    planned gifts as, 11
    reporting, 245

Deferred planned gift, 27

Demographics
    impact of, 40
    motivation and, 70–75

Demotivating factors, 84–86

Desires, of planned gift donors, 61–69

Development professionals
    actions of, 69
    advisors and, 160
    business cards for, 110

donors and, 2

e-mail and, 136

estate giving and, 160

exchanges of value and, 161–68

free advice and, 165–66

loved ones of donors and, 29

motivation of prospects and, 29

tax deduction information from,
  226

website, questions about,
  127–28

Direct mail, 111–16

  to ask for donations, 187–92

  urgency through, 190

Donor advisors. *See also* Professional
  advisors

  credibility of, 164

  cultivation of, 158–59

  development professionals and, 160

  exchanges of value and, 161–68,
    162–68

  fundraising goals of, 159

  nonprofit organizations, access to
    clients of, 162

  practices for working with,
    180–82

  referrals from, 161

  requirements of, 165

The Donor Bill of Rights, 28, 49

Donor-centered fundraising, 3

  illustration of, 15–17

Donor-centered marketing, 1–24

  care of donors in, 2–4

donor-centered fundraising, illustration of, 15–17

getting started, 253–76

marketing *versus,* 12

myths about planned giving, 9–11, 13

newsletters and, 121–22

percentage of Americans with
  planned gift, 5–9

planned gift marketing, 4–5

proactive *versus* reactive planned
  giving, 17–18

stewardship and, 236

timing of, 13–14

Donor-centered philanthropic
  planning, 286

Donors

  care of, 2–4

  community-based, 213

  defending, 249–50

  development professionals and, 2

  educating, 20

  history of, 204

  honoring wishes of, 248

  identifying, 25–57

  importance of gift, 185

  marketing recommendations from,
    228–29

  mission-only, 213

  planned gift, 27–31

  program-focused, 214

  reporting to, 245–46

  thanking, 237–39

  treatment of, 149–50

E

Economic comfort level, of planned
  givers, 29
Economy, future gifts and, 288
Education
  advertising, 151–53
  communication channel for,
    96–102
  through direct mail, 111–16
  of donors, 20
  through e-mail, 134–38
  events, 142–45
  existing materials, 109–11
  through face-to-face visits, 145–51
  fundamental strategic approach,
    95–96
  level, propensity and, 40, 74
  messages about, 103–9
  need for, 90–91
  through newsletters, 120–26
  of planned gift prospects, 89–156
  of professional advisors, 157–84
  social networking technology, 139–
    42
  through telephone
    communication, 116–20
  through websites, 126–34
Eisland, Elizabeth Tice, 250
Electronic newsletters (e-newsletters),
    134
Electronic screenings, 52
Elements, of marketing plan, 266–68
  budget, 268

  calendar, 268, 269
  key goals, 266
  key objectives, 267
  mission, 266
  outcomes, 268
  strategies and tactics, 267
  target markets, 266–67
Ellison, Roger, 52, 110, 150, 202, 270
E-mail, 134–38
  creating, 137–38
  development professionals and,
    136
  obtaining addresses, 137
  spam, 135
  timing of, 137
Emotions, in messages, 105–6
Endowment
  fund, 174–75
  important roles of, 286–87
  structures, 216
Estate gift, 33
  to annual giving, 34
  targeting donors, 34
Estate planning, 21, 85
  social networking and, 141
  taxes and, 83
Estate planning education series, 198
Estate size, ability and, 34, 37
Estate tax, 43
Events
  education through, 142–45
  face-to-face visits as, 150
  hosting, 143

planning, 144–45
for senior citizens, 143
Exchanges of value, 161–68
access, 162
bottom line, increasing, 166–67
credibility, 164
free advice, 165–66
philanthropy, 167–68
publicity, 162–64

F
Facebook, 139, 141, 142
Face-to-face visits, 32, 145–51
ask, 186, 200–220, 228
barriers to action in, 147
at events, 150
introductory, setting tone, 206–7
introductory, setting up, 202–3
pattern of, 149
trust and, 151
types of, 146–47
Family
care of, 82
nonprofit organizations and, 85
Federal Form 990, 28, 46
Fidelity Charitable Gift Fund, success
of, 166
Financial characteristics, impact of,
40
Financial Counseling Services (FCS),
170
Financial planners, 30–31
Financial security, perception of, 35

Fiscal management, of organizations
donors and, 28
Federal Form 990, 28
Fraternities, African Americans and,
77
Fraud, 247
Fredricks, Laura, 27, 221–223
Fundamental strategic approach,
95–96
Fundraising
approaches, 187
bait and switch in, 247
donor-centered, 3, 15–17
friend-raising and, 46
goals, 159
journalism and, 210
organization-focused, 3
planned giving as, 10
proactive, 18
readiness, gauging, 256
software, 250
over telephone, 192–200

G
Gee, Heather, 73, 77, 161
Gender
bequest giving and, 44
propensity and, 43
Generation X, 70, 71
Generosity, passion and, 52, 53
Get-acquainted session, 204
Gift planning, 54
events, 142–45

Gift planning programs, phases in, 255

Gift proposal, 210

Gifts, using telephone to ask for, 192–200

Gillon, John, 146, 210

Giving USA Foundation, 288

Golden Rule, 2

Governing board, social capital and, 45. *See also* Board, governing

GPD Academy, example, 285–90

Gratitude, as motivation, 76

Greaves, Steven C., 67, 215

Great generational cohort, 70, 71

Greenfield, James M., 244

Guide to Bequests (NRDC), 189

H

Handwritten notes, importance of, 112–13

Havens, JOhn J., 13–14, 75, 77

Headlines, writing, 152

"Health and Retirement Study," 6, 33

Hispanics
  charitable bequests by, 31
  motivation of, 72

Hoeffel, James, 204–5

Holistic approach, to planned giving, 17

Honesty, importance of, 62

Hospitals
  donations to, 48
  fundraising and, 15–16

I

Immortality, as motivation, 83

Inflation, charitable bequest and, 13

Informal focus groups, 150

Information, pros and cons of, 49–50

Intergenerational wealth transfer, 14

Internal Case for Donor-Centered Philanthropic Planning, 259
  elements of, 260
  purpose of, 259
  sample of, 285–90

Internal stewardship, 246–50

Internet conferencing, 151

Introductory visit
  development professional's role in, 203
  setting up, 202–3
  tone, setting, 206–7
  wrapping up, 208–9

J

James III, Russell N., 6, 15, 34, 39–40

Janney, Scott R.P., 42, 159–160, 165, 168, 170, 172, 176, 180

Jay, Elaine, 186, 229, 240

Jargon, avoiding, 129

Joint marketing, 159

Journalism, fundraising and, 210

K

Kendrick, John B., 82

Key goals, of planned giving program, 266

Key objectives, of target market, 267
KISS (Keep It Simple and Stupid)
    technique, 103
Komen, Susan G., 63
Kramer, Donald W., 114

L
Language
    jargon, avoiding, 129
    organization-focused, 15
    power of, 97
    power words, 97–102
Leadership, confidence in, 28
Lecture series, 110
Legacy
    net worth and, 217
    promotion of, 228–29
    recognition group, 240
    of science, 211–13
    university, 207
Legacy Leaders Million-Dollar
    Challenge (NRDC), 188, 189
Legacy society membership, 240
    behind-the-scene tours for, 244
    brand identity of, 242
    criteria for, 241–42
    death of member in, 244
Legal documents, 220
Life estate, legacy society membership
    and, 241
Life expectancy, cultural changes and,
    43
Life-income gifts, 172

Life-note, 105
LinkedIn, 139, 142
Liquid asset, tax deduction and, 26
Little Rock Council, 171–72
Luncheons, for planned gift donors, 244

M
Makous, Bruce, 200, 216
Manipulation, 60
Marketing
    to Baby Boomer generation, 72
    background, 17
    channels, 90–91
    creativity in, 266
    direct mail and, 114–15
    donations based on, 64
    donor-centered, 1–24
    donor-centered marketing versus, 12
    evaluating, 271
    impact of newsletter, 121
    joint, 159
    KISS, 103
    messages, 103–9
    multifaceted effort, 27
    passive, 229
    planned gift, 4–5
    recommendations from donors,
        228–29
    steps in, 19–22
    through storytelling, 106–7
Marketing effort, evaluating, 270–74
    areas for measure, 270–71
    process activity, 272–73

Marketing plan, building, 265–69
  elements of, 266–68
Messages
  authority, 107, 108
  consistency in, 107
  credibility in, 104
  emotions in, 105–6
  marketing, 103–9
  principles of, 107
  reciprocity, 107
  scarcity, 107, 108
Melvin, Ann T., 122, 137
Millennial generation, 70, 71
Minority groups, charitable bequests
  by, 31
Mission, of organization, 266
Mission-only donors, 213
Modeling, by professional advisors, 180
Model Standards of Practice for the
  Charitable Gift Planner (PPP), 28
Moore, David B, 36, 110, 142
Motivation
  bequest-specific, 81–84
  categories, 75
  demographic factors impacting,
    70–75
  gratitude as, 76
  immortality as, 83
  manipulation versus inspiration
    versus, 60
  for philanthropy, 213
  of planned gift donors, 59–88
  prestige as, 78
  publicity as, 162–64

regional differences and, 74
  religion as, 74
Motivational groups, 214
Mulia-Howell, Michelle, 191
Multiyear pledge funding, 216
Murphy, Phillip J., 1, 18, 263
MySpace, 139

N
Named funds, 216
Namesake scholarship fund, 64
National Conference on Planned
  Giving, 241
National Institute on Aging, 6
National Resources Defense Council
  (NRDC), 188
Net worth, legacy and, 217
Newsletters, 120–26
  cultivation and, 159
  electronic, 125, 134
  listing donors in, 237
  marketing impact of, 121
  themes in, 123–24
Nonprofit organizations, 4
  access to advisor's clients, 162
  advisor community and, 158
  Baby Boomers and, 71
  community life and, 33
  credibility of, 164
  data collection by, 53
  family and, 85
  gender and, 43
  giver's relationship with, 39
  giving back to, 78

planned gift and, 6, 9

priority-prospect equation and, 31

reciprocity and, 107

reputation, building, 163

steps for telephone contact, 199–200

websites for, 110, 126–27

O

Organizational acceptance, gaining, 255–57

Organizational factors, 79–81
of motivation, 75

Organization-focused fundraising, 3

Organization-focused language, 15

Organizations
brand name of, 65
budget limits and, 150–51
credibility of, 61
direct-response approaches, testing for, 194
donor advisors and, 162
e-mail from, 134
fiscal management of, 28
fundraising approaches by, 11
generational transfer and, 15
geographic obstacles for, 150–51
governing board of, 45
informal focus groups by, 150
lecture series and, 110
nonprofit, 4
planned gift marketing for, 4–5
planned giver databases, 36

preparing for donor-centered marketing, 254–55

professionalism of, 79

trust and, 48

volunteer and staff leaders of, 19

websites and, 17

Outcomes, for marketing plan, 268

"Over-the-transom" gifts, 187

P

Partnership for Philanthropic Planning, 11, 14, 69, 75, 254, 291

Passion, generosity and, 52, 53

Passive marketing, 229

Personal interaction, importance of, 201

Personalization, of thank-you letters, 238

Personalized letters, 195

Philanthropic legacy, 185

Philanthropic planning, donor-centered, 286

Philanthropic process
advice in, 166
credibility in, 164
professional advisors in, 157
trust in, 48

Philanthropic values, of Baby Boomer generation, 13

Philanthropy, 167–68
advisors' facilitation of, 182–83
of African Americans, 73
database of advisors in, 161
motivations for, 75, 213

Photographs, power of, 129

Planned gift dollar worksheet, 291–94

Planned gift donors
bequest-specific motives, 81–84
comfort zone of, 68
demographic factors impacting motivation, 70–75
demotivating factors of, 84–86
desires of, 61–69
general individual motives, 75–78
hope and, 63–64
interests of, 69
lifestyles of, 68
manipulation *versus* motivation *versus* inspiration, 60
motivation, identifying, 59–88
organizational factors, 79–81
recognition of, 240–44
risk and, 63

Planned gift program, potential worksheet, 277–81

Planned gift prospects
cultivation of, 89–156
education of, 89–156

Planned gifts
costs of, 148
deferred, 27
as deferred gifts, 11
expectation of ask for, 186
formula for, 216
identify donors of, 25–57
percentage of Americans with, 5–9

percentage of people asking for, 90
prospects for, 26–27
reasons for, 76
sense of community inspiring, 77
soliciting, 198
volunteer team to secure, 176
willingness to consider, 8

Planned givers
advisors and, 30–31
basic data on, 50–51
characteristics of, 27–31
databases for, 36
economic comfort level of, 29
factors impacting ability, 33–37
factors impacting propensity, 38–44
factors impacting social capital, 45–49
information pros and cons, 49–50
loved ones and, 29
priority-prospect equation, 31–33
prospect information, 38
senior citizens as, 34–35
trust and relationship building with, 38
wealth information, gathering, 36

Planned giving
best time for, 14
brand identity, creating, 92–95
cheat sheets, 264
circular process, 30
effective program, 17
familiarity with term, 90, 153
holistic approach to, 17

myths about, 9–11, 13

nonprofit definition of, 89

outcomes of program, 271–72

proactive *versus* reactive, 17–18

program evaluation, 270

successful programs, stepping stones to, 19–22

work groups and, 172

Planned Giving Advisory Council, 160, 169–75

members and, 177–79

Planned giving committee, 173

Planned Giving Course, 26

Planning, events, 144–45

Power words, 97–102

Practices, for working with professional advisors, 180–82

challenging process, 181

enabling others, 181

encouraging heart, 181–82

modeling, 180

shared vision, inspiring, 180

Preparation, for donor-centered marketing, 253–76

case for support, 257–63

marketing effort, evaluating, 270–74

marketing plan, building, 265–69

organizational acceptance, gaining, 255–57

organizations, 254–55

staff acceptance, gaining, 263–65

Prestige, as motivator, 78

Print advertisements, 152–53

Priority-prospect equation, 31–33

Proactive fundraising, 18

Proactive planned giving reactive *versus,* 17–18

Process activity, measurement of, 272–73

Professional advisors

building relationships with, 158–60

cultivation of, 157–84

defining and evolving roles of, 176–77

education of, 157–84

exchanges of value and, 161–68

limited experience, making up for, 169

Planned Giving Advisory Council and, 169–75, 177–79

practices for working with, 180–82

Professional advisory council, 172

Professionalism, of organizations, 79

Program-focused donors, 214

Propensity, factors impacting, 38–44

age, 41–43

children and grandchildren, 40

education level and, 40, 74

gender, 43

Prospect information, 38

Prospects

basic data on, 50–51

face-to-face visits with, 146

identification of, 271

life story of, 207

personal interaction with, 201

Prospects (*continued*)

planned gift (*See* Planned gift prospects)

for planned giving, 26–27

rating, 52–55

social networking and, 140–42

surveying, 52

telephone contact with, 117

Prospect screening group, 37

Protocols, importance of, 265

Publicity, 162–64

Purposeful conversation, 203

R

Rating, prospects, 52–55

Reactive planned giving, proactive *versus,* 17–18

Real estate gifts, 11

Realized net gift income, 271

Reciprocity

in messaging, 107

nonprofit organizations and, 107

Recognition

benefits of, 240

importance of, 181

of planned gift donors, 240–44

wishes of donor regarding, 242

Referrals, from donor advisors, 161

Relationship building, planned givers and, 38

Relationships

bottom line, building, 168

building with service and face time, 91–92

with professional advisors, 158–60

stewardship and, 235

Religion, charitable giving and, 74

Remember a Charity consortium (UK), 9, 86

Reporting, to donors, 245–46

Reputation, of nonprofit organization, 163

Revocable gifts, 234

Risk, planned gift donors and, 63

Rooney, Patrick M., 74

Rothey, Rebecca, 94, 110

S

Sagrestano, Brian M., 53–54, 71, 121–122, 191, 259–260

Sargeant, Adrian, 75, 78–81, 83–84, 104, 106, 186, 229, 240

Scarcity, in messaging, 107, 108

Scenarios, for requesting gifts, 217–19, 220–26

Schervish, Paul G., 13–14, 75, 77

Screening, prospects, 52–55

electronic, 52

Screening system, 36

Seeley, Mark R., 203

Senior citizens

hosting events for, 143

as planned givers, 34–35

Shang, Jen, 75, 78–81, 83–84, 104, 106

Silent generational cohort, 70, 71

Social capital
  building, 47
  factors impacting, 45–49
  importance of, 32–33
  organization's governing board and, 45
  trust building and, 49
Social networking technology, 139–42
  for prospects, 140–42
Software, fundraising, 250
Sororities, African Americans and, 77
Spam, 135
Staff acceptance, gaining, 263–65
Stelter, Larry, 7–8, 26, 41, 121,123–124, 273
Stewardship, 233–52
  defined, 234
  donor-centered marketing and, 236
  internal, 246–50
  planned gift donors, recognizing, 240–44
  positive feelings from, 234–36
  relationship enhancement through, 235
  reporting to donors, 245–46
  thanking donors, 237–39
Storytelling, marketing through, 106–7
Survey of Donors (NCPG), 240

T
Target markets, 266–67
  key objectives of, 267

Tax advisors, 30–31
Tax deduction, 226
  liquid asset and, 26
Taxes
  appreciated stock and, 64
  avoidance of, 83
  charitable lead annuity trusts and, 42
  estate, 43
  estate planning and, 83
  minimization of, 83
Team, 173, 174
  solicitation of gifts by, 176–77
  volunteer, 176
Telephone, 116–20
  ask for gifts over, 192–200
  cost effective nature of, 199
  enrolling prospects over, 198
  fundraising models, 199
  as information-gathering tool, 119
  open-ended questions on, 195
  steps for nonprofit organizations, 199–200
  volunteers, 192
Testimonials, 123
Thanking donors, 237–39
  reasons for, 237
Thank-you letters, 237, 238
  attributes of, 238–39
  formal, 238
  package, 190
  personalization of, 238

Third-party endorsement, 105

Timing

of donor-centered marketing, 13–14

of e-mail messages, 137

Tokens of appreciation, for legacy society members, 243

annual event, 243

birthday and holiday cards, 243

membership gift, 243

special newsletters and communications, 243

Tone, of introductory visit, 206–7

Troutman, David C., 246

Trust

in charities, 48

crisis in, 49

through face-to-face visits, 151

face-to-face visits to build, 146

organizations and, 48

philanthropic process and, 48

planned givers and, 38

social capital and, 49

Twitter, 139

U

United States, percentage of planned gift in, 5–9

United Way, 174–75

professional advisory committee of, 178

Universities

giving back to, 78

legacy, 207

telephone volunteers for, 192–200

Urgency, through direct mail appeal, 190

V

Value, exchanges of, 161–68

access, 162

bottom line, increasing, 166–67

credibility, 164

free advice, 165–66

philanthropy, 167–68

publicity, 162–64

Values, philanthropic, 13

Video telephony, 151

Vision, shared, 180

Volunteer groups, 173

committee, 173

council, 173

team, 173

W

Wahlers, Robert E., 38, 159–160, 259–260

Wealth information, gathering, 36

Wealth management, 159

Wealth transfer

intergenerational, 14

positive impact of, 14

Websites, 126–34

for nonprofit organizations,
110
photographs on, 129
for planned giving, 17
promoting, 133–34
Wills, 42

Women
gift planning and, 44
high-income, 44
Woodard, Larry C., 172
Work groups, planned giving and,
172